'Demonstrating how nations are continuing projects rather than natural human groupings has been central to recent scholarship in cultural and political studies. Reworking geography as territory, and proclaiming the naturalness of national space are crucial parts of such projects. Greece's nineteenth-century geographical self-invention took place in the context of the Greeks' supposed foundational role in European civilization and of enormously complex local and regional cultural histories. Robert Shannan Peckham reveals the vital role played by geography – as material space and as intellectual activity – in Greece's self-making. Written with elegance and a sure grasp of an impressive range of sources, *National Histories, Natural States* is a significant substantive work of cultural geography and a timely contribution to our understanding of the geopolitics of Southeastern Europe.'

Denis E. Cosgrove, Alexander von Humboldt Professor of Geography at the University of California, Los Angeles

'This book cuts a swathe through two hundred years of Greek exceptionalism. With firmness and sensitivity Robert Shannan Peckham lays bare the processes by which 'Modern' Greece came to identify itself, and to be accepted, as the direct inheritor of an ancient civilization. In *National Histories, Natural States* the construction of Greek identity between the 1780s and the 1920s is shown to be an inextricable part of the historical process that saw the terminal decline of the Ottoman Empire and the foundation of the modern Balkan nation-states. Peckham ranges with confidence across the disciplines of history, cultural studies, geography, archaeology and literature to place Greek practice in each of these in close relation to cognate practices culled from British, French, German, Italian, Spanish and Russian sources. In an entirely new way, *National Histories, Natural States* puts Modern Greece, and Modern Greek Studies, "on the map".'

Roderick Beaton, Koraes Professor of Modern Greek and Byzantine History, Language and Literature, King's College London

For Rebecca

NATIONAL HISTORIES, NATURAL STATES

NATIONALISM AND THE POLITICS OF PLACE IN GREECE

ROBERT SHANNAN PECKHAM

BLOOMSBURY ACADEMIC

LONDON • NEW YORK • OXFORD • NEW DELHI • SYDNEY

BLOOMSBURY ACADEMIC
Bloomsbury Publishing Plc
50 Bedford Square, London, WC1B 3DP, UK
1385 Broadway, New York, NY 10018, USA
29 Earlsfort Terrace, Dublin 2, Ireland

BLOOMSBURY, BLOOMSBURY ACADEMIC and the Diana logo
are trademarks of Bloomsbury Publishing Plc

First published in Great Britain by I.B. Tauris 2001
Paperback edition published by Bloomsbury Academic 2021

A catalogue record for this book is available from the British Library.

A catalog record for this book is available from the Library of Congress.

ISBN: HB: 978-1-8606-4641-6
PB: 978-1-3501-8014-7

Typeset by The Midlands Book Typesetting Co, Loughborough, Leicestershire

To find out more about our authors and books visit
www.bloomsbury.com and sign up for our newsletters.

Contents

Maps

Acknowledgement is made to the following sources:

'Greece' adapted from R.J. Crampton, *Eastern Europe in the Twentieth Century*, Routledge, 1997, p.390.

'The Ottoman Empire' adapted from J. Goodwin, *Lords of the Horizons*, Vintage, 2000, pp.viii–ix.

'The Expansion of the Greek State' from R. Clogg, *A Concise History of Greece*, Cambridge University Press, 1992, p.43.

'Frontier fictions' adapted from Clogg, op. cit.

Acknowledgements

Many of the ideas developed in this book were tested in public lectures, conference papers and seminar workshops at the Universities of Birmingham, Cambridge, Harvard, King's College London, Oxford, Royal Holloway and Bedford New College and University College London. I have benefited from the comments and discussions that ensued and would like to thank, in particular, Dimitris Tziovas, Gerry Kearns, Peter Mackridge, Gordon Clark and, above all, Denis Cosgrove to whom I owe special thanks.

Sections of the book have appeared in *Kambos: Cambridge Papers in Modern Greek* (1995), *Ecumene* (1996), *Political Geography* (2000), *Journal of Historical Geography* (in press), and *Journal of Mediterranean Studies* (2000); I am grateful to the editors of all five publications. Part of Chapter One was first presented as a paper in the session on "Hybridities" at the AAG conference in Charlotte, North Carolina, in April 1996, and I would like to thank the panel organizers Nancy Duncan and Joanne Sharp. A version of Chapter Five was similarly given as a lecture in the international conference on national memory in Southeast Europe held on the island of Halki, Greece, in June 1999, and organized by the Centre for Democracy and Reconciliation in Southeast Europe; I am grateful to Maria Todorova for her invitation, and to my godfather Costa Carras for his unstinting support.

In writing a book that covers such expansive tracts of knowledge, I have drawn upon the work of many scholars. They are too numerous to list here, but wherever possible, I have sought to acknowledge them in the course of the book.

National Histories, Natural States was begun at St. Catharine's College, Cambridge and completed at St. Peter's College, Oxford. A Fellowship from the Alexander S. Onassis Public Benefit Foundation in 1996 enabled me to carry out archival research in Athens and I am glad to take this opportunity of thanking the Foundation for its support. I would also like to acknowledge my debt here to Erik Holm and the trustees of the Eleni Nakou Foundation for generously supporting my research with a grant. In particular, however, I am grateful to the Masters and Fellows of both St. Catharine's and St. Peter's for providing me with stimulating environments in which to pursue my research. I am especially indebted to Simon Gaunt for his advice and friendship and to Geoffrey Kantaris who showed me the ropes.

From its inception in 1995, the Interdisciplinary Group on Greek Worlds at Cambridge has been an exciting forum for discussion; it would not have been possible without the wise council of Pat Easterling and the generous support of the A.G. Leventis Foundation; my thanks, in particular, to Dino Leventis. David Holton allowed me to test many of the ideas presented in this book as lectures in the Faculty of Modern and Medieval Languages and I am grateful to him, as well as to my students at Cambridge. Over the years of thinking through and writing this book I have benefited from conversations with family, friends and colleagues and it is a pleasure to acknowledge them here: Roddy Beaton, Philip Carabott, Paul Cartledge, Richard Clogg, Jim and Nancy Duncan, Geoffrey Gilbert, Andonis Papayannis and Michael Peckham. During the last stages of writing this book Yannis Sakellarakis reminded me that archaeologists get their hands dirty. My cousin Steven Runciman first inspired my enthusiasm for Greek worlds; his life and work remain an inspiration.

Sadly, this book was completed after the death of two teachers and close friends to whom I am much indebted. Sidney Greenbaum and Kostis Moskof both stood, like the Alexandrian poet C.P. Cavafy, at a slight angle to the universe. It is no exaggeration to say that without them this book would never have been written. It was Kostis, in particular, who encouraged me to develop my geographical imaginings during an unforgettable Easter spent at the Monastery of Stavronikita on Mount Athos.

Robert Shannan Peckham
St Peter's College, Oxford

Introduction

Two tendencies have become apparent in the process of political recon-figuration that characterizes the beginning of the twenty-first century. On the one hand, migrations and the emergence of ostensibly multi-cultural societies are challenging received ideas about the homogeneity of national cultures. On the other hand, recent years have witnessed the militant "place-bound politics of contemporary nationalisms"[1] that continues to undermine widely held convictions in "the end of history" heralded by Western globalization and an escalating "global cultural flow".[2] The fostering of local and regional identities and the drive for devolution sit uneasily with an ever-increasing centripetal pull.

But are these centrifugal and centripetal forces, in fact, contradic-tory? Are contemporary ideas about collective identities a throwback to essentializing nationalist conceptions of the "nation" and the "region" as "bounded objects in the natural world"? If this is the case, how exactly have these conceptions been severed from the cultural and political processes that engendered them?[3]

This book sets out to explore these questions from an historical perspective. *National Histories, Natural States* is intended as a contribu-tion to ongoing debates about nationhood and nationalism. The term "nationalism" is taken here to encompass both "the related phenomena of national identity (or nationality) and consciousness, and collectivities based on them – nations", as well as the ideological frame-work within which identity is articulated.[4] My purpose in writing the book has been to elucidate the relationship between nation formation, place and the geographical imagination. More specifically, in the pages that follow I argue that modern Greece provides a useful case study that sheds light on the processes through which nations are imagina-tively engineered, and in so doing, underscores the ideological function of cultural narratives in the construction and naturalization of national identity. In exploring the ways in which such narratives were

fabricated to tie disparate histories and territories together, the intention is not, as one commentator has recently remarked in a different
context, "to measure their authenticity against some historical yard-
stick", but rather, "to tease out the complexities of representing a viable
geo-political basis for a collection of territories recently emerged from
colonial domination".[5]

Within this general theoretical orientation the book has three central
aims. Firstly, it sets out to investigate the specific political and cultural
contexts and contingencies within which practices such as geography,
folklore, archaeology and literature were developed. A major concern
of the book is to demonstrate how such practices served to consolidate
territories within the state and legitimate claims to the so-called "unredeemed lands" beyond its borders. Emphasis is placed on the
interrelationships between these activities, to show how professedly
distinct systems of knowledge were inseparable from broader cultural,
social and political formations. A glance at a Greek periodical or newspaper of the mid 1880s, for example, vividly lays bare the multiple
connections between literature and other developing fields of enquiry:
articles on geographical themes are framed by descriptions of archaeological research, short stories, discussions of folkloric material and
political articles.

Secondly, while there are numerous varieties of nationalist experience, this book yields insights into nationalism as a territorial ideology
in Southeast Europe. The concept of the nation (understood here, not
as an organic entity, but rather as an "imagined community"[6]) functioned as a validating framework within which space was defined in late
nineteenth and early twentieth-century Greece. To be sure, from one
perspective it could be argued that nationalism "is nothing if not a
mode of constructing and interpreting social space", while "the notion
of a 'national territory' lies at the root of both the process of national
formation and the rise of nationalism, historically as well as
analytically".[7]

Thirdly, the book maintains that new cultural forms which emerged
during this period contained powerful structures of resistance and were
never fully determined by the institutions that defined them as
national.[8] This counter-discourse of the nation is an important theme
in the book and my aim is to show how, even during periods of militant
nationalism, the nation remains an unstable category, susceptible to
reworkings. Rather than focusing on nationalism as an invariable
cultural process that constructs a coherent and stable order, this book
emphasizes nationalism's internal tensions and underlines the often
discordant political visions that it contains.[9]

The focus is on nationalism as an equivocal force of integration and
disintegration, where the compulsions to assimilate and segregate

frequently contradict one another,[10] as well as on the ambivalence that characterizes the institutions of the nation-state.[11] The book demonstrates how the idea of an unproblematic national identity involves the subjugation of rival identities. In so arguing, it is hard not to make poignant comparisons with contemporary Southeast Europe. As Homi Bhabha reminds us:

> The hideous extremity of Serbian nationalism proves that the very idea of a pure, 'ethnically cleansed' national identity can only be achieved through the death, literal and figurative, of the complex interweavings of history, and the cultural contingent border-lines of modern nationhood.[12]

This process of dominance and sanitization which Bhabha describes can be construed as central to the idea of government as this developed in the nineteenth century. Societies were conceptualized as "objects to be surveyed, regulated and sanitized" in much the same way as colonized peoples were. To this extent, at least, "modernity itself can be understood as a colonialist project"; as a discursive exercise:

> entailing an ethnographically specific knowledge of particular populations, enabled by various methods of documentation, accounts of disorder or backwardness and conceptions of reform and advancement.[13]

Greek nationalism was articulated within the context of specific sociopolitical, economic and cultural developments. The argument presented in *National Histories, Natural States* is that the establishment of a Greek nation-state in the 1830s, carved out of the multi-ethnic Ottoman Empire and sanctioned through claims to the inheritance of ancient Hellas, raises broader issues about the relationship between geographical imaginations and the process of nation formation. From a country of isolated and largely self-governing rural communities an imported, centralized state system sought to nationalize space. State-sponsored practices such as folklore and archaeology endeavoured to gain dominance over the territory claimed by the state by framing relations with the land through a conceptual reorganization of the national space. Although "place" (*topos*) served as a key word in later nineteenth and early twentieth-century nationalist discourse, no attempt has yet been made to explore the relationship between political concerns for territory in Southeast Europe and the prevalent social and cultural preoccupations with place which found a forum in regional geographies, literature, folklore and archaeology. This is a serious omission since developments in comparative cultural studies have intimated the extent to which social life is embedded in space, as well as elucidating the relationship between space, power and knowledge.

During the nineteenth century Greece belonged to a region in which the process of "Europeanization" or "Westernization" was conspicuously played out and much debated. Within a clientelistic system inherited from the Ottomans, an elite sought to build a civil society, to appropriate the forms of modern Western life, and to suppress non-compliant peasant forces.[14] This book explores the constructions of a national space within the contexts of this self-conscious process of modernization and of a belligerent irredentist ideology. The piecemeal expansion of the state from 1863 to 1923 when it assumed its present frontiers (with the exception of the Dodecanese Islands which were ceded to Greece by Italy in 1947) added some 70 percent to Greece's land area and increased the population by more than a third. At a time when Southeast Europe is being politically and geographically reconfigured, the argument is put that we have much to learn about the mappings and re-mappings of the region over the last two hundred years, a period formative of the present Balkan crisis. As commentators have pointed out, with the break-up of Yugoslavia and the ensuing conflagration in the Balkans, the Empire has indeed struck back. *National Histories, Natural States* deals with wider processes that continue to have far-reaching repercussions. Although the book begins with an account of the mappings of Greece in the eighteenth and early nineteenth centuries, the main focus falls on the period roughly between 1870 and 1922.

In the pages that follow an attempt is made to map the processes involved in the imaginative construction of the nation across different cultural fields in order to show how the nation was both the object and product of interwoven institutional practices. The first two chapters sketch out an historical context for the rest of the book and concentrate largely on the years immediately before and after the establishment of the Greek Kingdom in 1830. Chapter One sets the scene by charting the emergence of a new concept of national territory that found expression in the writings of Greek intellectuals within the Ottoman Empire during the late eighteenth and early nineteenth centuries. The focus here is on the increasingly secular definitions of the nation which were formulated within broader debates about the interrelationship between language and territory, culture and environment. Pervading these debates were conflicting interpretations of "culture" (*politismos*) – a word that was coined during this period (1804). On the one hand, the *Volk* were celebrated as a repository of Greek history and national identity, organically linked to the land. On the other hand, the people had to be instructed in an arduous process of re-education. Nineteenth and twentieth-century concerns with nationalizing space, I suggest, need to be viewed within the light of culture's contested meanings.

Chapter Two considers the ways in which territory was incorporated into the independent Greek Kingdom following the War of Independence through a process of "naturalizing" the political history of the state's foundations. A reading of Panayiotis Soutsos's epistolary novel *Leandros* (1834) – among other texts – within the context of contemporary political, social and economic concerns, serves as a point of departure for exploring the ideological context of landscape production within a nationalist discourse. The symbolic structuring of space in the novel is inseparable, I argue, from the geographical construction of a national homeland and underlines the text's role in imagining a solution to the problems of the state's geographical, cultural and political fragmentation. The chapter provides an introduction to the book's main aim, which is to demonstrate how, during the second half of the nineteenth and early twentieth centuries, different practices sought to tie the newly acquired territories together in an effort to establish Greek culture's spatial integrity through history, as well as its historical integrity through space.

Chapter Three considers the meanings that accumulated around the concept of the "frontier" in Greek nationalist thought and focuses on the debates in Greece about the imperative to define the Greek Kingdom's boundaries. An analysis of these debates sheds light on a wider process: the naturalizing of boundaries in late nineteenth-century Europe. Attention is paid to the "cartographic anxiety"[15] which was born with the new state as the majority of Greeks had been left in Ottoman lands beyond the fledgling state's boundaries. This apprehension found expression in the proliferation of "frontier fictions". Divergent attitudes towards the position of Greece's boundaries, I maintain, reflected markedly different conceptions of Greek identity and the different terms (geographical, ethnographical, political, historical and cultural) on which Greek identity was argued.

The next five chapters are devoted to an examination of the different practices within which the Greek nation was mapped. Chapter Four considers the role of folklore in Greece and argues that folklore developed as a practice that aimed at unifying a national space. In so doing, it was mobilized to identify and abolish regional differences through a process of internal colonization. The aim is to show how the celebration of local, regional identities in Greece during this period was bound up with the "erasure of differences" upon which the nation's cultural uniformity rested.[16] To this extent, I argue, the folklorist was involved in eradicating the very traditions he sought to preserve.

Subsequent sections of the book develop these insights. Chapter Five explores the production of regional geographies and histories in

Greece within the context of the state's modernizing drive. The argument is put that the particularities of "place" were construed both as underpinning a territorial expansion and as a resistance to the homogenizing drive of a state-sponsored nationalism. Chapter Six focuses on works of prose fiction and considers, in particular, the importance of the island as a setting that provided an imagined resolution to the problems of the nation's indeterminate boundaries. Chapter Seven examines the ideological role of archaeology and the ways in which material and figurative excavations mutually reinforced and fed into each other, in the same way that fictive and physical mappings sustained the nation-building project. Chapter Eight considers the role of cartography and of formal geographical knowledge in legitimating claims to, and consolidating, territory. The rival claims over Macedonia by the Serbs, Greeks, Bulgarians and Turks prompted the so-called "map mania" in the 1870s as national antagonisms were played out in conflicting cartographic representations of the southern Balkans.

In adopting an interdisciplinary approach, the book is clearly indebted to those theoretical orientations that have been developed through disciplinary crossings between geography, the social sciences and comparative literary studies; a cross-fertilization that has contributed substantially to an understanding of culture as a dynamic process through which societies reciprocally define themselves and others.[17] *National Histories, Natural States* engages with and seeks to build upon a number of theoretical contributions in cultural and political geography: particularly the emphasis on social formation and the connections drawn between landscape and national identity. The application of literary theory and the textual model of landscape interpretation have suggested ways in which notions of textual communities joined by shared readings may be further developed to shed light on those processes of national imagining which Benedict Anderson has proposed. The theoretical argument of the book has also been sharpened through an engagement with the growing body of writing within comparative literary studies and cultural history that has sought to explore the meanings of place and space. *National Histories, Natural States* seeks to elucidate the spatial tropes that underlie new theoretical models, where "theorists are using the language and experience of space to build their arguments and to construct their political approaches".[18]

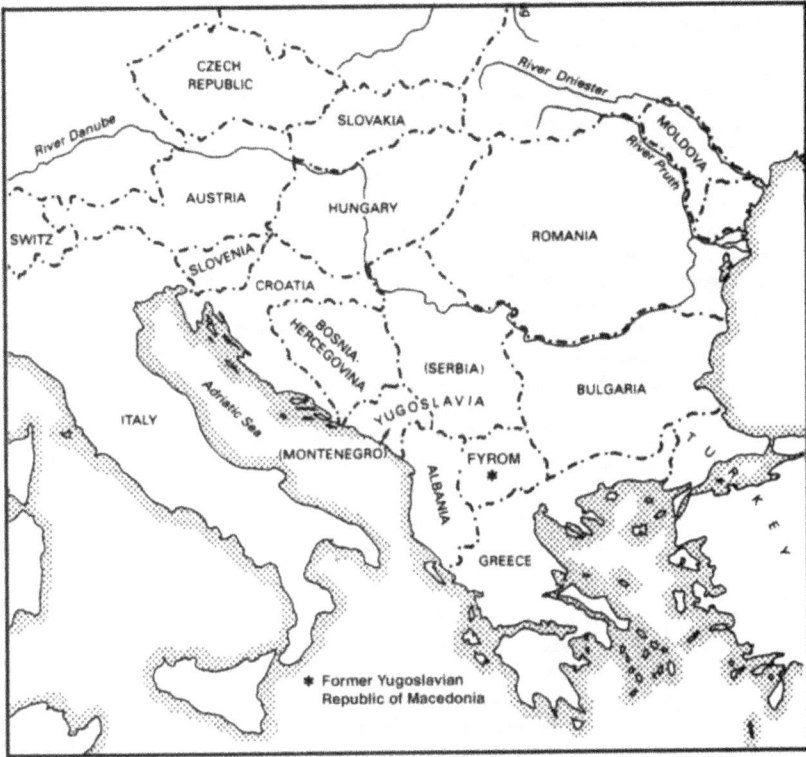

Greece

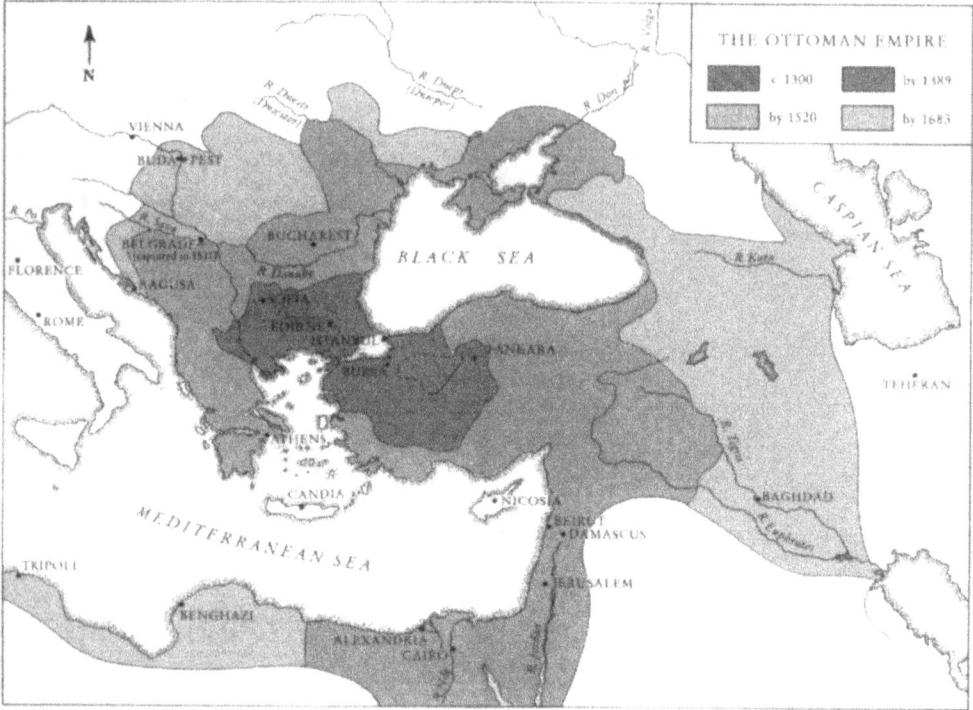

The Ottoman Empire, 1300–1700

Chapter One

Mapping the nation: language, geography and the new ethnography

In some form or another it is probable that every community through the ages, whether local, tribal, religious, or national, has pictured a homeland; a promised land of origin and return. From this perspective, it could be argued, the homeland is a transhistorical category that harks back to pre-modern and immemorial affiliations of people with territory. Certainly, this is how the motherland or fatherland was construed by emergent nationalist ideologies in late eighteenth and nineteenth-century Europe, when territorial claims were legitimated through reference to providential myths of the nation's pedigree and rootedness. As Konstantinos Oikonomos (1780–1857), an Orthodox cleric and champion of Greek independence, declared in a sermon delivered in 1819 to a Greek community at Ayvalik in Asia Minor and re-issued by the influential Greek journal *Estia* in the 1870s:

> Everyone claims that they have a fatherland (*patrida*), but unfortunately few understand what a homeland is...a homeland is the image of an earthly paradise which God gave man in the beginning to cultivate and to protect.[1]

In the same year as Oikonomos preached his sermon, in the preface to a Greek edition of Abbé Barthélemy's *Voyage du Jeune Anacharsis en Grèce* published in Vienna, the Greek translator declared that:

> there is nothing in the world more honourable, nor desirable, more sacred than the [Fatherland]...in short, patriots of all nations think of nothing else, breathe nothing else, have no other wish, than the advantage, the increase and the glory of the [Fatherland].[2]

1

But what is a "fatherland"? What defines a nation and gives a community legitimate rights to a homeland? Reflecting on definitions of the nation at the close of the nineteenth century, the political economist Walter Bagehot echoed St. Augustine's observations on the elusiveness of time as a graspable concept, when he concluded: "We know what it is when you do not ask us, but we cannot very quickly explain or define it".[3] The insistence with which the question "what it is a nation?" was posed in the course of the nineteenth century – the century, as Bagehot would have it, of "nation-making" – suggests that the contemporary preoccupation with the same question cannot readily be taken to herald the advent of a *post*-national era. In his portentous treatise *Degeneration* (1892), the Austrian Max Simon Nordau diagnosed the gathering "Dusk of Nations". A century later another dusk is being evoked; that twilight in which, as Hegel foresaw, Minerva's prophetic owl takes flight, "circling round nations and nationalism".[4]

The proliferation of global, transnational networks since the end of the Second World War has not, as was widely expected, led inevitably to the dissolution of national affiliations. In the early twenty-first century, as millions remain caught up in struggles over contested visions of homelands in the multi-ethnic state that was the former Soviet Union and on Greece's borders in Southeast Europe, questions about the relationship between state and nation, about rights to self-determination, about the connections between ethnicity, language, and territory, are being posed with ever-increasing urgency. If the resurgent nationalism sweeping through the Balkans with the break-up of Yugoslavia in 1991 has drawn attention to any single characteristic of nationalism, it is surely this: the importance of geographical awareness. At a time when some critics were writing the obituary of the nation and grandly proclaiming "the end of history", a nationalist upsurge has drawn attention back to the inseparable relationship between a people's territorial affiliations and the articulation of national identity; between the contingent symbols, "cultural shreds and patches used by nationalism" and the stark reality of political conflict.[5] As Benedict Anderson has remarked: "nationness is the most universally legitimate value in the political life of our time".[6] We continue to see the world through a "nationalising eye".[7]

1.2   THE STATE OF THE GREEK NATION

Before 1830 there was no Greek state. The Peloponnese, or Morea, and the districts of central Greece known as Roumeli formed part of the Ottoman Empire; an expansive multi-ethnic, religious and linguistic dominion that stretched (at least nominally in the early nineteenth century) from the tip of the Arabian peninsula at Aden, through North Africa, into the Balkans – a Turkish word meaning "mountains".[8] The territories of the Peloponnese, part of Roumeli, Evia, the islands of the Cyclades and a small portion of Epirus, which were later absorbed into the independent Greek Kingdom following the War of Independence in 1821, amounted to approximately 48,000 square kilometres which were governed by local Ottoman overlords under the suzerainty of the Sultan in Constantinople. The majority of the population, totalling some 750,000, were Greek – perhaps something in the region of 80 percent – but they lived in small, isolated communities.[9] In his memoirs Theodoros Kolokotronis (1770–1843), the fighter of the Greek War of Independence, observed that it was not until the French Revolution and Napoleon's occupation of the Ionian Islands in 1797, after the end of Venetian control, that the Greeks awoke to a more inclusive sense of national community. "The French Revolution and the doings of Napoleon", he declared, "opened the eyes of the world":[10]

> ...it was not until our rising that all the Greeks were brought into communication. There were men who knew of no place beyond a mile of their own locality. They thought of Zante [Zakynthos] as we now speak of the most distant parts of the world. They said it was in France.[11]

Before the domination of the eastern Mediterranean by the Ottoman Turks, the Greek populations constituted part of the Byzantine Empire, a vast multi-ethnic "commonwealth"[12] that at its height in the sixth century during the rule of Justinian I (reigned 527–565) included southern Spain, Italy, the Middle East, North Africa and the Balkans. The fall of Constantinople, the bastion of eastern Christianity, to the Ottomans under Mehmed II in May 1453 marked a decisive end to Byzantine pre-eminence and inaugurated a period of Ottoman consolidation in the region. In 1522 Rhodes was taken, followed by Cyprus in 1571 and Crete in 1669. Most Greek lands, with the exception of the Ionian Islands which remained Venetian, fell into Ottoman hands. In Greek historiography this long period is known as the *Tourkokratia*, the period of Turkish rule.

The vast majority of Greeks lived within the Ottoman Empire as *rayas* – a word meaning flock but designating subjects who were not members of the ruling Ottoman caste – under a system of administration that grouped populations into *millets*, or nations, organized on the basis of religious faith. The Orthodox *millet*, or *millet-i-Rum* (the "Greek" *millet*), although dominated by Greeks, embraced numerous ethnicities including Bulgarians, Romanians, Serbs, Vlachs, Albanians and Arabs. As Hans Vermeulen has observed:

> [U]ntil the beginning of the nineteenth century, the Slavs, Greeks and Vlahs still constituted one Christian community, united in the Rum millet. A peasant felt himself first of all as a member of a family, a village community and maybe a small culturally-distinguishable unit, and, secondly Rum.[13]

To this extent, the *millet* "reflected in microcosm the ethnic heterogeneity of the empire".[14] The issue of identity was itself contentious since numerous terms of self-definition were interwoven with, and complicated, the notion of "Greekness". The word *Romii*, although used to signify an adherent of the Ecumenical Patriarchate at Constantinople (whence *millet-i-Rum*), came to be used to designate Greeks. Towards the end of the eighteenth century the word *Ellines* or "Hellenes" began to re-establish itself.

Within the Empire Greeks assumed positions of authority. The so-called *Phanariots* were members of a Greek administrative elite within the Empire who took their name from the *Phanar* (Lighthouse) district on the Golden Horn in Constantinople, where the Patriarchate had moved at the beginning of the seventeenth century. From their courts at Bucharest and Jassy, which were open to cultural influences from Vienna (a city described by Adamantios Korais, despite his dislike of the Austrian Empire, as "the workshop of the literature of the Greeks"[15]) by way of the river Danube, Greek *hospodars*, or hereditary princes, had governed the Principalities of Wallachia and Moldavia (today's Romania) since the beginning of the eighteenth century.[16] If "South-eastern Europe was ruled by the Turks", Charles Eliot remarked, "its religion, education, commerce and finance were in the hands of the Greeks".[17] It was during the end of the eighteenth century that, for a number of reasons linked to social, cultural and political changes – not least the preoccupation in Europe with ancient Greece – that the Greeks began to articulate a clear awareness of their national identity and to conceptualize that identity in spatial terms as an organic affiliation to a distinct territory: Greece. As Elie Kedourie has remarked "Greek [nationalism] may be considered the first to appear outside Western Christendom, among a community ruled by non-Christians and itself hitherto violently hostile to all Western nations".[18]

1.3 LINGUISTIC COMMUNITIES

In Greece, as in Germany, ideas of a bounded national community were initially mapped out as a literary enterprise, "integration being achieved textually before being achieved politically".[19] The modern nation was affirmed through reference to an indigenous culture which, it was argued, had been forged by singular historical, cultural, and environmental conditions. Cultural representations played an important part in the process of laying claim to, and integrating, so-called "unredeemed" lands.[20] A fact which explains, in great part, the controversy that surrounds the Macedonian conflict today, a contest which has been fought largely over the interpretation of "cultural shreds and patches".[21]

The notion that there are linguistic communities whose borders define the nation, and that languages are peculiar to particular places, landscapes and peoples, constitutes a set of ideas about culture and the environment which circulated in the second half of the eighteenth and early nineteenth centuries, a period in which profound economic, social and political realignments within the Ottoman Empire contributed to a Greek cultural revival.[22] Montesquieu's (1689–1755) writings had been translated into Greek.[23] In his *De l'Esprit des Lois* (1748) Montesquieu had accentuated the climatic and geographical variations which shaped history and determined social behaviour, although he argued that these were not insuperable and it was the legislators' role to counteract them. His work was known to Adamantios Korais (1748–1833), one of the leaders of the Greek cultural revival who, as we shall see, was himself concerned with exploring the mutual relationship between peoples and places. Montesquieu had acknowledged the role of social practices and customs which were, he maintained, reciprocally influenced by societies in reaction to their physical surroundings. Johann Gottfried von Herder (1744–1803) was subsequently to stress the dynamic, constitutive role of language. For Herder distinct languages were immemorial and reflected discrete national communities. The *Volk* formed part of a linguistic community of shared traditions and collective memories which were embodied in folklore. Multi-ethnic political formations such as the Habsburg Empire or the Ottoman Empire that overrode the organic boundaries of the *Volk* were, as a consequence, aberrations. This view of the Ottoman Empire as an "unnatural" polity was widespread throughout the late nineteenth century. Edward Freeman, for example, argued in 1882 that "the Ottoman Turks are an artificial nation".[24]

These ideas were to have an important impact in Southeast Europe and an interest in ethnographic distributions was further promoted by the study of folklore and vernaculars. It was during the early decades of the nineteenth century, in particular, that linguistic affinity, rather than religion, became the dominant criterion of community; a tendency exemplified in Adrian Balbi's ethnographic atlas of the world (1828).[25] At least since the eighteenth century, language had been closely bound up for Greeks with definitions of the nation. Throughout Central and Southeast Europe, nationality and language consciousness became indissoluble. For the Slavic populations within the Austrian Empire, resistance to German hegemony was asserted through the espousal of national Slavic languages.[26] In 1792 Josef Dobrovsky's first systematic history of the Czech language and literature appeared, while Josef Jungmann's Czech-German dictionary was published between 1835 and 1839.[27] Herder had maintained that in the absence of political unity, the German language, as a medium of German culture, characterized Germanness. In Germany, as in Greece, nationhood was first and foremost "an ethnocultural fact".[28] The *Volkessprache* was not deemed politically important until the late eighteenth century, when the nation began to be envisaged in ethnolinguistic terms. The politicization of a German cultural identity was sown by the Napoleonic wars and with it, the idea of a German nation-state.[29]

In part because of the wide geographical distribution of the Greeks in diasporic communities within the Russian Empire, the Balkans and the eastern Mediterranean, language and religion, rather than affiliation to a distinct territory, became the chief determinants of Greek national identity. Grigorios Zalikoglou (1777–1827), the Greek translator of Rousseau who lived in Paris and wrote a posthumously published history of the Greek War of Independence (1828), entreated his fellow countryman to "guard our [i.e. the Greek] Language, if we want our nation and our faith to exist vigorously for all time", remarking in the preface to his popular Greek-French dictionary (1809), that language is:

> the only ancestral treasure that remains to us, the one certain pole which draws us together and embraces us, the one natural bond that unites us. Myriads of others share the same faith, but not having the same language will never become one with us...the language has guarded the nation.[30]

Greek remained the *lingua franca* of the Balkans to such an extent that the Habsburg authorities classified Balkan Orthodox merchants indiscriminately as Greeks.[31]

A few years after Zalikoglou's pronouncement, Korais, who was born in Smyrna and came from a Greek mercantile family, was to assert in the same vein that "nothing is more public than language; it obeys neither monarchy or oligarchy. Language, this is the nation."[32] A person could be exiled from his homeland and subjugated by an oppressive power but, according to Korais, he could never be banished from his linguistic inheritance since "language is one of the nation's most inalienable possessions".[33] Korais's assertions were made in the same spirit as the folklorist Jacob Grimm's remark that language "owes its birth and development to the fact that we are free; it is our history, our heritage".[34]

The Bulgarian *vûzrazhdane*, or late eighteenth-century national revival, too, and partly in response to Greek claims and the Hellenization of the *millet-i-Rum*, involved a similar championing of the Bulgarian vernacular. The Bulgarians, like other non-Greek members of the "Greek" *millet*, became increasingly exasperated by the Greek stranglehold over the Orthodox Church. Thus, in his *Slavonic-Bulgarian History of the Peoples, Tsars, Saints, and of all their Deeds and of the Bulgarian Way of Life,* the monk Paiisi Hilendarski (Paisy of Khilendar), chronicled the glorious deeds of the medieval tsars and saints and warned against the dangers of Hellenization, entreating his fellow Bulgarians to "keep close to your heart your race and your Bulgarian homeland":

> But, they say, the Greeks are wiser and more cultured, while the Bulgarians are simple and foolish and have no refined words. That is why, they say, we had better join the Greeks. But…there are many peoples wiser and more glorious than the Greeks. Is any Greek foolish enough to abandon his language and his teaching and his people as you abandon yours…? Bulgarians, do not deceive yourself, know your own nation and language by studying your own tongue.[35]

Such pleas were aimed at countering the process of Bulgarian absorption into Greek culture as intimated in Daniel of Moschopolis's *Introductory Instruction* (1762), a work which was explicitly conceived as a manual to teach Greek to non-Greek Orthodox Christians in the Balkans:

> Albanians, Wallachians, Bulgarians, speakers of other tongues, rejoice,
> And ready yourselves all to become Greeks.
> Abandoning your barbaric tongue, speech and customs,
> So that to your descendants they may appear as myths.[36]

In the late eighteenth century, dictionaries of Romanian appeared, while the argument of replacing Cyrillic by the Roman alphabet gained momentum.[37]

Particularly influential in the debate about a national Greek language was Dimitrios Katartzis (1730–1807), a Phanariot aristocrat and high court judge who was active in the court of Bucharest. Katartzis energetically promoted modern Greek, putting forward proposals for educational reforms between 1783 and 1791 in which he argued for the use of a Greek vernacular ("the domestic style of Constantinople") as the language of education and culture. In 1780

Katartzis declared that the Greek language was the most poetic of all languages, superior even to classical Greek, and the expression of the nation. In this light, he composed a grammar to provide a basis for his educational programme, placing Modern Greek on an even par with the ancient language.[38] Katartzis was "probably the first among authors writing in Modern Greek to use the Greek word for nation, *ethnos*, to describe a collectivity clearly delineated by its language and cultural heritage".[39]

The vigorous exchange between Neophytos Doukas (1760–1845) and Ignatius, Archbishop of Wallachia, further underlined the revolutionary implications of this politicization of culture, which the anonymous pamphlet entitled *Hellenic Nomarchy* (1806), published in Livorno, was quick to acknowledge. The publication stressed Karageorge's Serbian insurrection of 1804 against the Ottomans as an example for the Greeks to emulate.[40] Doukas's anxieties focused on the confined demographic distribution of Greeks. In his *Letter to the Ecumenical Patriarch of Constantinople Cyril*, which was published in Vienna in 1815, Doukas, who is somewhat misleadingly characterized as a reactionary on account of his use of Atticized Greek, called for a cultural mission to revitalize and extend the Greek nation through a process of linguistic assimilation; a process rejected vehemently by Ignatius. In particular, Doukas urged the Patriarch to send monks from Mount Athos to teach Greek in regions where it was not spoken:

> Just as our language has been, as it were, completely compressed and confined to the smallest possible area, so too has the Greek nation been reduced...Despite this, however, it could derive advantages in other respects if it receives the necessary attention; because no other nation can extend its language to the same degree as we can. On the one hand, through intermixture with those around us in Bulgaria, Wallachia, Albania, Asia and elsewhere, and on the other hand, because of the elegance and usefulness of our tongue.[41]

The Church, and particularly the Patriarchate in Constantinople, had played a key role in preserving Greek identity within the Ottoman Empire. The long established Patriarchal Academy, for example, contributed a decisive role in promoting the Greek language. While the ecclesiastical intelligentsia had dominated the educational system, it had further "helped to constrain the regional development of popular Greek in circumstances that would otherwise have promoted wider fragmentation of the kind that had begun in the most peripheral regions".[42]

For Doukas, a proponent of "archaic" Greek for whom the modern language was a humiliating symbol of national servitude, the Greek nation was pre-eminently a linguistic community and one which could readily assimilate other races through a process of cultural domination in which the Orthodox Church was destined to play a leading role. The Greeks controlled the higher reaches of the Orthodox ecclesiastical hierarchy, suppressing Serbian and Bulgarian attempts at independence. This emphasis on the importance of the Church as the disseminator of Greek was likewise stressed, albeit in more moderate terms, by the civil servant and diplomat Panayiotis Kodrikas (1762–1827) who, like Korais, lived for part of his life in Paris where he was a representative of the Ottoman Empire.[43] At the same time, however, Kodrikas could attack the position of Moisiodax, a champion for cultural change and the use of vernacular Greek, by casting aspersions upon his ethnic background:

> But he was a foreigner to the nation of the Greeks by birth and consequently had not tasted the milk of a Greek upbringing. For him the Greek language was a question of learning and study and not naturally acquired by habit and use since infancy…his hearing was not accustomed to the harmony of the language of the Modern Greeks.[44]

1.4   NEW GEOGRAPHIES

Although the idea of "natural frontiers" did not surface until the end of the eighteenth century – notably in the defence of France's borders made in 1792 by the revolutionary leader Georges Danton (1759–1794)[45] – in contrast to a trend towards defined boundaries in Western Europe, those in Eastern Europe and the Balkan lands of the Ottoman Empire "remained vague, shifting according to the interests of the local authorities".[46] It was not until the Treaty of Carlowitz between the Habsburg and Ottoman Empires in 1698, following Kara Mustafa's defeat before the walls of Vienna in September 1683, that a commission was established to map out the new frontier (1699–1701).[47] Maps were used in the negotiations to settle the Austro-Turkish frontier at the end of the century.[48]

Increasingly, however, during the eighteenth century language and territory were being linked in geographical literature produced chiefly by Phanariot Greeks in the Ottoman principalities of Wallachia and Moldavia. The Phanariot Iakovos Rizos Neroulos (1778–1849) underlined the importance of geographical knowledge in his *Histoire Moderne de la Grèce* (1825).[49] While they were influenced by liberal ideas of the Enlightenment and, later, by the French Revolution, Greek writers also articulated Romantic concerns for language as the expression of a

distinct national character which was organically attached to a particular place. A category of historical and geographical writing emerged
which focused on regional history and geography, combining the gathering of ethnographic data with a conviction in geography's moral and
religious purpose. As the critic K. Th. Dimaras has observed, this
interest in language and geography came close to Herder's
preoccupations.[50]

Two outstanding figures were the geographers Daniil Philippidis
(1755–1832) and Grigorios Konstantas (1758–1844), both clerics from
the village of Milies in Pelion, who formed part of Katartzis's circle.[51]
Their voluminous *Modern Geography*, which was published in Vienna in
1791, belongs to a body of eighteenth and early nineteenth-century
texts which strove to map out the homeland. In 1716 Chrysanthos
Notaras had published his *Introduction to Geography* in Vienna and in
1728 the metropolitan bishop, Meletios of Ioannina, produced his
seminal work of historical geography entitled *Ancient and New Geography*. Meletios was one of the first geographers to argue for the
importance of investigating ancient remains as a way of demonstrating
Greek cultural continuity. His encyclopaedic book ranged widely and
included descriptions of Africa and China, as well as Europe. In 1760
Yeoryios Fatzeas's *Geographical Grammar* appeared, which was a translation of a work by the mathematician Pat Gordon,[52] and in 1781 Iosipos
Moisiodax published the revised edition of his pioneering study of
mathematical geography, *Theory of Geography*, which consisted in large
part of lectures which he had given in the Princely Academy in Jassy.[53]

Philippidis and Konstantas's *Modern Geography*, which was published
a decade after Moisiodax's, drew the favourable notice of the distinguished geographer and cosmographer Jean Denis Barbié du Bocage
(1797), a founding member of the Paris Geographical Association and
the pupil of d'Anville, who had drawn up the maps for the third
edition of Barthélemy's *Voyage du Jeune Anacharsis en Grèce* in 1791 – the
account of an imaginary journey by Anacharsis the Younger though
Greece in the fourth century BC.[54] Korais, a correspondent of du
Bocage, had himself translated Hippocrates's *On Airs, Waters and Places*,
as well as Pausanias's *Description of Greece* and Strabo's *Geography*.[55]
Reviewing Korais's translation in the *Edinburgh Review*, one contemporary commented on the situation of modern Greece and noted that:
"An acquaintance with the great geographer is of the highest importance to those who travel through Greece and Asia Minor".[56]

Geographic knowledge was explicitly placed within the political
context of Greek subjection within the Ottoman Empire. In a speech
on the state of Greece which he delivered before the *Société des Observa-
teurs de l'Homme* in Paris in 1803 – one of the first anthropological
institutions which sought to study society and culture as part of natural

history and which included as a member the biologist and botanist Jean-Baptiste Lamarck (1744–1829)[57] – Korais specifically noted the production of geographical texts and maps as a sign of Greek rehabilitation:

> Geographical maps in Modern Greek have been known for several years, and geographical books have appeared in which one finds several districts of Greece described in detail.[58]

Undoubtedly, Korais's most detailed exploration of the relationship between peoples and places is contained in the extensive preface to his 1800 translation of Hippocrates's treatise *On Airs, Waters and Places*; a text which analyzes the effect of climate and region on people and details the different geophysical conditions of Europe and Asia. Korais extends the scope of Hippocrates's treatise by noting national differences and seeking to relate these, on the one hand, to climatic conditions and geography. Montesquieu, Korais believed, had been profoundly influenced by Hippocratic theories.[59] On the other hand, a country like China, or for that matter France, has a recognizably distinct national identity, he argues, even though the nation includes different climatic zones. Korais here maintains that "character" is constituted by both geophysical influences, as well as by a people's "spiritual" or "moral" energy.[60] He laments his poor knowledge of Greek geography and emphasizes the need for detailed topographic surveys:

> In the absence of any help that I might have derived from an actual inspection of the Greek places (*lieux*) where Hippocrates made his observations, I sought to make up for this failing by exacting all the enlightenment I could get from topographies of different countries of Europe and particularly of France...[61]

This interest in the relationship between culture and environment was fuelled by the connections between nature, culture and political freedom which were central to the European preoccupation with Greek culture from the second half of the eighteenth century. The German scholar and critic August Wilhelm von Schlegel (1767–1845), in a series of lectures delivered on dramatic art and literature in 1808 in Vienna, for example, asserted that the ancient Greeks were the finest product of a "natural education". Schlegel sought to relate Greek concerns for liberty to the auspicious climate.[62] Such views owed much to the archaeologist and art historian Johann Joachim Winckelmann's (1717–1768) writings, which played a large part in shifting emphasis from Rome further east to Greece as a republican ideal that represented the spirit of liberty. The discovery of Pompeii in 1748, a city founded as an ancient Greek colony, had renewed interest in Hellenic culture and Winckelmann strongly believed in the importance of the environment as a determinant of cultural identity. "To the Greek climate", he wrote, "we owe the production of Taste and from thence it spread at length over all the polite world".[63]

At the same time, travellers to Greece from the end of the eighteenth century and the beginning of the nineteenth century, such as Edward Dodwell, Sir William Gell and William Martin Leake, sought to combine antiquarian interests with accurate descriptions, both of ancient monuments and of the physical surroundings in which these were located.[64] In this sense, the French survey of 1828 (which is discussed in Chapter Two) belongs to a body of texts which increasingly sought to investigate Greek archaeological remains within the context of a more discursive description of place and culture. As we shall see in subsequent chapters of this book, the linkage of place and culture was to work its way into Greek thinking through the impact of German geographers such as Alexander von Humboldt (1769–1859) and Karl Ritter (1779–1859), who travelled around the Peloponnese in the company of his pupil, the archaeologist Ernst Curtius in 1837.[65]

The relationship between climate, landscape and Greece's cultural richness, however, posed several problems for writers and travellers of the eighteenth and early nineteenth century. If it was true that the benevolence of the Greek environment gave rise to Hellenic culture, how could the present-day Greeks have degenerated to a condition of subservience? If travellers like Robert Wood insisted that Homer's verse was an authentic transcription of Greece's geography and history, underlining the continuity of the Homeric landscapes which were still clearly recognizable, other commentators pointed to the conspicuous changes.[66] What was at stake was the Greek claim to represent Classical Greek culture and increasingly that claim was being asserted and contested in terms of the inter-dependence of the modern Greeks with the Greek landscape.

The title of Philippidis and Konstantas's work, *Modern Geography*, encapsulates the authors' desire to promote innovative scientific ideas from Europe. Like Katartzis, the authors of *Modern Geography* extolled the Greek language as the most beautiful of all languages, while a description of Greece is included between entries devoted to Britain, France and Germany. Their aim was to write in a language which would make their work accessible and give the Greeks "the possibility of redis-covering their physical space, of housing their history".[67] The spoken language is celebrated by Philippidis and Konstantas as the central defining characteristic of the nation. Accordingly, by rejecting the vernacular in favour of the ancient language, Greeks were undermining their own national identity. For Philippidis and Konstantas the Greek language was evidence of the Greek nation's distinctiveness, even while it demonstrated further proof of Greece's European status since, according to the authors, it shared common elements with English, via Celtic. As the geographer Antonios Miliarakis asserted in 1885:

> ...they belonged to the large body of teachers of the nation (*yenos*) who, during the years of Greece's slavery, created with much labour and in the face of many dangers, oases in the midst of the desert and wasteland, summoning the new generation to drink from the spring of knowledge, to find consolation in learning and moral rejuvenation in the cultivation of the verdant pasture of ancient memories.[68]

More particularly, their aim in writing *Modern Geography* was to fill the gap in geographical knowledge which was, in their view, an important national task since geography fostered a sense of national loyalty.

The relativist approach adopted by the authors of *Modern Geography* came out of the discovery of non-European languages which had made it possible to think of Europe as one amongst many civilizations, a realization that was inextricably bound up with the championing of national vernaculars and crucial for the development of the comparative ethnology of the Enlightenment.[69] Such a comparative perspective is evident when, reflecting on the reasons why the Ancient Greek language should have been corrupted into its present form of regional variations, Grigorios Paliouritis notes in his *Greek Archaeology* (1815) what the consequence would be if: "the French were to fall under the yoke of a foreign nation, and the seat of wisdom passed to Africa...".[70]

Towards the end of the eighteenth century, then, older conceptions of an all-embracing Orthodox Christian community in Southeast Europe were being redefined along ethnic lines into linguistic communities. Secular definitions of nations were replacing communities held together by a shared faith.[71] A tension became apparent between ideas of specific "territorial bonds of secular citizenship" and the religious-communal experience of the *millet*; a tension which was to have far-reaching repercussions well into the twentieth century.[72] The ethnic and linguistic subdivisions within the *millet-i-Rum* began to sharpen. In a Balkan society characterized by fluid social, economic and cultural exchanges the boundaries separating ethnicities were being "tightened, reified, or closed".[73] This shift is evident in the increasing number of Greek secular books being published: in 1725 eighty percent of books published were religious, by 1800 it had dropped to fifty-three percent.[74] A pre-national, ecumenical conception of Balkan culture and society, which the Romanian historian Nikolai Iorga called

"Byzance après Byzance",[75] is articulated in the poetry of Konstantinos Dapontes. The poet was born on the island of Skopelos in 1714 and served in the hospodar courts of the Principalities before becoming a monk on Mount Athos in 1753, where he assumed the name of Kaisarios. Dapontes's narrative poem *Garden of Graces* is an account of his nine years of wanderings with a section of the true cross to raise money for the Athonite monastery of Xeropotamou.[76]

Slowly, inter-state interactions and conflicts – notably the reverses experienced by the Ottomans during the Russo-Turkish campaigns that culminated in the Treaty of Küçük Kaynarca (1774) – together with a closer familiarity with the countries beyond the borders of Southeast Ottoman Europe, were stimulating new cultural and political perspectives.[77] The emergence of a secular intelligentsia and of an entrepreneurial elite in the towns, together with increasingly powerful rural notables, eroded traditional Ottoman concepts of authority and the *millet* system itself.[78] In the 1790s Rigas Velestinlis (1757–1798), the protomartyr of Greek independence, who had formerly served as secretary to Alexandros Ypsilantis, chief interpreter to the Ottoman Porte in Constantinople, had published his revolutionary proclamation, the *Declaration of the Rights of Man and the New Political Constitution of the Inhabitants of Roumeli, Asia Minor, the Archipelago, Moldavia and Wallachia*. This document, which was clearly influenced by the French constitutions of 1793 and 1795, envisaged the overthrow of the Ottoman Empire and its replacement with a multi-ethnic state modelled on the Byzantine Empire, in which Greek would be the official language and Greeks would dominate. Rigas, who had a life-long enthusiasm for geography and cartography, also produced a map in twelve sections engraved by Franz Müller and entitled *Map of Hellas Including its Islands and a Part of its Numerous Colonies in Europe and Asia Minor* (1797), which depicted a reconstituted Greek Empire and marked famous ancient and Byzantine Greek sites. Nine of the twelve sheets contained allusions to Barthélemy's *Voyage du Jeune Anacharsis en Grèce* (parts of which Rigas had translated[79]), while his own maps were based on du Bocage's atlas, as well as on information drawn from Meletios's geography and the work of Philippidis and Konstantas. It has been argued that the map "was designed for use in a military campaign" and one of Rigas's friends, Argentis, who had contributed to the cost of publishing Rigas's work, admitted that they had been produced "with the purpose of 'liberating the Morea'".[80]

In the newly founded academies at Jassy and Bucharest, as well as in the schools established in the prosperous Greek communities of Chios, Smyrna, and Ayvalik on the Asia Minor coast, and in the areas on the Black Sea recently annexed by Russia, the emphasis began to shift to the classics, mathematics, and natural sciences under the influence of

Enlightenment ideas and encouraged by an increasingly influential Greek mercantile bourgeoisie.[81] As Korais observed:

> ...schools are already being enlarged, and the study of foreign languages and even of those sciences which are taught in Europe is being introduced into them. The wealthy sponsor the printing of books translated from Italian, French, German, and English; they send to Europe at their expense young men eager to learn; they give their children a better education, not excepting girls...[82]

In particular, geography and history began to be taught in Greek schools by the end of the eighteenth century, notably in the Academies of Jassy and Bucharest, but also in Smyrna, Trieste, Athens, Chios and on the Ionian Islands. In the preface to his *Theory of Geography* Moisiodax declared: "Geography is one of the most necessary sciences and, consequently, must be taught in all schools".[83]

The preoccupation with the national community did not exclude more focused interests in localities. On the contrary, the one was closely related to the other. In their *Modern Geography* Philippidis and Konstantas paid attention to regional variations and, in particular, to their native Pelion in central Greece, from which they took their name "Dimitries" ("Dimitrias" being the ancient name for modern Volos):

> ...let others imitate us and let each person describe his own place of birth, not mathematically, or with geographical exactitude, noting longitudes and latitudes, because the unfortunate state of our nation doesn't permit that; not, I say, mathematically or geographically, but in a simple narrative, with each person describing what kind of land and towns his birth-place has, what kind of law, how many souls there are in each village, what sort of people live there, what customs, what religion, what trees, what revenue, what livestock, what seas encircle it, what other regions border it...[84]

Konstantas's regional patriotism was so strong that he declined the invitation to head the Patriarchal Academy in Constantinople in order to return to his homeland to build a school and teach.[85]

For Philippidis and Konstantas, mapping the nation was inseparable from the questions of language and writing; their project was to produce a *topography* of the nation in the radical sense of the word which combines both *topos* (place) and *grafia* (writing). The nation was a geographical and a "textual community" which was formed around shared readings; readings which defined it as a national identity and marked it off from other communities.[86]

Other local geographies were produced at the end of the eighteenth and beginning of the nineteenth centuries such as Nikitas Niphakis's history of the Mani (1791) and Argyris Philippidis's geography of Boeotia (1815). Konstantinos Koumas (1777–1836) urged clerics to describe the geography of their parishes[87] and in the preface to his translation of a German historical geography, he asserted:

> History and geography are closely related; that is why it is important to introduce the geographical description of the country about which one wishes to learn history...it is even more important when one learns history to have before one's eyes maps and to search for every country and place encountered in history.[88]

The journal *Learned Hermes* (1812), which was edited by Anthimos Gazis – the co-author of a school textbook of geography and Archimandrite of the Greek Church of St. George in Vienna – and abounds in geographical information, requested its readers to submit information on:

> ...archaeological data, that's to say inscriptions, research on the location of ancient towns in relation to new ones; observations on Strabo's geography, as well as those of Pausanias and Meletios; research on the history of a region or of a town and any suchlike that relates to the archaeology of Greece.[89]

Here, geography and history are seen as inseparable, and the passage registers a new awareness that the nation's past can only be retrieved through a recognition of its spatiality. As the same publication announced in a preface to a work by Metropolitan Cyril of Adrianople:

> To know ancient geography from which history also comes, we must begin by modern geography and must examine when the town in which we live was built and afterwards research ancient towns which have been destroyed; and above all, to obtain a complete geography of our homeland, every good patriot must offer a topography of his own birthplace, but drawn on maps with a description of its place, of its climate, and of its products, of the distance that separates it from another neighbouring town, of the ruins around it, of mountains and rivers etc.[90]

Geographical knowledge of specific places was projected onto a larger national conception of territory and history.[91] A Greek school manual at the beginning of the nineteenth century (1814) announced that every patriot had to be a geographer.[92] Geography was construed as imperative for economic success upon which the national revival itself was dependent. This was the view promoted by Nikolaos Papadopoulos in his "commercial geographical dictionary" of 1816 which formed part of a larger work entitled *Profit-Making Hermes*.[93] Thus, by the beginning of the nineteenth century a new geography was displacing "an inherited sense of space defined by a geography of faith, which was expressed in the descriptions of the Holy Land and other places of pilgrimage in the Orthodox East". The new geography marked a fundamental "reorientation to secular values" and promoted other models "for the future of Greek society".[94]

1.5   THE TORN HALVES OF CULTURE

As the folklorist Alki Kyriakidou-Nestoros has aptly observed, the attention in *Modern Geography* both to language and to local manners and customs provides an often-neglected historical context for the rise of nineteenth-century folklore and regional studies.[95] Not coincidentally, perhaps, Philippidis and Konstantas's work was rediscovered in the late 1870s at precisely the time when folkloric studies and regional histories were expanding against a background of national uprisings in the Balkans and of Russia's crushing victory over the Ottoman Empire in 1877–1878, which culminated in the creation of an independent Bulgaria following the Treaty of Berlin in 1878. Thus, in 1879 Stephanos Krinos published a section of *Modern Geography* in Athens, while in 1885 the historian and geographer Antonios Miliarakis wrote an appreciative article in *Estia* in which he singled out the authors' audacity in describing Greece's "political...situation under the servitude and oppressive system of Turkish government".[96] Niphakis's geography was republished in 1855, as was Argyris Philippidis's in 1878.

As Kyriakou-Nestoros has also noted, in the eighteenth and nineteenth centuries, deep-rooted and conflicting interpretations of culture pervaded debates about the relationship between language, place and the nation.[97] On the one hand, the *Volk* was celebrated as a repository of Greek history and national identity, organically linked to the land. In this sense, "the Volkesgeist [was] constitutive, and the state merely expressive of nationhood".[98] On the other hand, the people had to be instructed by intellectuals in order to begin a painful process of re-education after centuries of intellectual deprivation under the Ottomans. Korais was one of the first to advocate the model of the nation-state for Greece; he was convinced that the Greeks had been liberated twenty years too early since they had not reached a requisite level of education.[99] It was with a clear pedagogical end in sight that over a period of twenty years he promoted his *Greek Library* of ancient Greek texts. For Korais, enlightened nations were those with a consciousness of their linguistic heritage. Greece could only be liberated if the language was rejuvenated first. While he stressed the organic relation between language and nation, employing the analogy of a suckling child, Korais repeatedly emphasized the role of the intelligentsia:

> The intelligentsia are naturally the lawmakers of the language which the nation speaks, but they are (I say it again) lawmakers of a democratic thing. The correction of the language belongs to them, but the language is the possession of the whole nation, and a holy possession.[100]

This contradiction in conceptions of culture can be traced through Herder's thinking, too. While Herder argued that language was the medium in which the character of a people was engraved, he simultaneously maintained that language was constitutive. As J.P. Stern has observed:

> Thus a language is seen under two aspects, as manifesting two functions: it describes, and refers to, what is already given (say, in the history of a nation), but at the same time a language constitutes, and is asserted as, the basic condition of a people or a state, and as such it contributes to a present or future attainment of that people's political goals.[101]

The nineteenth century was the great age of vernacularizing lexicographers, grammarians and philologists.[102] The impetus to define and theorize a coherent, national idiom anticipated and served as a stimulus to political integration within the institutions of a sovereign Greek state. The remarkable production of grammars, dictionaries and linguistic treatises by such figures as Zalikoglou, Doukas, Athanasios Christopoulos, Ioannis Vilaras, Katartzis and others, in the years immediately preceding the Greek War of Independence, should be seen as a supremely national endeavour. If it is evidence of Greek culture's increasing secularization, of an expanding readership and a new scope of intellectual activity which encompassed geography, politics and the sciences, it should also be seen in nationalist terms. As the Corfiot Nikolaos Sofianos (1500– after 1552) remarked as early as the mid-sixteenth century in the dedication to Book One of his *Grammar*, written in Latin and published in Venice, a centre of Greek learning:

> When I saw that most nations...in our time honour their (spoken) languages with enthusiasm not only by writing things worthy of note in them...but by diligently reducing them to the rules of Grammar, I

myself began to wonder whether it would be worth my while if I brought our language, which we Greeks use for everyday purposes, back to order and rule...[103]

The overtly political vocabulary employed by Sofianos in the context of linguistic restoration underlines the connections between the political community and the state of language. Sofianos himself had prepared a map of Greece (*Ellas*) based on Ptolemy with toponyms drawn from ancient authors such as Herodotus, Thucydides, Strabo and Pausanias, but he also drew a table in which he endeavoured to identify these with modern place-names.[104] As one recent critic has remarked of Korais's philological preoccupations:

> Korais's desire to refashion the formal organization and the boundaries of modern Greek grammar can be seen, not just metaphorically but politically, as an act of (re)instituting the boundaries of Greece itself as a *modern* culture.[105]

The problems of linguistic and political integration are treated explicitly by the playwright Dimitrios Hatzi-Aslan Vyzandios (1790–1853), in his satirical play *Babel or the Regional Corruption of the Greek Language*, published in 1836. Set in 1827 in a taverna in Nafplion, the then capital of the fledgling state, a group of seven Greeks celebrate the victory of the joint British, French and Russian fleet, under Admiral Sir Edward Codrington, over the Turco-Egyptian navy at Navarino. The revellers, who come from different regions of Greece and speak in different dialects and include an Albanian with little command of Greek, soon end up in a brawl as a result of misunderstandings – the most notorious being when one compatriot accuses another of sheep rustling, but is misinterpreted as accusing him of eating excrement. What Vyzandios's comedy highlights is the extent to which language functions as a key index of similitude and difference. The altercation between the Greeks in the taverna stands as an ironic reflection on the collective push to bring about "rule and order": to establish a unifying system of linguistic *and* political representation out of cultural and geographical diversity, as well as competing political allegiances. In his preface to the second edition of the play, Vyzandios attributed this linguistic fragmentation and "the pitiful state to which the Greek language has been debased" to the years of Greece's enslavement under Ottoman tyranny.[106] It was precisely this inheritance – the undefined or fragmented geographical and political nature of the Greek nation – which gave prominence to cultural narratives and representations of nationhood. .

Practices such as geography, literature and folklore were thus defined on one level as institutions that promoted an ideal of the nation's communion. On another level, however, the purpose was to give expression to the people's distinct character which had always existed, even in non-verbal forms such as popular customs and traditions. The concern in Greece during the nineteenth and twentieth centuries with nationalizing space needs to be viewed, this book suggests, in the light of culture's contested meanings. In 1805, with the financial support of the Zosimas brothers, wealthy merchants from Ioannina, the implacable educator Korais launched his *Greek Library*, following the publication of Heliodorus's novel *Aithiopika*. In his introduction to this work published in the form of a letter to his friend Alexandros Vassiliou, Korais celebrated the novel as an innovation of the ancient Greeks and, noting the absence of a Greek word for the French *roman*, he proposed the term *mythistoria*, a term which remained in usage until the mid century when it came to be replaced by *mythistorema*.[107] As Iakovos Pitsipios (1802–1869) was later to declare of Korais in a pre-publication announcement for his novel *The Orphan of Chios* (1834): "This notorious critic...recognized the truth that moral novels are necessary to every nation".[108] Korais's wide ranging introduction to the *Aithiopika*, in which he urges the young to seize the opportunity for education as a weapon in the national struggle to liberate Greek lands, constitutes a series of reflections on the relation between novel, language, and nation. Furthermore, in the same year that the edition of Heliodorus's novel was published, in a letter to Vassiliou who had undertaken a translation of Korais's *Mémoire sur L'État Actuel de la Civilisation dans la Grèce* (1803), and who was having difficulty in finding a word for "civilization" in Greek, Korais had evoked the term *politismos*. This seems to be the first modern usage of the Greek word for "culture" and "civilization".[109] At the beginning of the nineteenth century, then, prose-fiction, culture, nation and the struggle to liberate a national territory were becoming indivisibly yoked, so that no one part could be detached from the others. The process of conceptual definition was inextricably bound up with the establishment of clearly delimited political boundaries for the national community; a connection accentuated by the etymology of the verbs *kathorizo* and *prosdiorizo* in Greek which are variations of the verbs *orizo* and *periorizo* meaning to "bound", "define" or "delimit". Herein, it could be argued, lay both the exceptional authority and impotence of the writer in modern Greece. It is both the acceptance and rejection of this fraught legacy in the nineteenth and early twentieth centuries – the conviction that all narrations must *necessarily* be national – that this book sets out to explore.

Chapter Two

Cultural landscapes and the formation of the Greek state

2.1 NATURAL HISTORIES

During the second half of the eighteenth century, for a number of interrelated socio-political reasons, the idea of Greece as a distinct geographical, political and cultural space found expression in the production of geographical, historical and philological works produced by Greeks in the Ottoman Empire and in the diasporic communities outside it. The War of Independence in the 1820s, however, presented the architects of the fledgling Greek state with a number of practical problems, the most pressing of which was how to forge a unified polity out of a politically and culturally fragmented country.

In this context, landscape – defined as "a cultural image, a pictorial way of re-presenting, structuring or symbolizing surroundings"[1] – functioned as a powerful ideological tool in conceptualizing Greece as a fixed, objective and natural entity. In the nascent Greek state, torn by internal divisions and composed as it was of a substantial immigrant population, the naturalization of the land was central to the forging of a new communal identity.[2] This rhetoric of landscape has increasingly become the focus of critical enquiry within cultural geography where the emphasis has been on symbolic process, text and narrative. Particular importance has been placed on the ways in which "landscape masks the artifice and ideological nature of its form and content".[3] As Stephen Daniels has observed in his study of landscape and national identity in the United States and England:

> National identities are co-ordinated, often largely defined, by legends and landscapes, by stories of golden ages, enduring traditions, heroic deeds and dramatic destinies located in ancient or promised homelands with hallowed sites and scenery.[4]

In Greece the notion of a clearly bounded national space was naturalized so that a nationalist discourse, with its emphasis on a collective,
national affiliation, evaporated into the landscape and the state's
origins were effaced and re-written as components of a "natural"
history in an enterprise of mythic narration that projected the
invented as incontrovertible fact.[5] The production of such Greek landscapes was bound up with the material appropriation and utilization of
the land, as well as with legislative initiatives aimed at creating a
national territory that would be coherent and unified. Landscape
became a way of imagining the nation[6] and it functioned "as a concept
of high tension"[7] in the construction and maintenance of a Greek
national identity:

> Landscapes, whether focusing on single monuments or framing
> stretches of scenery, provide visible shape; they picture the nation.[8]

2.2   NATIONALIZING SPACE: PANAYIOTIS SOUTSOS'S
LEANDROS

Panayiotis Soutsos's (1806–1868) *Leandros* has claims to be the first
novel published in independent Greece, in 1834, the year in which the
capital of the infant Kingdom was formally and symbolically shifted
from Nafplion to Athens. In the prologue to this Greek "foundational
fiction",[9] the author – the scion of a Greek princely family which had
ruled the Ottoman Principality of Moldavia in the years immediately
before the War of Independence – places his writing within the broad
context of the embryonic Kingdom's progress towards political consolidation. In doing so, he suggests that his epistolary novel should be
read as more than a poetic drama set, as one critic has asserted, "in the
inner world of Romantic sentimentality".[10]

The novel's main action takes place in Athens and Nafplion, while
the love-sick protagonist, at the behest of his friend and confidante
Harilaos, later journeys around the newly established Kingdom for two
months in an attempt to console his tormented mind. Admittedly, the
reader is given only the briefest glimpses of post-independent Greece,
such as the young King Otto's enthusiastic reception by the populace
in Nafplion (Greece's then capital) in February 1833, the macabre
spectacle of an execution, and the town's labyrinthine streets recently
named after heroes of the War of Independence. Lord Elgin's plun-
dering of the Parthenon from 1800 to 1805 is mentioned, but there are
few direct references to the housing problems that plagued the new
capital or to the political factionalism in the war-ravaged and depopu-
lated Greek lands which disenchanted contemporary foreign

observers, such as the British travellers George Finlay, John Hartley and William Mure. Twelve years of hostilities from 1821, when the Greeks had risen in revolt against the Ottoman Empire, had devastated the country. On the entreaties of Sultan Mahmud II, Ibrahim Pasha, the adopted son of the Pasha of Egypt, Mehmet Ali, had landed in the southern Peloponnese with the reformed Egyptian forces – the so-called *Nezamiye* or "Ordered Army" – in 1825 (the year of Soutsos's own arrival in Greece) and had undertaken a "scorched earth" campaign that left the regions he passed through prostrate: vineyards, orchards and olive groves were burned, and villages razed. As Finlay noted:

> All agricultural stock was extirpated, houses, barns, and stables were destroyed, fruit trees and vineyards rooted up, the very forests from which the dwellings might have been re-constructed, were every where burned down, lest they should afford shelter to the unsub-dued populations.[11]

In the wake of the Egyptian invasion, plague spread through the Peloponnese. Mure declared that the "site, with rare exception, of every Greek city, town or village, from Athens down to the poorest mountain hamlet presents in fact one confused mass of rubbish".[12]

Conversely, Soutsos depicts a recognizable and generalized Romantic landscape reminiscent of the pastoral representations that adorn the walls of the heroine's room in his brother Alexandros Soutsos's (1803–1863) political novel, *The Exile of 1831* (1835):

> On the walls were paintings representing pastoral landscapes, shep-herds grazing their flocks in verdant valleys, waterfalls gushing in ravines, eagles flying above the desert and ships tossing in the waves of a boundless ocean.[13]

In *Leandros*, ruins of the distant Classical past merge with the ruins left by the tumultuous years of the War of Independence in which Panayi-otis had lost his brother, Dimitris. Together with his kinsman, Alexandros Rizos Rangavis (1809–1892), Panayiotis Soutsos was one of the founding members of the Archaeological Society of Athens (1837), and in the novel, landscape is evoked as a rich repository of the nation's past.[14] Allusions are made throughout to the historical Greek heirlooms interred within the national space. Taking leave of Athens, the protagonist invokes the Attic earth which "holds in its bowels" abundant white marble pillars, silver coins and urns.[15] As the epony-mous hero journeys around the Greek Kingdom from Athens to Nafplion, Hydra, Salamis and Megara, particular topographies recall ancient Greek texts, so that the landscape becomes an aide-mémoire and is ideologically linked to battles, both ancient and modern, and to shrines and birthplaces of Greek heroes. Thus, on his visit to Salamis, the scene of the great naval victory by the Greeks during the Persian Wars in the fifth century BC, the protagonist celebrates the feats of a modern Greek hero, Yeoryios Kariskos or Karaïskakis, a general who fought in the Greek War of Independence and was killed at the relief of the siege of the Acropolis in Athens in 1827. Leandros imagines the warrior's tomb standing guard over Greece's frontiers so that the legendary figure of the War of Independence is symbolically incorporated into the very foundations of the nascent state. The regenerative and heroic sacrifice in reclaiming the national territory finds its equivalence in Leandros's own sacrifice when he takes his life in the concluding pages of the novel. Political and fictional martyrs, the novel suggests, may be related, while Soutsos's narrative promotes an ideal of martyrdom around which the "just cause and longevity of a national identity is forged".[16] Echoing Herder, the Greek landscape is described as the theatre of Greek history – a particularly poignant observation at a time when dramas of the Greek War of Independence were popular on the London stage.[17]

Space in Soutsos's novel is symbolically structured and naturalized as a cultural landscape whose history is systematically activated with the narrator's readings.[18] This naturalization becomes integral to the creation of a communal identity, diverting attention away from the political conflicts that were convulsing Greece and evoking, instead, the stable, unified, "natural" history of the Kingdom.[19] The symbolic structuring of space is inseparable from the geographical construction of a national Greek homeland and, as such, Soutsos's landscape constitutes an essential part of the iconography of nationhood; part of "those shared ideas and memories and feelings which bind a people together".[20] In 1830 Korais, whom the Soutsos brothers had visited in the 1820s in Paris, had pleaded for "renewed struggles" in order "to redeem the old boundaries of ancient Hellas".[21] As if in answer to Korais's solicitation, Soutsos's tour of the recently liberated Greek territories in *Leandros* is a symbolic gesture of territorial consolidation; a conceptual mapping which, as Artemis Leontis has recently argued, engenders a particular "topography of Hellenism".[22] The hero's peregrination is simultaneously a return to Greek "poetic spaces": to the sacred repository of Greek memories in the land. As Anthony Smith has observed:

> The homeland is not just the setting of the national drama, but is a major protagonist, and its natural features take on historical significance for the people. So lakes, mountains, rivers and valleys can all be turned into symbols.[23]

Moreover, the "homeland", as a project of self-renewal, is "achieved by externalizing the struggle for collective identity in acts of environmental manipulation and by attaining mastery over a recalcitrant nature...so the monuments and geographical features of the land became *national* monuments and features".[24]

Leandros was published in its first form, with the title *My Wanderings*, as a series of letters in the newspaper *Ilios* and signed with the pseudonym "Wanderer".[25] The hero moves around the newly established Kingdom in a manner reminiscent of a tour by an eighteenth-century European classical scholar, or philhellene. Soutsos sought to reclaim the Greek landscape which European Romantic writing had appropriated and converted into a universal topos in much the same way that Orientalist writings had evoked the Orient as "a *topos*, a set of references, a congeries of characteristics, that seems to have its origin in a quotation, or a fragment of a text, or a citation from someone else's work...or some bit of previous imagining, or an amalgam of all these".[26] Soutsos likens Leandros's journey to Columbus's discovery of the New World. In so doing, he echoes Goethe's description of Winckelmann as a Columbus who envisaged the New World before he discovered it, as well as Keats's description in "On First Looking into Chapman's Homer" of Cortez the explorer. At the same time, the characterization anticipates the archaeologist Ernst Curtius's account of the British traveller to Greece, William Martin Leake, as "the Columbus of the ancient world".[27] The difference being that the Greek landscape reverberates, for Soutsos, not only with ancient history, but with the recent struggle of the nation's liberation:

> Leandros sees Greece full of joy, through the magical prism of his enthusiasm; he paints its ancient monuments, the victories of the modern Greeks...[28]

On his tour of Greece, Leandros symbolically activates the sacred sites he visits and embeds them in a unified cultural and geographical space. In a still deeply divided Greece, however, Leandros's cultural tour furnishes a model for, rather than a model of, what it purports to represent;[29] the hero's mapping is an attempt to find an imagined solution to concerns about the state's geographical, cultural and political fragmentation. Soutsos's novel can be seen as an endeavour to legitimate the territory being enclosed through its re-presentation in fiction. In short, then, Leandros suggests both the "worldliness of literary texts and the imaginativeness of geographical texts",[30] as well as pointing both to "the environmental values and perceptions of a culture"[31] and highlighting the ideological context of landscape production within a nationalist discourse.

2.3   PICTURING THE NATION

It should be remembered that Greece won her independence at a time when landscape, particularly in England, was one of the principal ways in which the nation pictured itself.[32] In Greece, too, a tradition of national landscape painting developed after the War of Independence. Pictorial images of the Greeks' re-appropriation of their homeland gave expression to a growing sense of political and cultural community. Landscape paintings reiterated and reinforced the nationalist idea of Greece as a country legitimated through its glorious history. As in Soutsos's novel *Leandros*, Greece was pictured in these representations as an aesthetic construction.[33]

An essentially foreign tradition of landscape painting co-existed with the naïve representations of the War of Independence by such artists as Alexandros Iaias and Panayiotis Zographos. The latter was commissioned by the Greek military hero General Makriyannis in the 1830s to commemorate, in a series of twenty-five pictures, specific events from the war – an event in which the artist had himself participated.[34] Zographos, who painted murals in Kastoria and Pelion, worked in a primitive style with oil on wood panels and was clearly inspired by the "two-dimensional ascending perspective of Byzantine portable icons".[35]

In the wake of Otto's arrival in Greece, a number of distinguished Bavarian artists made their way to Athens.[36] Peter von Hess (1792–1871), for example, painted historical compositions and was commissioned by King Ludwig I of Bavaria, Otto's father, to decorate the Galleries of the Hofgarten in Munich with scenes from the Greek War of Independence. Other artists included the landscape painters Carl Rottmann (1797–1850), Ludwig Lange (1817–1878) and Carl Krazeisen (1794–1878) who depicted battle scenes from the War of Independence during a mission to Greece in the late 1820s.[37]

Independent Greece, as an imagined community, thus became closely entangled with nationalist discourses elsewhere in Europe where Neoclassicism merged with Romantic nationalism. This was particularly true in the Prussia of Wilhelm II (reigned 1786–1797), where the Greek Revival was linked to an emergent German nationalism. In Bavaria Ludwig I commissioned the architect Leo von Klenze (1784–1864) to transform Munich from a peripheral court city into a grand capital, at much the same time as Klenze was advising Otto on the monumental reconstruction of his new capital, Athens. German representations of Greek landscapes were thus inspired by and, in turn, fed into an ascendant Neoclassicism. The German connection, reinforced with Otto's ascension to the throne of Greece, was to prove important since the Greek artists who dominated the nineteenth century, and included Theodoros Vryzakis (1814–1878), Nikiphoros

Lytras (1832–1904), Nikolaos Gyzis (1842–1901) and Yeoryios Iako-vidis (1853–1932), all studied in Munich.[38]

Moreover, in France during the Restoration (1815–1830) Eugène Delacroix's (1798–1863) depictions of the Greek War of Independence, drawn from travel reports and newspaper articles, as well as the work of prominent Liberal artists, implicitly identified the revolutionary Greeks with the ideological inheritance of revolutionary France.[39]

The newly founded Polytechnic in Athens (1836) – later to be renamed the School of Fine Arts (1843)[40] – was a spur to artistic production, and amongst the first generation to attend was Vryzakis. The painter's father was killed in the War of Independence and Vryz-akis was brought up in the orphanage established by Capodistrias on Aegina, before studying in Athens and later in Bavaria under von Hess, with a scholarship from Ludwig.[41] The vast majority of Vryzakis's land-scapes are inspired by the War of Independence and celebrate the recovery by the Greek revolutionaries of their ancient homeland. They depict scenes such as "The Exodus from Missolonghi" (1852) and "The Reception of Lord Byron at Missolonghi" (1861); works painted in a formal Neoclassical style reminiscent of Jacques-Louis David (1748–1825). In the late 1840s Vryzakis visited Greece with the aim of touring sites associated with the War of Independence and interviewing veterans of the Revolution.

In the "The Encampment of Karaïskakis" (1855), which is repro-duced on the cover of this book, the Greek military heroes, Karaïskakis and Makriyannis, stand on the summit of a commanding hillock looking out confidently over an empty plain towards the Athenian Acropolis. By their side a Greek flag flutters in the breeze. In the centre of the composition, a warrior dressed in traditional Greek attire with a *fustanella*, or pleated skirt, and a cluster of knives protruding from his belt, leans against a marble pillar. A rifle is slung over his shoulder. Behind him, to the left, two Greek warriors are conspicuously heaving ancient stones to fortify their position. The fight for Greek freedom, Vryzakis suggests in "The Encampment of Karaïskakis", rests upon the Ancient past, just as that past is being incorporated into the present through the active heroism of the Greek warriors.

The connection between the present struggle and the ancient past is, in fact, made in numerous paintings of Greek fighters from the 1830s who are depicted leaning against ruins of ancient columns. The presence of an Orthodox priest in the right-hand corner of Vryzakis's work, who is blessing a soldier as he goes off to fight, further underlines the syncretic nature of Greek identity which is made up of both Ancient and Byzantine vestiges, just as the warriors decked out in traditional Greek costumes mingle with soldiers in European dress.

The painting evokes the idea of an intimate male fraternity, an integrated and convivial community. While the vertical outcrop suggests a hierarchical relationship between the commanders and the soldiers below, the focus is on the group positioned around the column, picked out by the sunlight, in the centre of the composition. In the final analysis, the painting, reminds us, as Anderson has observed, that the nation is "conceived as a deep, horizontal comradeship".[42]

The setting, far from being a backdrop, is central to the meaning of the painting, which has less to do with military contestation (the enemy forces are conspicuous by their absence), than with the symbolic re-appropriation of "Greece". In Vryzakis's idealized representation of the Greek War of Independence, internal factions and feudings have been banished. The reclaiming of the land by the Greeks, the work hints, is at once a physical re-appropriation – underlined by the soldiers heaving stones, or brandishing a shovel, and by their preparations to fight – but is also bound up in age-old Greek cultural practices such as the recitation of stories and the playing of folk tunes. The group clustered around the central figure, which includes a musician strumming on a lute and men smoking pipes, is reminiscent of other works where the fighters are imagined as an ideal community. Vryzakis's painting engages, for example, with the Belgium-born Henri Decaisne's (1799–1842) "Failure of a Military Operation" (1826), where a group of Greek warriors are positioned on a rocky outcrop with a distant vista of burning land and escaping refugees.[43] The juxtaposition of the figures in the foreground and the vista behind echoes the landscapes of Claude Lorrain (1600–1682) as popularized in paintings by travellers to Greece. The scene is raised to a universal and transhistorical phenomenon. Although on one level it is clearly a historical composition, the historical reality is transformed into a myth which, as Roland Barthes noted, "deprives the object of which it speaks of all History".[44] National space is dramatized as "archaic and mythical" and the nation's "modern territoriality" is represented in terms of Tradition: "the difference of space returns as the Sameness of time, turning Territory into Tradition, turning the People into One."[45] Contemporary technologies (namely the spyglass, the guns and European dress) are countered by the ancient, even timeless rituals enacted in the painting: the roasting of a lamb on a spit, the telling of stories, the playing of music. In the background the empty, barren plain, reminiscent of Carl Rottmann's desolate Greek landscapes, represents a space waiting to be claimed and stands out against the crowd of warriors in the foreground of the composition. The landscape has been emptied of all problematic content, reminding us, as Soutsos's novel does, that the process of exclusion is integral to the nationalist enterprise.[46] Finally, in contrast to the bleak open vista of uncultivated land, a flask of water is conspicuously placed by Vryzakis under the central ruined column, while in the bottom right-hand corner a Greek soldier is filling a cup with wine. The water and wine intimate fertility, communion, the rejuvenation of the dried and empty landscape by the heroic Greeks and the reactivation of those values embodied in the ruins of the glorious classical past.

Although it has been argued that the most tangible link between the modern Greek and his glorious past was his language,[47] this book endeavours to show how landscape was produced and maintained as another – arguably the most important – link between the past and the present. By the same token, while many of the texts considered in this study are literary, it is important to bear in mind that the process of imagining, with which this study is concerned, involves other non-literary discourses;[48] indeed, that the process of nation-building is predicated on the transformation of the material environment into a symbolic space.

2.4   THE REORGANIZATION OF THE LAND

Landscape representations in independent Greece were informed by urgent political, social and economic concerns. When Soutsos wrote *Leandros* the land question was a controversial political issue on a number of fronts. As one historian has written: "Success in healing the awful wounds of war and in initiating the process of social and economic development would surely depend in large measure upon wise and efficient utilization of the land of Greece".[49] While the Kingdom's boundaries remained vulnerable, within the state itself there were three main threats to the Kingdom's integrity. The first was the pressing question of land partition following the Turkish exodus, which, according to one contemporary observer, left some 45 percent of all cultivated lands in mainland Greece in the possession of the state.[50] According to Finlay the distribution of a portion of uncultivated lands to those of no property "according to a fixed scale of civil or military service during the revolution" was a matter of urgency.[51]

Under Ottoman rule, land holdings were divided into a complex system of state, semi-public and private ownership regulated by Islamic law. The state lands belonging to the Sultan were known as *miri*, while the *timars* consisted of lands parcelled out as military fiefdoms, the *wakf* was land held by holy or charitable foundations, and the *mulk* designated private land holdings. In addition, peasant tenancies and sharecropping arrangements existed and from the sixteenth century large landed estates known as *chiftliks* developed, encouraged in part by European demands in agricultural produce such as wheat, cotton and wool.[52] By the eighteenth century, with the disintegration of the *timar* system and the rise of a new provincial elite, or *ayan*, the internal cohesion of the Ottoman Empire was being threatened.[53]

During the early years of the Greek Revolution, confiscated Turkish holdings were claimed by the Greek government as "national estates" to be exploited as collateral for foreign loans, although no coherent policy was formulated to justify this appropriation of land. It was not until much later in the nineteenth century – not, in fact, until after 1871 – that the Greek government took some effective measure in distributing the national estates. According to one British writer in 1854 "the cultivators of the soil" in Greece were "retained in a state of medieval barbarism".[54] The lack of detailed demographic data and information about land registration made attempts to administer it difficult. Although the principle had been laid down by Count Ioannis Capodistrias, Greece's first president (1828–1831), that all those who served in the war should be given land vacated by the Ottoman Turks, only approximately a sixth of Greeks were landowners, the rest being tenants.[55] Panayiotis's brother Alexandros Soutsos was actively involved in the land question since he was appointed a member of the committee in charge of surveying the national lands by Capodistrias.[56]

Secondly, there remained sharply pronounced regional differences. As John Petropulos has remarked:

> In view of the geographical barriers of sea and mountains, it is not surprising that localism and sectionalism should have been strong. The force of nationalism in 1821 was still new, and town, village, or district still commanded primary loyalty. Traditionally, administration had conformed to geography and had intensified sectionalism. What became independent Greece had never constituted a single unit within the Ottoman empire. Not even each of its acknowledged geographical divisions had enjoyed administrative unity. Moreover, Ottoman rule had favored sectionalism in two ways – by allowing communities and regions a large degree of autonomy and by never attempting to introduce any widespread uniformity of administration.[57]

There had been no experience of central government in the lands that made up the Greek Kingdom. Regions were characterized by distinct dialects and legal usages. Some areas remained strongly tribal. The population was ethnically mixed with a sizeable Albanian population in Attica, the Argolid, Akarnania and the islands of the Saronic Gulf.[58] Loyalty to a national government was, at best, weak and local chieftains or *kapitanii*, together with the landowners, frustrated government attempts to unify the state. A survey team sent by Capodistrias to identify private and state-owned lands in the Valtos eparchy of Akarnania, cited difficulties and obstacles it faced, some villages even refusing to admit the survey committee.[59] Finlay emphasized the local loyalty:

> No social feature is more remarkable, and perhaps none less agreeable to strangers, than a species of local patriotism, which draws a marked line of distinction between the immediate society of which each separate community consists. The Greek rarely speaks of his nation, yet he speaks continually, and with enthusiasm, of his country – an epithet which he applies to his native village. Whether his birth-place be the barren mountains of Suli, the rocky islands of Hydra or Psara, or the marshes of Missolonghi – still it contains for him every endearing and patriotic association which other nations find in their more enlarged signification of country.

Rooted as they were in the family and the village, Finlay was doubtful whether such patriotic feelings were "capable of further extension without some diminution of their force".[60]

Rebellions in the provinces were endemic. In the southern Peloponnese, the Maniots, under the leadership of Petrobey, resisted attempts by Capodistrias's government to raise taxes. They later rose against the Bavarians in 1834 and in 1838 with a mixture of grievances, as did the populations of Messinia, Aitoloakarnania and Hydra. Capodistrias himself was assassinated on his way to a Sunday service at the Church of St. Spyridon in Nafplion in October 1831 at the hands of Yeoryios and Konstantinos Mavromichalis, disgruntled members of the powerful clan that dominated the Mani.[61]

These sharp divisions, which stemmed from differences among the ruling elite of the Peloponnese, the islands and Roumeli, were soon to lead to civil war. Contending representative bodies were established in the Peloponnese, in Missolonghi under the protection of Alexandros Mavrocordatos and in eastern Roumeli, where the regional overlord was Theodoros Negris.[62] Smaller disputes were subsumed within these larger antagonisms,[63] even while military leaders clashed with the civilian leaders, many of whom were Phanariots. As Frédéric Thiersch, who had been sent by King Ludwig of Bavaria to report on the condition of Greece, observed in 1833: "Aucun peuple n'est composé de parties tellement différente de civilisation, de moeurs et d'intérêt que celui qui habite le royaume de la Grèce".[64] On assuming the presidency in 1828, Capodistrias had embarked upon a programme of centralizing political power to give the new state coherence, but in doing so he seriously underestimated the strength of particularisms. The civil war that followed his death has been described as "the longest and most damaging of any yet known in Greece". [65]

On the arrival of the Bavarians a new three-tiered administrative system of province, prefecture and municipality was set out in a decree, "On the Administrative Division of the Country" (15 April 1833), largely masterminded by the Regent, Georg Ludwig von Maurer, a professor of law at the University of Munich. This was essentially an externally directed, state imposed system of government which rode roughshod over traditional allegiances and communal self-government.[66] As Nikolaos Pandazopoulos has argued, von Maurer's professed aim was to turn Greece into a replica of Belgium and Holland. As such, his system was predicated on eliminating entrenched communal structures.[67] Under the Ministry of the Interior, a Public Economy Office, headed by the French Saint Simonist Gustave d'Eichthal (1804–1886), was established which laboured to retrieve all state assets, develop a national industry, and encourage agricultural initiatives.[68]

The new administrative system sought to diminish the autonomy of local communities (*kinotites*) and eradicate regional legal customs by integrating them into municipalities. Pressure was applied on rural hamlets to merge with larger villages into functional administrative units of two hundred or more residents.[69] Attempts were made to transform what had, in effect, been a provincial backwater of the expansive Ottoman Empire, with a population living in dispersed agricultural communities, into a centralized European sovereign state.

The process of unification was legitimated through state-sponsored practices such as geography, folklore, literature and archaeology that strove to demonstrate both Greek culture's spatial integrity through history, as well as its historical integrity through space.[70] Moreover, the reconfiguration of space coincided with the first systematic field measurements of Greece which were undertaken by the French Expeditionary Force, under the leadership of General Maison (1828–1829). This formed part of an ambitious interdisciplinary survey of the Peloponnese – a scaled-down version of the mapping of Egypt in the *Description de l'Égypte*, commissioned by Napoleon and published in twenty-three volumes between 1809 and 1828.[71] The Greek survey, in fact, announced that the object of the expeditionary force was to collect "des materieux de toute nature pour la publication d'un ouvrage du genre de celui de la Commission d'Égypte".[72] Different areas of investigation were assigned to different teams. Thus, Dubois, the Curator of the Egyptian Museum, was in charge of the archaeological section, while the architect Abel Blouet headed the body in charge of architecture and sculpture and Bory de Saint-Vincent, who had accompanied the French expedition to Australia in 1800, had responsibility for the division concerned with the natural sciences. Topographic research was conducted, which led to the publication as part of the survey of the first trigonometric map of the Peloponnese prepared by J.J. Pelet in 1832.[73]

Similarly, in 1834, the year in which Soutsos's novel was published, a topographical survey was begun in central Greece in order to fix the Greco-Ottoman borders definitively which led to the publication in Argos of a map of the mainland borders of Greece.[74] The national school curriculum established in the same year gave priority to ancient and modern geographies which were taught in parallel.[75]

These mappings prefigure the modernizing drive of the nineteenth century that sought to establish a homogenous, unified national space out of the devastated and divided Ottoman province which Greece had been. As Capodistrias declared in 1830, it was a momentous task to create a state out of "a country in which the scheme of social order is scarcely traced out, and in which anarchy finds a perpetual refuge in the recesses of the mountains".[76] And yet, as Richard Clogg has argued, this attempt to graft a new order onto deeply rooted local structures was to have profound consequences:

It was this grafting of the forms, but not the substance, of Western constitutional government onto an essentially traditional society, with a very different value system from that prevailing in the West, that was to create within Greece a fundamental political tension that has continued for much of [Greece's] post-independence history.[77]

The tension between a plurality of local and particular cultures, and a stable and unified national culture which was promoted by the centralizing state system, was to characterize Greek institutions throughout the nineteenth and into the twentieth century. As I have already argued in Chapter One, this tension reflected radically different meanings of culture as popularly emergent on the one hand, and on the other, as a process of enculturation spearheaded by an educated elite.

2.5 MONUMENTAL LANDSCAPES

From the establishment of the independent Greek Kingdom in the 1830s, space was nationalized through the promotion of monumental landscapes that helped bind together the territories liberated from the Ottoman Empire.[78] A government archaeological department was founded in 1834 with the Bavarian Ludwig Ross as its director (1834–1836). All of the great Greek populated cities of the eastern Mediterranean such as Constantinople, Smyrna and Alexandria, however, remained outside the borders of the fledgling state. While the population of the Greek state amounted to under one million, three times as many Greeks remained in "unredeemed" lands under Ottoman control or in the Ionian Islands which formed part of a British protectorate.[79]

33

Plans were drawn up for the rebuilding of Nafplion, Patras, Argos, Sparta, Chalcis and Hermoupolis. Athens, however, was chosen as the state's capital over other towns in December 1834, largely on account of its Classical pre-eminence. The Ministry of the Interior recommended the move in view of "the ancient monuments of the city" and "the world-wide fame of Athens for thousands of years". [80]

A programme of urban regeneration was initiated that centred on the construction of Neoclassical buildings such as the University designed by the Danish architect Christian Hansen, the Military Hospital designed by Wilhelm von Weiler and the Archaeological Museum designed by Ludwig Lange.[81] This was a programme that articulated a heroic version of the past and strove to efface Greece's Ottoman legacy by celebrating a continuity with ancient Greece. As one contemporary commentator remarked in 1830: "Architecture is all the time engaged in this aim, opening up streets, leveling, and rectifying as much as possible everywhere, in order to correct the city's former ugliness which can please only barbarians, and to contribute here, indeed, to the nursing of the place".[82] To this extent, as one critic has recently observed, the pursuit of a national urban form was a correlative of the search for a "national character" undertaken by nineteenth-century jurists, archaeologists, and folklorists.[83] The architects Stamatios Kleanthis (1802–1862) and Eduard Schaubert (1804–1860) were commissioned in 1832 to lay out a design for the city which focused on prominent ancient sites, creating "a new plan equal to the ancient fame and glory of this city and worthy of the century in which we live".[84] Although it was never implemented, the plan sought to standardize the "disordered" space of the Ottoman city by instituting a system of grids centred on public squares with the palace placed strategically at the node. The architect and painter Leo von Klenze, a passionate advocate of Greek and Hellenistic architecture, arrived in Athens in 1834 as architectural adviser to the King and undertook a clearing of the Acropolis and a dismantling of all the medieval buildings on it; in 1835 the Acropolis was opened to visitors. Von Klenze was perhaps the chief proponent of German Neoclassicism and the architect of the Glyptothek (1816–1830) in Munich, as well as the Propylaeon (1846–1863) and the Walhalla Temple (1831–1842) near Regensberg.[85] At the same time, Karl Friedrich Schinkel (1781–1841), the state architect of Prussia who transformed Berlin with a series of monuments in a rationalist Greek style, although he never actually visited Greece, drew up extravagant plans for a royal dream-palace on the summit of the Acropolis in 1834.[86] In the event, the palace was built by Friedrich von Gärtner and erected between 1836 and 1843. It was not, however, until the 1860s, following George's accession to the throne as King George I, that a plan for the city was drawn up and implemented.

Thus, Greek national identity was closely bound up with interpretations of the nation's archaeological and architectural inheritance. From the foundation of the state:

> New settlements were planned. Old ones were to be restored, redesigned, and expanded. New legislation covered the use and appropriation of space, and was constantly enriched with further regulations.[87]

The terms of the debate over Greek cultural continuity in the nineteenth century had, furthermore, been established by the Austrian historian Jacob Fallmerayer (1790–1861). In the first volume of his history of the Peloponnese (1830) he had argued against cultural continuity, citing the distribution of non-Greek, Slavic toponyms in support of his argument that the Greeks were not the descendants of the Hellenes. Fallmerayer's thesis was to influence mid nineteenth-century mappings of Greece and the Balkans such as Wilhelm Müller's influential ethno-geography of 1842.[88] Not surprisingly, perhaps, great attention was paid by Greek intellectuals to toponyms. Following independence, Greece was divided up into ten administrative provinces with ancient names such as Arkadia, Lakonia, Messinia and Argolis. Symbolic importance was attached to re-establishing such ancient place-names, even while modern toponyms which had become associated with the War of Independence such as Missolonghi, Hydra, Spetses and Psara were celebrated. The preoccupation with toponyms was to continue into the twentieth century. In 1897 the Ministry of the Interior set up a commission to examine the names of municipalities,[89] while a further committee was convened to consider toponyms in 1909.[90]

One of the principal features of nationalism is the association of shared historical memories with a homeland and the translation of space into distinct cultural landscapes that affirm the national community's ties to the land.[91] In early nineteenth-century Greece, the transformation of space into a cultural landscape was bound up with institutional endeavours to map the national territory. While the apparatuses of state power extended political control over specific territories, practices such as literature, archaeology and geography struggled for imaginative domination and aestheticized the new territories.[92] The formation of Greece involved more than military conquest and the physical appropriation of the land; it also entailed a process of imagining through which a politically, socially and geographically fragmented territory was surveyed, represented and recorded in ways that legitimated the national space. The emphasis here is on representation, text, narrative and symbol; in short, on nationalism as a cultural process.

The expansion of the Greek State, 1832–1947

Christos Christovasilis
(Epiros)

Alexandros Papadiamantis
& Alexandros Moraïtidis
(Skiathos)

Yeoryios Vizyinos
(Eastern Thrace)

Argyris Eftaliotis
(Lesvos)

Dimitrios Vikelas
(Chios)

YUGOSLAVIA

BULGARIA

1920-22

ALBANIA

TURKEY

1920-22

DODECANESE
ISLANDS
(to Italy, 1912)
(to Greece, 1947)

1832
1864
1881
1913
1920

Ioannis Kondylakis (Crete)

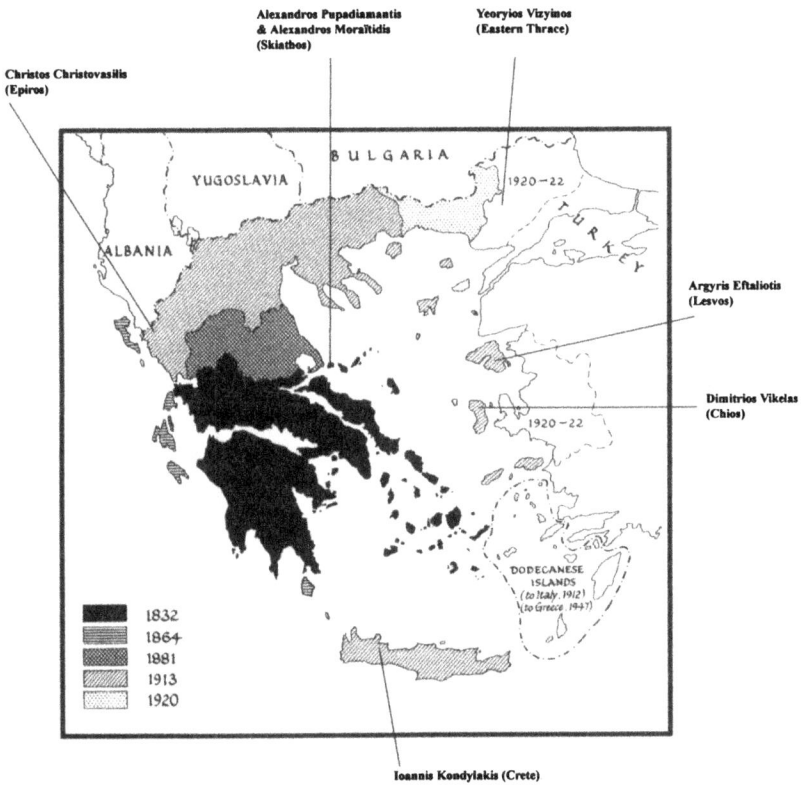

Frontier fictions

Chapter Three

Frontier fictions

3.1 CARTOGRAPHIC ANXIETIES

With the foundation of the Greek Kingdom in the early 1830s, the majority of Greeks had been left in Ottoman lands beyond the fledgling state's boundaries. From at least the second half of the nineteenth century irredentism, known as the "Great Idea", remained the nation's dominant ideology. This was a vision of a greater Greece that drew its inspiration from the splendours of the Byzantine Empire; a vision of territorial expansion in which all the Greek-populated areas of the Near East would be included within a unified Greek state, with its centre in the imperial city of Constantinople, the "New Rome". The term "Great Idea" was first clearly articulated by the politician Ioannis Kolettis (1774–1847) in an address before the Greek National Assembly (1844):[1]

> The Greek Kingdom is not the whole of Greece, but only a part, the smallest and poorest part. A native of Greece is not only someone who lives within this kingdom, but also one who lives in Ioannina, in Thessaly, in Serres, in Andrianople, in Constantinople, in Trebizond, in Crete, in Samos and in any land associated with Greek history or the Greek race...[2]

Acknowledging Greece's irredentist ambitions, King George I, who assumed the throne after Otto's deposition in 1862, grandly adopted the title "King of the Hellenes" – rather than King of Greece – thus confirming his sovereignty not only over Greece but over all the Greeks who dwelt outside the narrow boundaries of the Kingdom. Greek claims in the Balkans were inseparable from the vision of an enlarged Greek state that encompassed Crete, Macedonia, the Aegean islands, Cyprus, the coastal territory of Asia Minor, and areas on the Black

Sea.[3] The boundaries of this enlarged state were vague, but the coastal strip of Asia Minor centring on Smyrna, a commercial hub of the eastern Mediterranean to which many Greeks emigrated from the Aegean islands and the Greek Kingdom during the late nineteenth century, was conceived, together with Constantinople, as the core of the imperialist vision.[4]

Some three decades after Kolettis articulated his vision of the "great fatherland", the US Minister to Greece, Charles Tuckerman (who believed that Greece's misfortunes were the result of the country's circum-scribed boundaries) expatiated on the "Great Idea" when he noted:

> Briefly defined the Great Idea means that the Greek mind is to regenerate the East – that it is the destiny of Hellenism to Hellenize that vast stretch of territory which by natural laws the Greeks believe to be theirs, and which is chiefly inhabited by people claiming to be descended from Hellenic stock, professing the Orthodox or Greek faith, or speaking the language.[5]

As another foreign observer remarked, Greece combined the appetite of Russia with the dimensions of Switzerland.[6]

The idea of territorial expansion, predicated on the resurrection of a glorious medieval past, was not unique to Greece. In 1844, the same year as Kolettis delivered his speech on the "Great Idea", the Serbian statesman Ilija Garašanin (1812–1874), who was twice prime minister (1852, 1861–1867), articulated his vision of a greater Serbia in a project known as the *Načertanije* or "Plan". This envisaged the incorpo-ration into a single kingdom of all lands that were considered predominantly Serbian and Orthodox, including Bosnia, Herzegovina, Kosovo, Montenegro, and northern Albania.[7] Garašanin's vision of a unified Serbia rested upon a belief in the restoration of Stefan Dušan's (1308–1355) Medieval Balkan empire.[8] It was a vision that determined Serbian national policy until 1918.[9]

An indication of the fervour which Greek irredentist dreams inspired in contemporaries is the admission by the writer, academic and diplomat Alexandros Rizos Rangavis in his autobiography (1894) that in 1861 he had planned an invasion of the Ottoman Empire with friends, in the hope of exploiting the French campaign in the Near East to extend Greek territory.[10] Rangavis was later to represent Greece at the Berlin conference in 1878. The vehemence for the "Great Idea" is described by the writer Demosthenes Voutiras (1872–1958) in his novella *Langas* (1903), one of the few works of prose fiction to tackle the public reactions to Greece's disastrous "Thirty Days War" of 1897 against the Ottoman Empire. In this work, eager patriots in the capital follow the war on maps.

A "cartographic anxiety" was born with the new state. The French archaeologist Victor Bérard began his survey of contemporary Hellenism by posing the question: "What exactly are the real frontiers of Hellenism [...]?"[11] Debates about the place and significance of national boundaries had raged from the foundation of the Greek state and continued until the Asia Minor Disaster of 1922, when the dreams of a greater Greece, vigorously championed by the Prime Minister Eleftherios Venizelos (1864–1936), embracing two continents (Europe and Asia) and five seas (Ionian, Aegean, Mediterranean, Marmara and the Black Sea), were shattered by the decisive Kemalist offensive. The fact that the richest Greek communities remained outside Greece, together with a resentment felt against educated Greeks who moved to the Kingdom after Independence, led to a controversy in the National Assembly over who should be considered a "native" Greek, or *authochthon*, as opposed to *heterochthons*, or Greeks from outside the confines of the Kingdom. This tension between what Ion Dragoumis termed the "Helladic" and the "Hellenic" was to persist throughout the nineteenth century. As Dragoumis himself declared: "The Greeks of Greece, let us call them *Helladiki*, identified in their minds the Greek state, the Greek Kingdom, the small Greece, with the Greek nation. They forgot the Greek nation, *Romiosyni* and Hellenism".[12] From a Hellenic, as opposed to a Helladic, perspective, then, the Greek War of Independence was perceived as a marginal occurrence that took place, as one *heterochthon* Greek remarked in 1860, in a remote and unfamiliar province of the Ottoman Empire.[13] The idea of a consolidated, clearly demarcated national space sat uncomfortably beside a messianic vision of expansion outwards, conceived in Ratzelian terms as an organic territorial growth.[14]

In the first revolutionary constitution of Epidaurus (1822), Greek citizenship was defined in the following terms: "Greeks are the *autochthonous* inhabitants of the realm of Greece who believe in Christ".[15] Attempts were subsequently made to pass legislation aimed at preventing Greeks of the exterior from holding office. Paparrigopoulos himself had been dismissed from his government appointment in the Ministry of Justice in 1845 because he happened to be a *heterochthon*, born as he was in Constantinople. The Constitution promulgated at the assembly of Troezene following Greek Independence (1827) asserted, more obscurely, that Greece's provinces should be defined as all those regions "which raised or will raise arms against the Ottoman dynasty".[16]

Greece's boundaries were redefined on five occasions between 1832 and 1924, but during the same period numerous arguments were put forward to support alternative boundary lines. As one commentator observed in the middle of the nineteenth century: "No European state...has such strange, non-existent, unsettling and actually vague boundaries as Greece has with the Ottoman state".[17] The British Ambassador to the Sublime Porte,[18] Stratford Canning, who met with his French and Russian counterparts on the island of Poros in September 1828 to consider various proposals for the frontiers of Greece, recommended a boundary extending from Arta to Volos and including the islands of Samos and Crete, as well as Evia.[19] Capodistrias advocated as the state's frontier a line running from Preveza in the west to Lamia, although this was the very minimum and he initially pressed for a Greece that extended into Albania from the West to Thessaloniki:

> If we are guided by history, by the ancient remains which have been saved and by the opinion of travellers and geographers, this country [Greece] ought to have its northern border begin at the mouth of the Vijosë and extend along the length of the river to its source and then across the mountains of Zagoria and Metsovo and Olympos to the Gulf of Thessaloniki.[20]

As he put it more vaguely in a note to Sir Robert Horton, Under-Secretary for the Colonies under Canning and Goderich:

> The Greek nation consists of people who have never ceased, since the fall of Constantinople, to profess the Orthodox religion, to speak their ancestral language, and who have remained under the spiritual or temporal jurisdiction of their Church, no matter what part of Turkey they inhabit. The limits of Greece have been defined for four centuries by rights which neither time nor misfortunes of all kings, nor conquests have ever been able to abolish. They have been defined since 1821 by the blood shed in the massacres of Cydonies, Cyprus, Chios, Crete, Psara, Messolonghi; and in the numerous battles on land and sea which have brought honour to this gallant nation.[21]

Adamantios Korais, as we have seen, had ambiguously urged, in 1830, for "renewed struggles to redeem the old boundaries of ancient Hellas".[22] For Korais these "old boundaries" implicitly contained any place where the Greek language was spoken, a view shared by Neophytos Doukas who claimed "almost all of those living between the Pruth and Nile Rivers as Greek" and remarked in 1811 that "when I pronounce the sweet name of the Hellenes I do not mean only those few inhabiting the lands of ancient Greece, but simply the whole area in which the modern tongue of the Greeks is spoken".[23] The Arta to Volos line was revoked in 1829, but finally settled upon in 1832, with

41

the exclusion of Samos and Crete which the Poros conference had previously recommended.[24] As late as 1867, however, Dimitrios Vernardakis (1834–1907) was repeating Capodistrias's arguments,[25] while Nikolaos Saripolos, Professor of Law at the University of Athens, declared in 1877 that the Kingdom's natural boundaries extended from Crete and Cyprus to the Black Sea and Asia Minor with the capital at Constantinople.[26] In his 1885 article on Philippidis and Konstantas's *Modern Geography*, Miliarakis remarked that in their book the two geographers had been the first "to trace out the truthful boundaries of Greece".[27] In fact, the section of *Modern Geography* devoted to Greece begins with a declaration that the country is much larger than Europeans claim or than the ancient geographers maintained, stretching as it does from mainland Greece through the East in the swathes of territory Hellenized by Alexander the Great. Different "Greeces" are identified and the geographers assert that "Greece" proper extends from Methoni at the southwest tip of the Peloponnese to the Black Sea in the northeast.[28]

The question remained: where were Greece's boundaries to be fixed? In the 1870s and 1880s, with the weakening of the Ottoman Empire, the spread of Pan-Slavism in the Balkans, together with the spectre of Bulgarian aggrandizement and the escalating tension in Macedonia, the issue became a pressing one. Since the justification for the existence of the Greek state rested largely on claims of cultural continuity, it was logical that the frontiers of the Greek state should follow the line of old Greece. The Athenian schoolteacher Dionysios Pyrros (1774–1853), in his *Methodic Geography of the Entire Habitable World* published in 1818, had argued, therefore, that Greece should conform to the boundaries of ancient Greece, wherever they were deemed to be. Macedonia was excluded from many early mappings of the nation, although Yeoryios Kozakis-Typaldos, writing in 1839, bemoaned Greece's continued subjection. Nevertheless, Konstantinos Paparrigopoulos in 1849 could allude to the Macedonians as a hybrid race, although his view was to change and four years later he asserted the Greekness of the Macedonians.[29] Summing up in 1885, Dimitrios Vikelas (1835–1908) exclaimed:

> Our efforts and our aspirations are directed towards the formation of a Greek State whose northern boundary would begin from the point in the Adriatic which is above Corfu and would extend as far as the Aegean at Chalkidiki, including the Greek part of Macedonia; the island of Crete would form the southern limit of this state.[30]

If, as Peter Sahlins has argued, territorial boundaries are drawn to distinguish a collective identity from that which lies outside it,[31] divergent attitudes towards the positions of Greece's boundaries reflected markedly different conceptions of Greek identity and the different terms (geographical, ethnographical, political, historical and cultural) on which Greek identity was argued.

3.2   THE PROCRUSTEAN BODY

The lack of consensus about the nation's geography, about the location of its centre and periphery, suggests its fundamental instability; "a cramped body", as one foreign commentator noted, lying "uneasily upon the Procrustean bed which diplomacy had cynically constructed for it".[32] The equivocal borders between the nation and state undermined the integrity of Greece's own body. Images of the nation's bodily mutilation were to persist into the twentieth century. The fighter of the War of Independence, Theodoros Kolokotronis, declared that the narrow boundaries of the Liliputian state were analogous to a dwarf's shoe set upon the foot of a giant.[33] The politician and writer Ion Dragoumis (1878–1920) was later to declare that the tight-fitting uniform of the state could not be made to accommodate the expansive body of the nation:

> The state is the shirt which a nation, worthy of political independence, can wear and which sometimes doesn't completely cover it. Parts frequently remain uncovered by the shirt. Perhaps the politicians of the state want to cut off those parts? It could be, however, that the shirt might not be worn and yet the nation is still able to live and somehow or other progress.[34]

By the same token, territorial and bodily amputations – the trauma of national dismemberment and the painful wrenching of body parts – were inextricably bound up in literary and geographical texts, particularly in the early twentieth century at the prospect of "losing" Macedonia and following the Greek defeat in Anatolia in 1922. Some of the most poignant scenes in Stratis Myrivilis's (1890–1969) novel *The Schoolmistress with the Golden Eyes* (1933) take place in a military hospital in Asia Minor during Greece's defeat where a soldier, Stratis Vranas, has his gangrenous leg amputated. His comrade Leonis Drivas, the protagonist of the novel, like the doctors, cannot summon the courage to tell the dying man that he has lost his limb. While an explicit connection is made between the amputation of the soldier's leg and the felling of the giant oak tree in Alexandros Papadiamantis's (1851–1911) short story "Beneath the Royal Oak" (1901), an implicit connection is also established between the severance of the limb and the truncation of historic Greek lands from the main body of the nation that followed the Catastrophe.[35] As the Frenchman Édouard Driault observed in his work on Greek irredentism in 1920: "Quand le corps est mutilé, sans alimentation, il a la fièvre et s'agite pour vivre".[36]

The excision of Vranas's leg has deep resonance in Greek literature. The dismemberment anticipates, for example, the one-legged protagonist Vangelis who returns to his village at Easter from the Balkan Wars in Angelos Sikelianos's (1884–1951) poem "In St. Luke's Monastery", published two years afterwards in 1935; and it recalls Kostis Palamas's (1859–1943) short story "The Death of a Hero" (1891), in which the handsome, robust hero, Mitrios Roumeliotis, slips on cobblestones on his way to the Good Friday service, injuring his leg which festers and finally kills him. As the narrator remarks: "Only one thought filled him with dread, froze his blood and turned him to stone. His heart stopped cold at the prospect of being left crippled. The injury to his leg was more terrible to him than any misfortune."[37] In his nationalist novel *The Blood of Martyrs and Heroes* (1907), Dragoumis described the death of Pavlos Melas – the Commander-in-Chief of the Greek bands in the areas of Kastoria and Monastir who was killed by Turkish troops in 1904 – in a chapter significantly entitled "The Death of the Hero" that harks back to Palamas's story. As Melas himself remarked, Macedonia was "the lung of Greece" and the prospect of its loss constituted a form of mutilation.[38] Myrivilis was to acknowledge a connection between Palamas and his protagonist Vranas when he evoked Palamas as the poetic equivalent of the statesman Venizelos who championed Greek irredentist ambitions; "he was", the writer noted, "Papadiamantis's oak tree".[39] There are clear echoes, too, of Mitrios Roumeliotis in Myrivilis's own novella *Vasilis Arvanitis* (1943), where the eponymous hero injures his leg with fatal consequences when he falls into a ditch, "collapsing", the narrator adds "like an uprooted oak tree".[40]

At the same time, the Greek state was conceptualized during the nineteenth century as an insalubrious imposition that deformed the natural, capacious physique of the nation, forcing its limbs out of joint. In his introduction to a French translation of a lecture on Hellenism delivered in 1876 by the Greek Foreign Minister, Étienne Vlasto quoted the words of a French critic who compared Greece to a deformed body:

> Greece (as she has been created by the Great Powers), is not a nation; she is the rudimentary structure of a nation...Greece is an enormous head on a small debilitated body, a head, moreover, which is in a state of perpetual confusion...she is the section of a mutilated body fidgeting to be joined back to the other scattered limbs.[41]

The grotesque symbolism in this description of Greece as a butchered torso struggling to reassemble its disjointed limbs is reminiscent of a hallucinatory scene by Hieronymous Bosch. Greece is dramatized as a creation of international diplomacy, a product of political laboratories rather than an authentic, integrated anatomy with organic frontiers. As Charles Stewart has observed, traditional folk conceptions of monstrosity in Greece involve a combination of animal and human features and in the bodily inversions that characterize Greek *exotika*, or demons, the feet are "the most frequently distorted parts of the body": "Physical deformity or crookedness contrasts with the straight and the well-formed". The Modern Greek word for beautiful, *omorfos*, means literally "well formed" and the word for ugly, *aschimos*, signifies that which is "without form".[42] Lest we forget, in popular Greek folklore, the devil is said to be crippled in the legs – sometimes, indeed, referred to as the one-footed (*to monopodi*), while straight long legs carry erotic connotations, symbolizing health and fertility.[43] In short, then, the body provided a poignant political metaphor, since, as Mary Douglas has famously observed, it "is a model which stands for any bounded system", even while "the functions of its different parts and their relations afford a source of symbols for other complex structures".[44] A close relation was sustained between the contestation of national boundaries and the equivocal nature of bodily parameters.[45]

3.3   READINGS OF THE PAST

The debate about where Greece's boundaries were to be drawn was closely bound up with readings of the nation's past, both ancient, Byzantine and modern. Greece's independence had been legitimized largely through a conscious appeal to the Ancient Greek inheritance. Yet, from the middle of the century this emphasis on Greece's Classical legacy, centred geographically on the Peloponnese and Attica, began to give way as the Medieval, Byzantine past was rediscovered and increasingly celebrated. In 1893, for example, the collection of artefacts from the Christian Archaeological Society was publicly displayed in the recently completed National Archaeological Museum (the Byzantine Museum in Athens, however, was not formally opened until 1930).[46] The man at the centre of the "map mania" in the 1870s, Konstantinos Paparrigopoulos (1815–1891), a professor of history at the University of Athens, was the person largely responsible for the reassessment of Byzantium and for articulating a tripartite vision of Greek history that stretched, uninterrupted, from Ancient Greece, through Byzantium, to the modern period. The shift in attitude to Macedonia owes much to

Paparrigopoulos's *History of the Greek Nation* which was published in five volumes between 1860 and 1874,[47] and in which "Byzantium and Kolettis's conception of the Great Idea [came] together as components of the political culture of 'Romantic Hellenism'".[48] Geography, at least from the 1880s, worked in the service of this imperialist vision of a Romantic Hellenism.[49]

The purpose of textbooks on ancient geography, as the educationalist Politimi Kouskouri remarked in 1854, was to demonstrate to contemporary Greeks what a modest portion of their ancestral lands they now occupied.[50] Increasingly, Greek geographers sought to undermine the boundaries that marked off the Greek Kingdom from the regions of "enslaved Greece" in a hope that their geographies would, in the words of Antonios Miliarakis, foster a "spirit of fraternity between all Greeks, free and enslaved".[51] In his geography textbook of 1880 Spyridon Moraitidis declared that:

> In the fourth grade we show our students the totality of Greek lands....We teach them that these lands are Greek, that is to say that they are in the possession of and inhabited by people who are close to us, who are of the same origin, have the same religion and speak the same language as us. But a part of them (we point to the land delimited by the boundary) is free, because the King of the Greeks, George, reigns there, that we Greeks have chosen as a king; and a part (we show the rest of the Greek lands in Europe and Asia) are subject of the King of the Turks, the Sultan.[52]

In the 1880s the distinction between Greece and the Greek lands began to break down. The Balkans was increasingly envisaged as a Greek peninsula that extended to Asia Minor.[53] Thus, Antonios Antoniadis (1836–1905) asserted in his *Geography of Greece and Greek Lands* (1888):

> The Greek peninsula and neighbouring Asia Minor resemble each other to such an extent in terms of their climatic conditions, and used to be and still are inhabited by the same people; they are so close and have such identical beliefs and ideas that they seem to be destined almost by nature to form a single state.[54]

This line of reasoning was to continue in the arguments put forward to legitimate the Greek military presence in Asia Minor after 1919. Thus, in a lecture given in Paris in 1920, the economist and Minister of Foreign Affairs, Nikolaos Politis, evoked the findings of the German geographer, A. Philippson, to argue that the coastal areas of Asia Minor were not only Greek culturally, but belonged to Greece on geographical and geological grounds as well. Asia Minor was:

...une contrée égéenne, parfaitement semblable à la forme des régions grecques et étroitement rattachée par la nature et l'histoire avec la mer et la Grèce au delà de la mer.[55]

3.4 THE INVISIBLE SEAM: BETWEEN EAST AND WEST

For foreign travellers, Greece was a frontier land at once Balkan and Mediterranean, Christian but distinctly Eastern. Henri Belle, who served as First Secretary in the French Embassy between 1861 and 1863, had likened Greece to a European frontier territory; a more familiar equivalent, as he put it, to the Wild West.[56] And in perhaps the most far-fetched comparison, George Cochrane concluded his two-volume *Wanderings in Greece* (1837) with a chapter entitled "The Colonization of Greece", in which "the waste lands of Greece" were depicted as frontier territory ripe for colonization by intrepid Englishmen.[57] As another foreign observer noted of the Bavarians in 1835, "Greece to them is a new colony".[58] Mihail Mitsakis (1863–1916), writing in 1890 in a sketch about the gold rush at the mines in Lavrion (known as the *Lavriatika*) near Sounion, remarked that Greece had been turned into an American frontier territory, or a miniature California.[59]

For Greeks, the preoccupation with defining Greece's boundaries was closely bound up with questions about Greece's identity as a Western or Eastern nation, a tension aptly summed up in Markos Renieris's article published in 1842 and entitled "What is Greece?" which began with the question: "What is Greece? Orient or Occident?"[60] For Renieris, employing a geographical metaphor, any politician who failed to address this issue resembled: "a sailor who sailed in the ocean without map and compasses".[61]

Greece was conceived as occupying a strategic frontier region; a buffer zone against the Muslim East that nonetheless ran the risk of "contamination" by the very forces it sought to keep at bay. Fears of contamination by the East were to dominate every aspect of Greece's cultural life until the late 1880s including the perceived need to cleanse or "purify" the language and to obviate Ottoman legacies in modern Greek institutions. There were those, however, who held that because of this pivotal position, Greece represented the vanguard of European enlightenment and was destined to fulfil a messianic role disseminating European civilization into Asia. Greece's irredentist ambitions were partly grounded upon a conviction of the nation's advanced level of civilization in relation to the brutishness of the Ottoman Empire, a position of superiority which Édouard About had endorsed in his study *La Nouvelle Carte d'Europe* (1860). A reaction to this essentially Occidentalist view of Hellenic culture, however, took place towards the end of the century, particularly in literature, as a conspicuous attempt to resist European influences.[62]

Yet the projection of Greece as a frontier zone – a vital link, a fault-line, a seam – preponderated. Konstantinos Oikonomos had employed a characteristic sartorial metaphor to describe the cultural relationship of the Greek world with enlightened Europe as early as 1816 in the preface to his translation of Molière's *L'Avare*:

> We cut and stitch the fabrics of enlightened Europe according to the usage of our compatriots; so much more aptly must we apply the compositions of the wise Europeans to our customs. Only blessed is he who can join them together and adapt them as is proper.[63]

Greece was envisaged as being located on a cultural join or imaginary seam between Europe and the East. Metaphors of conjoining and stitching pervaded discussions of Greece's ambivalent geographical position between Europe and Asia, just as in the language of territorial consolidation, the term *enosis* (or joining) signifies the territorial unification with the fatherland. As Renieris asserted: "Ancient Greece found herself between Europe and Asia, between West and East, no less than modern Greece."[64] In the same article Renieris traced a complex movement in which Greece is explicitly gendered and made to contain her opposite in a homo-erotic coupling with herself that produces a hybrid Byzantine culture:

> Greece, by her nature, by her civilization and by historical mission, is West not East...During the age of decline and corruption, at the time of the Byzantines, she seemed to transfigure herself into her opposite.[65]

For many Greek writers, Greece's hybridity as part-West and part-East was the nation's distinctive characteristic. The notion of Greece's in-betweenness was extended by Saripolos in his book *Le Passé, le Present et l'Avenir de la Grèce* (1866) to include the Greeks as a racial group who were – he argued – Indo-Pelasgic in contrast to the Indo-Germanic race and therefore in a better position to civilize the East. Greece's irredentist mission as a civilizing force in the East was given its clearest expression by Kolettis before the Greek National Assembly in 1844 when he declared:

> By her geographical position Greece is the centre of Europe; between East and West, she has been predestined to enlighten first

the West, through her own fall, and then the East, through her own resurrection.[66]

In Kolettis's biblical vision, Greece was both central and peripheral. She was central precisely because she was situated on the frontier, thereby assuming, inevitably, the role of gatekeeper to the East and West. Underlying the representations of Greece's interstitial, mediating position between East and West lay a conviction that Europe itself was defined by an opposition. In other words, Greece was European because, in a heavily gendered metaphor, she gave birth to the very distinction of East and West, a notion reproduced by Edward Said who has argued that the ancient Greeks in their representation of the Persians as Others were the first Orientalists;[67] a view prefigured in Renieris's own conclusions that ancient Greek conflicts with the East anticipated nineteenth-century campaigns such as Napolean's invasion of Egypt.

Nineteenth-century Greece provides a particularly striking case study that elucidates the ways in which identity formation is bound up with a contradictory economy of sameness and difference, comparison and differentiation. In certain significant ways, the Greek debate parallels the nineteenth-century Russian preoccupation about whether Russia belonged to Europe and Asia. Both countries laid claim to the Byzantine heritage. Russian nationalists assigned Russia a civilizing vocation in the East and Russian identity was, likewise, defined against both Europe and Asia. As Mark Bassin has observed in words that might just as well be used of Greece: "at the same time that Russia turned *away* from the West towards Asia, it was apparently doing so as a representative of this very West".[68] Like Greece, Russia's destiny was determined, it was claimed, precisely by its position on the fissure that marked off the East from the West, the Occident from the Orient, astride Fallmerayer's wall which the Austrian historian had posited as marking off the European from the non-European. It was a dichotomy symbolized in the imperial double-headed eagle that looked both ways, separate gazes conjoined in the same body; a symbol of both aversion and desire. Russian and Greek identities were founded upon a distinction, or difference, which was vigorously promoted as a unifying national legacy.

3.5 FRONTIER FICTIONS: WRITERS, HEROES AND FRONTIERSMEN

The frontier functioned as an important *topos* in Greek fiction. The physical protection of the state's frontiers found its equivalence in the struggle to safeguard a national Greek culture from corrosive foreign incursions. Although Rangavis's historical novel *The Lord of the Morea* (1850) had focused on the struggle over the control of "old" Greece, many contemporaneous writers such as Grigorios Palaiologos (1794–1844) or Pitsipios had ranged freely between Greece and other "unredeemed" territories of the Ottoman Empire in their fiction. The hero of Palaiologos's picaresque novel *The Polypath* (1839), for example, journeys from Constantinople across Europe to England where he meets a perplexed Englishman who 'enquires of the Greek how he can be Greek since he was born in Turkey. A fellow countryman answers that the Greeks and Turks are the equivalent of the Scots and the English, sharing everything except their religion:

> "But how is it that you are Greek", the Englishman enquired of me in all seriousness, "since you were born in Turkey?". "What has that got to do with it?", the other answered earnestly. "Turks and Greeks are identical, just as the English are with the Scots. They share the same language, the same customs, and they differ only slightly when it comes to religion; but just as the Scots wish to break away from the English, so do the Greeks wish to detach themselves from the Turks." [69]

Pavlos Kalligas's (1814–1896) novel *Thanos Vlekas* (1855) begins on Greece's northern boundary and while the eponymous hero seeks refuge across the border in the Ottoman Empire, he is symbolically killed by dissatisfied peasants on his brother's estate in the Peloponnese, the heartland of the old Kingdom. Similarly, Vikelas's novel *Loukis Laras* (1879) ranges geographically from the island of Chios in the eastern Aegean to Europe.

Writers in the 1880s, however, increasingly turned to life at the frontiers. In a process of inversion, the peripheries were promoted as the centre of an authentic Greek cultural life so that plots coalesced around the frontier and geography structured narratives. With a few exceptions – notably of Andreas Karkavitsas (1866–1922), who was born in the Peloponnese – writers during this period came from and wrote about the outlying regions of the Kingdom. Thus, Yeoryios Vizyinos (1849–1896) came from Eastern Thrace, Papadiamantis from Skiathos, Ioannis Kondylakis (1862–1920) from Crete, Christos Christovasilis (1861–1937) from Epirus, and Argyris Eftaliotis (1849–1923) from Lesvos. They had little to say about the Peloponnese, the core of the original state carved out of the Ottoman Empire in the 1820s.

In the course of the nineteenth century, fiction, in Greece as elsewhere, began to wrest the nation "from other geographical matrixes that were just as capable of generating narrative – and that indeed clashed with each other throughout the eighteenth century".[70] As

Franco Moretti has also observed, the historical novel offered nine-teenth-century Europe a "phenomenology of the border" at a moment when borders were "simultaneously hardening, and being challenged as 'unnatural' by the various nationalist waves – and when, as a consequence, the need to represent the territorial divisions of Europe [grew] suddenly stronger".[71] The celebration of the margins was by no means unique to Greece. In Britain, for example, if the character of the nation found expression in the domesticated space of the "garden of England", it was in "the wild and upland margins of the kingdom" that the seeds of British nationhood lay: those "marginal" lands where "the national parks and areas of upland wilderness to be preserved for the nation" are found today.[72] The promotion of the frontier was closely bound up with theories of dialectical regeneration, which are further discussed in Chapter Four. "Literary language, the language of the cities", the Orientalist and comparative philologist Friedrich Max Müller (1823–1900) had argued, "decays as it develops away from experience and must be reinvigorated by input from the regional frontiers where the forms of speech should still touch the forms of experience".[73] Ironically, however, frontier fictions were promoted by increasingly centralized, state-sponsored institutions, so that the excluded centre, with its core reading public, underscored and gave meaning to the periphery, just as the periphery furnished a space from which the centre could imagine itself.

At exactly this time, in 1875, the scholars Yorgos Sathas (1842–1914) and Émile Legrand (1841–1904) published the romance *Diyenis Akritis*, which they had uncovered five years previously in the monastery of Sumelia near Trebizond, in the Ottoman Empire on the Black Sea. The epic tells the story of the eponymous Byzantine warrior, a frontiersman living on the turbulent borders of the Byzantine and the Arab Empires. His name, *Akritis*, means borderer or frontiersman. In their preface, Sathas and Legrand sought to place the publication of the romance in a contemporary context of Greek cultural activities, including the founding of *syllogi*, or literary societies in the Ottoman Empire, and the circulation of historical, philological and folkloric works. They argued that the vigorous promotion of Greek language and literature, as opposed to costly military campaigns, was a surer and safer way of ensuring the successful outcome of Greek expansionist policies in the East, even while the exploits of the Byzantine hero were compared to glorious feats of the heroes of the War of Independence. As one commentator declared, Diyenis Akritis is an heroic frontiersman "who fought to preserve the Hellenic Christian state of Byzantium from the ceaseless incursions, raids and oppression of harsh tyrants and brig-ands of another race, to uphold and extend freedom and justice for the people".[74] At his inaugural lecture as Rector of the University of

Athens in 1907, the folklorist Nikolaos Politis (1852–1921) declared similarly that the Akritic epic was "the national epic of the modern Greek" and added:

> To put the matter in its appropriately proud context, in Degenes Akrites the desires and ideals of the Hellenic nation reach their peak, because in this man the long centuries of ceaseless struggle by the Hellenic against the Islamic world are symbolized.[75]

The figure of Diyenis Akritis, the frontiersman, served as a fitting symbolic double for the writer's own double-role which was predicated on both protecting the nation-state and in opening up new spaces for incorporation within it.[76] Indeed, Karkavitsas wrote a long story based on Diyenis's heroic exploits, which included sections of the demotic folk poems within it.[77] Literature was both defensive *and* offensive; it sought to integrate the national space, to consolidate a national culture and at the same time to extend the state's frontiers. In this respect, literature's role was Janus-faced; to safeguard the nation's frontiers from being overwhelmed by foreign influences and to stake out unredeemed Greek lands.[78] As Psycharis (1854–1920) famously declared in *My Journey* (1888): "A nation in order to become a nation requires two things: to enlarge its frontiers and to create its own literature".[79]

From the 1880s analogies, often negative, were increasingly drawn between the writer's activities and the heroic deeds of the War of Independence. The celebration of the heroes of the 1820s, who against all odds had carved an independent Greek Kingdom out of the Ottoman Empire, merged with an idealization of the *kleft* as symbol of Greek freedom, and more generally, with an affirmation of the values of *pallikarismos*, or masculine bravery. Just as "brigandage merged into the irredentist struggle and gave it a distinct character and colour", so the kleft was construed as a "patriotic" outlaw who dwelt, albeit in a highly metaphorical sense, on the borderlands of the state.[80] By the mid-nineteenth century *agonistai*, or fighters, had "became objects of veneration, not unlike their counterparts in the conquered American West, who participated in the Wild West Shows".[81]

The national aspect of the freedom-loving and proud frontier fighter who challenged constituted authority had been celebrated amongst others by Dora d'Istria, a Romanian princess of Albanian extraction who was granted Greek nationality in the 1860s, and who "dwelt upon the activities of the Greek guerrillas as the embodiment of Hellenic valour".[82] The klefts were increasingly distinguished from the later brigands who defied the authority of Athens, while their self reliance and bravery were affirmed with the publication of collections of kleftic songs and anthologies of folk poetry. By the mid-century, for example, the klefts were celebrated as national fighters by the diplomat and writer Lambros Enialis[83] and constituted the subject matter of popular theatre.[84] The publication in the 1870s of Anastasios N. Goudas's (1816–1882) eight-volumed *Parallel Lives of Men who Distinguished Themselves during the Regeneration of Greece* marked the culmination of a long process of heroification.[85] By the 1880s the kleftic ideal had become inextricably bound up with nationalist ideology.[86] Both Konstantinos Paparrigopoulos and Spyridon Trikoupis (1788–1873) extolled the virtues of the kleft as against the common brigand, a difference underlined by Henry F. Tozer.[87] The ensuing furore in the British Press that followed the Dilessi murders in the spring of 1870 had dramatically highlighted the debate over the identity of the kleft. Finlay, for example, was led to assert of the klefts that:

> despite sentiment and ballads, [they] were neither more nor less than brigands, who habitually plundered Christians and accidentally murdered Mussulmans. It is a mere euphemism to call them patriots, and an egregious error to suppose they had not a great share in perpetuating the barbarism which gave them birth.[88]

However, Greeks such as Goudas strove to differentiate between the common bandit or brigand and kleft, arguing that brigandage was extrinsic to the Greek character and brigands were either foreign or a pernicious legacy of centuries of Ottoman oppression:

> If, however, one were carefully to go through the ancient and modern history of Greece, he would not find it difficult, if not to induce the West to alter its opinion entirely, then at least to persuade it that by using the word 'brigandage' (*listia*) it frequently confuses the Greeks' inherent honour and patriotism – the so-called *pallikarismos* – with it.
>
> But, however eager the Hellene may be to become a kleft in order to exercise his *pallikarismos* at complete liberty in the mountains, to the same degree it is in his nature to reject brigandage (*listia*)...[89]

The celebration of the kleft and frontiersman as a protector of national Greek space was thus bound up with a nostalgia for the heroic struggle for independence and with a concomitant desire to regain the impetus for expansion. In this sense the move to the frontier marked a journey back through temporal layers to an "original" heroic history. As Moretti has observed of the historical novel, space became time in proximity to the border.[90] "Behold our decline since 1821", wrote the influential journalist Vyzandios, "where are the Greek dreams of fifty years ago?"[91] Karkavitsas's short story "Homeland", published in the volume *Old Loves* (1900), a collection of short stories written between 1883 and 1897, draws a similar parallel between the disillusion of post-1897 Greece and the heroic idealism of 1821, while exposing the traditional rivalry between the Roumeliots and the Peloponnesians. The tale focuses on a chance encounter, after many years, between two friends, Petroletsos and Yorgakis Lambropoulos, the first from Roumeli (or central Greece) and the second from the Peloponnese. Whereas the impoverished and wandering Petroletsos has sacrificed all material comforts and personal happiness in order to fight for national freedom, his friend Yorgakis has exploited historical circumstances to amass a fortune and to realize his personal happiness at the nation's expense. The tale ends with Petroletsos's apostrophized vision of the Homeland who appears before him to affirm the enduring value of his sacrifice.[92]

In another of Karkavitsas's tales, entitled "New Gods", written in 1889 and published in the collection *Short Stories* (1892), the heroic reminiscences of Himaras who fought against the Turks during the War of Independence are contrasted with the professional militia who have been sent to the mountain village of Vounihora by the government to combat banditry. The old warrior's heavy flintlock gun compares poorly with the modern weapon with which the sergeant of the gendarmerie, Papatheodorakopoulos, is equipped. New technologies and the soldier's professional attitude to fighting no longer leave room for received ideas of heroism enshrined in popular songs and local traditions, while regional differences between the adversarial mountain-dwellers and the passive lowland-dwellers have been undermined, since Papatheodorakopoulos comes from the lowlands. As the narrator remarks:

> The competition between the weapons was, for Himara, a struggle of the past with the present, of the past generation, of the great and the admired, and the new generation, of the completely unimportant, the humble and puerile, which could only grow to manhood and prosper under the shadow of the old.[93]

Such fictions registered an anxiety about the state's relationship with the nation, as well as about the marginalization of the frontiersman in an increasingly centralized kingdom where city values were moving out to claim the country. The mountain frontier was projected as a repository of authentic Greek identity and historical memories which were in danger of being lost. And if the city sought to control the rejuvenating frontier zones, conversely the wilderness was mapped onto the city. Thus, the protagonist of Mitsakis's short story "The Reed-Pipe" (1890) is an old man from the mountains of Roumeli who plays folk tunes on his pipe, carved out of an eagle's bone, outside the Royal Gardens in central Athens. The commotion of the capital is here juxtaposed against the heroic traditions of rural Greece which are the subject of the player's tunes: the life of the stables, the solitude of the sheep folds, the idylls of the rural life. Mitsakis's pipe player possesses the ruddy complexion of a mountain shepherd and the narrator envisages him in former years as a kleft warrior. Significantly, soldiers stop to listen to him in Athens and an implicit contrast is drawn between the erstwhile warrior in the wilds of mainland Greece and the modern uniformed fighters in the institution of the army. In contrast to the mechanical cacophony of the trams, the pipe-player's music expresses the "heart and feeling of an entire people".[94] As the narrator remarks:

> seeing him, such a stranger to the world in which he finds himself, such a stranger to the surroundings which envelope him, the urge comes upon you immediately to push your way through the human crowd, to grab him then and there as he sits with his reed-pipe and his cape, to carry him off at once, far from the horse-cabs and trams...to some mountain of Roumeli.[95]

Mitsakis's sketch dwells at some length on the alie(nation) of the pipe player; on his displacement to an urban milieu in which he becomes a spectacle for the passers-by. Life on the frontier finds its urban equivalence in social marginalization. In this way, Mitsakis's text suggests how the boundary that secures the limits of the nation "may imperceptibly turn into a contentious *internal* liminality that provides a place from which to speak both of, and as, the minority, the exilic, the marginal, and the emergent".[96] Ironically, "real" Greek values, which were embodied in the people, were being relegated to the margins of the city; to those working-class slums on the Athenian outskirts. Perhaps not unsurprisingly, in this light, many of the writers who set their fiction in Athens chose to write about precisely these marginal, working-class areas on the edge of the city such as the districts of Ayios Philipos, Thesio, Gazi, Yerani, Psiri and Vathia. In many of these narratives the protagonists from the frontiers of the Greek state find themselves marginalized in Athens. Just as the outlying, frontier regions of the nation-state were celebrated in much rural fiction as a place where national Greek culture was produced, or re-produced, so the frontier of the capital was defined as a place where an indigenous Greek culture was manifest, in contrast to the superficial and foreign modernity of the centre with the royal palace at the hub. It was a further irony, too, that this slum literature owed much to European preoccupations with the urban poor in the final decades of the century that found expression in England, for example, in the slum fiction of

George Gissing and Walter Besant in the 1880s and of Rudyard Kipling, Arthur Morrison, and Somerset Maugham in the 1890s. By the same token, Mitsakis's tale reflects the ways in which the country was being brought to an urban readership, for, like the country tunes of the pipe-player, Greek rural fictions were yarns spun for an urban public.[97] "Ethography" was the term applied to this genre of "folkloric realism", set, for the most part, in the Greek countryside.[98] In short, Mitsakis's text draws attention to a fundamental contradiction at the heart of frontier fictions: such fictions were "not just stories 'of' the border, but of its erasure", narrations of the nation that told of the peripheries' integration into the homogenous space of the nation-state. The frontier was blotted out at the very moment of its celebration.[99]

The turn to the frontier, I have suggested, marked a turn to the past so that continuities across space involved continuities through time. The rural peripheries were construed as sites where historical memories accumulated; this preoccupation with the nation's glorious past. and its heroic narratives of foundation merged with the obligation to resist foreign contamination. Y. Flessas, in the preface to his novel *The Adventures of a Greek* (1860), declared that his intention was to write about the men of 1821 because it was both a theme wholly forgotten and a fitting theme in the context of the translated texts then swamping Greece. Ironically, tales of the Greek War of Independence were also popular outside Greece. In Britain, Vikelas's novel *Loukis Laras*, subtitled "reminiscences of a Chiote merchant during the War of Independence" appeared in a version by John Gennadius (1881), while Mrs Edmonds's translation of Kolokotronis's memoirs, entitled *Kolokotrones, the Klepht and the Warrior: Sixty Years of Peril and Daring: an Autobiography*, was published in 1892.[100] A year earlier an article by Rennell Rodd had been printed in *The Nineteenth Century* with the title "'The Poet of the Klephts: Aristoteles Valaoritis". Trikoupis's voluminous *History of the Greek Revolution* was published in London, while W. Alison Phillips's *The War of Greek Independence 1821–1833* appeared in 1897, the same year that Xenos's novel *Andronike: The Heroine of the Greek Revolution* was reprinted in the United States, from the original English translation of 1861.[101]

Although the writing of the generation of the 1880s is often viewed as a reaction against the historical novel, historical material played a central role in the work of these writers and important continuities existed with early nineteenth-century fiction. Historians claimed an epic status for their historical accounts. Paparrigopoulos, for example, in his five-volumed *History of the Greek Nation*, sets out a mythic narration of Greece's progress from antiquity, intimating the nation's glorious destiny. Conversely, writers of fiction sought authority for their work by couching their texts in historical references.[102] As the critic Mario Vitti has remarked, much ethographic fiction served a similar function to the historical novel, striving "to inculcate national pride, to strengthen the unifying dreams of the nation".[103]

The turn of the century also saw the publication of numerous histories by writers of prose fiction. Inspired by his travels in central mainland Greece and by his readings of Finlay and Trikoupis, Karkavitsas wrote historical essays, and Dimitrios Kambouroglou published a history of Athens (1889–1896). Kondylakis published his *History of the Cretan Revolution* (1893) and Papadiamantis translated both General Gordon and Finlay's histories of the War of Independence. Papadiamantis was encouraged to do so by his friend Yannis Vlachoyiannis (1867–1945), who went on to edit the memoirs of General Makriyannis, first serialized in an Athenian newspaper in 1904 and published in book form in 1907.[104] Many of the memoirs of the War of Independence published in the last decades of the century were associated with the activities of the historian Pavlos Lambros (1820–1887), a judge of the 1883 short story competition.[105]

Following Flessas's example and Stefanopoulos's conviction that the heroic exploits of 1821 furnished Greek writers with material that outshone any other national history, the War of Independence was recalled as a heroic struggle in much fiction of the 1880s and 1890s. Vikelas's novel *Loukis Laras* (1879), which is set during the War of Independence, was distributed free to new subscribers of the influential journal *Estia* as a momentous "national work".[106] By implication, the carving out of a literary space found its equivalence in the carving out of the nation-state's territory. Numerous short stories and novels by, amongst others, Drosinis, Eftaliotis, Karkavitsas, Kondylakis, V. Nikalaïdis, Papadiamantis and Vlachoyannis took historical or folkloric accounts of episodes from the War of Independence as their point of departure.[107] Indeed, Papadiamantis's short story "Christos Milionis" (1885), which is often taken to mark a bridge between his earlier work and his later ethographic short stories, draws on a Greek folk song and focuses on the defiant exploits of the celebrated kleftic hero against the Turks. In a review of Vlachoyiannis's historical short stories, Palamas praised them for the manner in which they gave expression to the "unquenchable flame of the national soul".[108]

Other examples of such heroic narratives of the nation-state's foundation are the Souliot stories of the writers Kostas Krystallis (1863–1894) and Christovasilis. The former, who was born an Ottoman subject in Epirus and escaped to Greece in 1887 after being denounced to the authorities for writing a stirringly patriotic collection of poetry, *The Shadows of Hades*, published a collection of short stories in 1894, the year of his death. This collection contains one story entitled "The

Notebook of Yerokalamiou" which consists of entries in a diary kept from the 1821 Revolution to 1881, which saw the freeing of Thessaly and left Epirus still in Ottoman control.[109] Another of Krystallis's stories, "The Young Souliot", is about a Greek who kills a Turkish pasha. In the "The Fête of Kastritsa" the narrator stresses the glories of Byzantine Epirus, and in the "The Icon" the protagonist's "great ideas" (*megales idees*) are explicitly associated with the heroic struggle of George Kastriotis or Scanderbeg, the charismatic Albanian leader, against Murad II and Mohammed II's attempts to subject the Balkans to Ottoman rule.

Like Krystallis, Christovasilis came from Epirus and published numerous collections of patriotic short stories around the turn of the century. In "My Best New Year", for example, he notes that the tale was written in 1889 while he was in Thessaly and Athens, condemned to death by the Turks in Ioannina. The local drama is set in an encompassing context of national struggle against the Ottomans.[110] What such writing does is to resuscitate earlier homologies from the time of the War of Independence in which the political role of print was projected as a form of fighting, and the might of the pen likened to that of the sword.[111] Or, as Ioannis Typaldos-Alfonsatos remarked in 1860, Alexander the Great had extended the frontiers of Hellenism, not by the might of weapons (*opla*), but by the dissemination of Greek letters (*grammata*).[112]

In the 1890s and early 1900s, as the struggle between Greece, the Ottoman Empire and Bulgaria over the possession of Macedonia intensified, emphasis was increasingly placed on literature's moral directive to raise the people from their thraldom and to inculcate a sense of national awareness, preparing future citizens for their ineluctable national destiny. In this spirit, a pamphlet published by *The National Language*, a society promoting Greek education outside Greece, asserted in 1905: "The nation's great weapon in Macedonia is the school". From the 1860s cultural societies had been established with increasing frequency within the Ottoman Empire with the aim of promoting Greek culture as "the executive organs of the great national plan".[113] In 1879 the Literary Society of Parnassos organized a conference of societies in which 72 societies participated from within the frontiers of the Greek state and 41 from Europe and the Ottoman Empire,[114] thus affirming Eric Hobsbawm's observation that "the progress of schools and universities measure that of nationalism, just as schools and especially universities became its most conscious champions".[115] Fighting could take place on different fronts and literature was enmeshed with other institutions, such as the economy. Aristidis Oikonomos, writing in the *Economic Review* in 1877, for example, asserted that "whoever thinks that the "Great Idea" is purely a military affair, is forgetting the kinds of weapons which our industrial century created".[116] The important role of literature and education were emphasized by John Gennadius in his preface to the English edition of Kolokotronis's memoirs:

> The culture of the Greek language and the study of Greek literature have undoubtedly had, at all times and places, and still have, as an immediate result, the awakening of a sense of individual dignity and of national freedom.[117]

In summary, the nation had to be *written*; it had to be mapped out on paper and read, before it could be actualized politically. In this sense, Greek writers assumed a double task: they strove both to reveal the practices that characterized the nation and to instruct; to provide manuals for the enfranchisement of the national subject.

The double task assigned to literature as an adversarial and protective discourse both resulted from and, in turn, contributed to a complex of ideas about the meaning and place of frontiers. On the one hand, literature's function was popularly conceived as pushing the frontiers of the nation-state outwards with the purpose of fulfilling an expansionist national destiny. Simultaneously, however, literature was construed as a defensive practice involved in preserving the present nation-state as it existed against imminent external threats. In the first case, the frontier was projected as a temporary line of demarcation which would inevitably shift eastwards with the acquisition of new territories. The tension over the double role of literature mirrored that of the role of the army. While some maintained that the army should bolster Greece's aspirations, others such as Rangavis (as Foreign Minister in 1856) asserted that the Greek army should be nothing more than an internal peace-keeping force since the national frontiers were guaranteed by the Protecting Powers.[118] The argument was even put that the Greeks of both the Kingdom and the Empire would eventually assume formal control of the Ottoman Empire and run it as a Christian Empire – Kolettis's "great fatherland" in the model first advocated by Rigas Velestinlis. Even while Panayiotis Soutsos's protagonist, Leandros, stakes out the ancient boundaries of the new Kingdom, the same author – inspired by the ideas of Saint Simon – could equally remark that boundaries were contingent and one day they would evaporate altogether as Greece merged with Europe in a vision not dissimilar to Yorgos Theotokas's (1905–1966) aerial mapping of the harmonious European "garden":

> Let us hope that one day in Europe there won't be any more need for nations, frontiers, custom-duties, trade limits. Europe, of which

the different parts are already connected by customs, by needs, by sympathies and by its enlightenment, Europe will be one society. Centuries are the equivalent of years in the age of nations. In two years of nations all that has been previously said will happen.[119]

3.6 THE SOCIAL PSYCHOLOGY OF EXPANSION

If, as Ernest Gellner has asserted, "nationalism is the principle that holds that political and cultural boundaries should be congruent", anxieties over the congruence and incongruence of boundaries in Greece were repeatedly expressed.[120] The writer's task, no less than the geographer's, was simultaneously to document the nation's life and to imagine it as it might be.

In 1893 Frederick Jackson Turner delivered his paper "The Significance of the Frontier in American History" before the American Historical Association at Chicago, where the World's Columbian Exposition was in full swing. In 1897 Friedrich Ratzel (1844–1904), who enjoyed great popularity in Greece at the turn of the century, published his *Political Geography*, in which the state was construed as a biological organism and its expansion was a natural life force or *lebensraum*.[121] And in 1907 Curzon had celebrated the "ennobling and invigorating stimulus" of frontiers which saved young men "from the corroding ease and the morbid excitements of Western civilization":

> Frontiers are indeed the razor's edge on which hang suspended the modern issues of war or peace, of life or death to nations. Just as the protection of the home is the most vital care of the private citizen, so the integrity of her borders is the condition of the existence of the State.[122]

As David Trotter has remarked, such writers "could be said to have sketched a social psychology which locks subjectivity into the politics of expansion".[123] In Greece the drive to claim new territories eastwards was bound up in a similar "social psychology" and writing, as this chapter has sought to demonstrate, no less than geography, was inextricably bound up with the politics of expansion and integration.

There was, of course, an important counter-discourse that questioned the rejuvenating power of the frontier and the integrity of the national culture being enclosed. In 1896, the year that the first Olympic Games was held in Athens and on the eve of Greece's disastrous war with the Ottoman Empire, Karkavitsas published his novel *The Beggar*. From 1895 Karkavitsas had become a full-time military doctor and drew, in his writing, upon the experience of his earlier

travels and postings around Greece. *The Beggar* is set in frontier territory in the recently liberated province of Thessaly (1881) under Mount
Olympos. Rather than focusing on heroic resistance to outside threats,
however, Karkavitsas is concerned with the fundamental disunity of the
society and culture enclosed within these boundaries which are championed as national. The Greek state is presented as corrupt and its
population degenerate, while cultural continuity exists, the narrator
insists, not between ancient and modern Greece, but between the newly
liberated Greek lands and the Turkish institutions which governed
them for centuries. One of the chief characters in the novel, Petros
Valahas, is a customs officer dispatched to "the last customs station in
the Kingdom", in the village of Nychteremi. Valahas is significantly
from old Greece, and more particularly, from Missolonghi, with its rich
and heroic history. If the downtrodden villagers are disillusioned with
the new Greek administration, nothing has changed since Thessaly's
annexation. The villagers live in squalid shacks with their animals and
the novel suggests that, despite the redrawing of frontiers, old frontiers
and attitudes persist within the ostensibly unified state. The Turks in
the narrative are not the real enemies, rather the Greeks are at war
with themselves. It is this anxiety – the spectre of internal disunity – as
much as the expansionist ideology of the "Great Idea", that shaped
those developing institutions of the modern Greek state through which
the "unredeemed" territories were consolidated.

Chapter Four

Folklores of modernity

4.1 MODERNIZATION

One influential view of the process of nation-building suggests that it is an activity initiated from a political centre. In France, for example, Eugen Weber, amongst others, has argued that it was not until after 1870 that local regional identities were displaced. During this period the provinces were opened up by roads and railways. State-sponsored institutions such as compulsory primary education and military conscription fostered a unified and standardized national culture, thus transforming peasants into Frenchmen.[1] Doubt remains, however, about the speed with which, even in France, local affiliations and a sense of place disintegrated under the impact of an abstract national loyalty[2] that forged what Ernest Gellner has called a "common or single conceptual currency".[3] In Greece the lag between the adoption of a modern national identity and the abandonment of a traditional local identity – between peasants and Greeks – was far more pronounced. In the absence of conclusive research on regional Greece, however, it is impossible to assess with any certainty the degree to which a "modern" national identity was diffused outwards and, recipro-cally, to determine the extent to which rural populations accepted the formal means of national integration. As John Lawson observed in his *Modern Greek Folklore and Ancient Greek Religion* (1910), when he reflected on the question of Greek national identity:

> If he [a Greek] be asked what is his nation land (*patrida*), his answer will be, not Greece nor any of the larger divisions of it, but the particular town or hamlet in which he happened to be born...[4]

Tensions persisted between the centre and the periphery, between the nation and local levels of politics – tensions that continue to be felt in

Greece today.[5] As Miller observed at the turn of the century: "The magnate of each local district is often the determining factor in the election of deputies to parliament."[6] What concerns us here, however, is nationalism as the promotion of a homogenous "centrally sustained" high culture which, as Gellner noted, is projected as the natural repository of political legitimacy. Moreover, the cultures which nationalism claims to be defending are "often its own inventions, modified out of all recognition".[7] At the beginning of the twentieth century the Greek socialist Yorgos Skliros (1878–1919) was to argue, in similar terms, that the very concept of fatherland and nation were being duplicitously mobilized by the bourgeoisie to promote its own interests.[8]

Debates about the relationship between cultural formation and national identity, as Chapter One has suggested, were anticipated in the contradictions that pervade late eighteenth and nineteenth-century thinking about the nation. To what extent was culture popularly emergent? To what degree was it imposed in a process of enculturation? These questions were to inform folklore as an emerging discipline in the late nineteenth century predicated upon a celebration of rural Greek peasant culture and, concomitantly, upon the demonstration of the state's territorial and historical integrity.

The years between 1870 and 1920 marked an important change in perceptions of place in Greece, less dramatic, certainly, than those elsewhere, but nonetheless fundamental.[9] "Land" began to be appreciated as "countryside".[10] This transformation was bound up with changing conditions of production and consumption within society, and in Greece, with changing structures of land tenure.[11] In the 1880s and 1890s the influence of local leaders diminished substantially.[12] Emphasis began to be placed on the concept of a "national centre", a term which gained increasing currency.[13] The country's endemic brigandage, a legacy of the pre-revolutionary period, was slowly brought under control, although this led to a spiralling of crime as brigand chiefs were crushed, leaving a void, and as young men drifted from the rural areas to the capital. Indeed, from the 1870s Greece had the highest homicide rate in Europe.[14] By and large, however, travel became safer and Murray's *Handbook* for 1884 declared that, with the exception of the frontier regions, Greece posed no dangers for travellers; although British newspapers continued to report attacks on travellers by brigands, especially in the frontier territories.[15] This situation was a marked contrast to the uproar that had greeted news of the Dilessi murders in April 1870, when a party of English aristocrats was abducted by brigands on an outing to visit the historic battlefield of Marathon, and four members of the group were murdered, causing international outrage.[16]

Under Charilaos Trikoupis's (1832–1896) administrations in the 1880s and 1890s, the Greek provinces were penetrated economically through the construction of roads and a railway network, as well as the building of the Corinth Canal which was formally opened in 1893.[17] Before 1880 it had taken three days to complete the 85 kilometre journey from Athens to Corinth, hugging the coastal path along the Saronic Gulf.[18] A railway line from Athens to Piraeus was constructed in 1867–1869 and electrified in 1904, although the main Piraeus-Athens-Larissa line was not built until 1902–1909. From 1885 Athens was linked by railway with Kifissia, Faliro, Lavrio, and Corinth. In 1907 the capital was connected by rail with both the Peloponnese and Thessaly, although it was not until 1916 that Greece was linked up by rail with the rest of Europe.[19] Writing in 1893 R.A.H. Bickford-Smith noted that there were seven railway companies and a total of 911 kilometres of railway with 504 kilometres under construction, as compared to Bulgaria's 402 kilometres of track and Serbia's 549 kilometres.[20] By 1905 there were 1,332 kilometres of track in Greece. In contrast to the other regions of the Mediterranean, however, travel in Greece depended mainly on horse-power. In the 1860s railways had come to Southern Italy and a line was built across Sardinia in the 1870s. By the 1880s Sicily, Egypt, and Algeria were all served by railways.[21] Transport within the Greek capital was by horse tram, steam train, and bus. The first motorcar circulated in Athens in 1896, the year in which the Olympic Games were hosted in the Greek capital. On the eve of the Balkan wars there were only 150 cars and 805 kilometres of carriageway in the country.[22] In 1893 Greece had 186 telegraph offices and 8,958 kilometres of wire managed by the Eastern Telegraph Company based on Syros, although there were still no telephones.[23] Other major public works were undertaken, notably the draining of Lake Copais by a British company which recovered some 1,200 hectares of fertile land for cultivation. As Nikos Mouzelis has remarked:

> The territorial and population growth, the influx of foreign capital, the development of an extensive transport system, the creation of a unified internal market and the establishment of an institutional framework facilitating state intervention in the economy, provided some of the basic preconditions for the development of capitalism in the Greek social formation.[24]

If Trikoupis's modernizing drive stimulated the circulation of capital through the regions and led to the establishment of provincial banks,[25] it also encouraged the rise of the newspaper in Greece as a medium of communication which responded to the demands of a new urban public. By 1893 there were 131 newspapers[26] and in 1895 Dragoumis quipped that there were more newspapers than there were readers.[27] As Vikelas observed in 1885, attempting to sum up the changes:

Greece has not remained stationary since 1871. Her frontiers have been extended; the population has increased; the cities have expanded, industry and commerce have developed, railroads have been constructed, and the inauguration of a line from Athens to Megara and from Volos to Larissa has recently been announced; in Corinth they're now occupied in transforming the Peloponnese into an island; at Lavria they're exploiting the treasure of the earth...the number of schools and pupils has steadily increased.[28]

While the period from 1880 to 1922 saw the unification of the state and the growth of a labour force and of a consumer market, the Greek case, nevertheless, differs markedly from other European countries. The 1851 census in Britain, for example, showed that for the first time the majority of the population lived in cities.[29] Although the cases of Germany and France were different, in contrast to the relatively attenuated agricultural sectors elsewhere, Greece remained a predominantly agrarian society with substantial pockets of economic backwardness. In France at the turn of the century, 67 percent of the population continued to live off the land.[30] In Greece the separation between the spheres of production and consumption from the 1870s was even less pronounced. People retained contact with the villages, while cities were still small and even after Trikoupis's reforms communications remained poor. Nor was the process of modernization as thorough as in the French case. In 1893 an estimated 78 percent of the population was rural, similar to that of Romania, although less than that of Italy[31] and as late as 1938, 60 percent of the Greek population still depended on agriculture, as compared to 40 percent in Italy, 5 percent in England, but 75 percent in Yugoslavia.[32]

Notwithstanding this, the growth of urban centres in Greece was notable. In 1834 the population of Athens was some 10,000; by 1870 it had reached 43,000 (not including the surrounding villages). The greatest period of urban migration fell somewhere between 1870 and 1890. By 1896 the population of Athens was well over 100,000, making it the third largest city in Southeast Europe, after Bucharest and Constantinople.[33] In 1853 Patras was the only town in the Peloponnese with a population of over 5,000. By 1907 there were ten such towns.[34]

4.2 SURVIVALS: BACK TO NATURE

In Greece the last decades of the century witnessed a "back to nature" movement, bound up with an interest in folklore, which was, in part, a reaction against the pace of urbanization and progress. Attention was shifted onto those unfamiliar elements within the national space itself.

It was in the wild, outlying, rural regions of the nation-state that authentic national traditions lived on. The prevailing views of foreign observers greatly influenced the way in which Greeks saw themselves, a fact noted by the writer Dimitrios Chatzopoulos (1872–1936) in 1901 in an article in which he ridiculed Greek writers for endeavouring to satisfy European appetites for stereotypical folkloric narratives which bore no resemblance to the realities of modern Greece. He wearily noted how an Englishwoman arrived in Athens and, to the consterna-tion of a local inhabitant, lamented that she was unable to find a single brigand.[35]

Occupying the furthest limits of Europe, the Greeks were perceived by travellers as "the aborigines" of the continent.[36] Char-acteristically, in his survey of Greece at the turn of the century, Miller observed that "among the country-folk, as a rule, the best qualities, physical and moral, of the race are to be found", adding that "while the Greeks, especially in the remote country districts, are a long-lived race, there are signs of physical deterioration among those who have always been town dwellers".[37] The explorer and archaeologist James Theodore Bent, who studied the local traditions and customs on the Aegean islands in the late 1880s, drew an explicit connection between the Greek and the Celt when he observed that "for a pure Greek, as for a pure Celt, you must search in mountain villages and unfrequented bye-paths".[38] Similarly, the folklorist Rennell Rodd insisted that it was among "the dwellers of the upland pastures, whose lives contrast so markedly with the keen working mind, the restless, fretful activity of...the little trader of the coast towns" that unadulterated Hellenic customs were still alive.[39] Much the same sentiments were expressed by the journalist H.N. Brailsford, who travelled through Macedonia shortly after the Ilinden Uprising of 1903. "The true Greece is to be sought in the Highlands and the Isles", he declared, "where Hellenism is still married to its barren rocks and the waves that cradled it, it lives triumphant and unspoiled. Its decadence is only in the ghettos and bazaars and the breathless city lanes".[40]

The Greek "aborigines" on the "edge" of Europe thus fulfilled an equivalent symbolic role in relation to British travellers as the Celtic fringe did. This preoccupation with the manner and customs of "the country-folk" registered an anxiety about the disappearance of a rural way of life under the onslaught of a cosmopolitan modernity.[41] As John Pentland Mahaffy announced in his popular travel book *Rambles and Studies in Greece*, the very title of which is reminiscent of British folk-loric preoccupations, genuine national character was in danger of disappearing before a "great tide of sameness":

If he [the traveller] desires to study national character, and peculiar manners and customs, he will find in the hardy mountaineers of Greece one of the most unreformed societies, hardly yet affected by the great tide of sameness which is invading all Europe in dress, fabrics, and usages.[42]

Influenced by such outsiders' perceptions of their own culture, Greek folklorists worked within a nationalist ideology: their task, as formulated by Nikolaos Politis, the man who coined the Greek word for folklore (*laografia*) in 1884, was the search to establish the continuity of Greek culture from antiquity through time and across space.[43] As Michael Herzfeld has remarked "the very name 'Hellenes' was an artefact that, for Politis, claimed all the territories in which it was found for the Greek nation".[44]

National character was defined succinctly, in 1880, by Richard Claverhouse Jebb, Professor of Greek at the University of Glasgow and later Regius Professor of Greek at Cambridge, in a lecture on Greece delivered before the Philosophical Institution at Edinburgh, as "broadly-marked tendencies or aptitude traceable through every period of [the nation's] history...the persistency of such broad traits vouches at least for a continuous tradition of those institutions and usages, those ways of thinking and feeling, which give essential unity to an originally composite nationality".[45] Jebb's pronouncements reflected a wider preoccupation in Britain and elsewhere with tracing the nation's ancient origins.[46] This idea of a "continuous tradition" articulated by Jebb was reflected in a tripartite model of national culture which was applied across disciplines. In 1873, for example, Henry Sweet proposed the division of English into Old, Middle and Modern, while a similar notion of cultural continuum was asserted in Greece by Konstantinos Paparrigopoulos and Spyridon Zambelios (1815–1881). In Britain, institutions such as the Folk-Lore Society (1878), the National Trust (1895) and the magazine *Country Life* (1897) were established to bolster the sense, in Jebb's words, of an "originally composite nationality", while the late Victorian era saw numerous heritage initiatives aimed to promote the "essential unity" of the national life: the foundation of the Society for the Protection of Ancient Buildings (1877), the first local laws to preserve endangered plants (1888) and the inception of the Victorian County History (1899).

"Englishness",[47] no less than "Frenchness"– as Eugen Weber has argued[48] – or, for that matter, "Greekness", was closely bound up with the celebration of local, regional identities. The regions betokened pre-industrial moral values that were being lost.[49] They were construed as underpinning a national identity and providing a bulwark against the deleterious progress of modernity that threatened to dismantle the organic national culture rooted in the land. Regional studies sought to record regional customs, legends and dialects in the same way that different flora, fauna and landscape morphologies were catalogued. Writing in his autobiography about the folkloric movement in Greece, Yeoryios Drosinis observed that the object was "to find themes from outside the cosmopolitan centres of city life in the freedom of the Greek life of the mountains and the sea".[50] In Greece at the very moment of unification or modernization, there was a pronounced focus on local knowledge which found its expression in folkloric studies, in regional literature, and in the publication of numerous local histories and geographies. The concern with popular culture, which had been ignored as Greece's unspoken Oriental legacy, was increasingly celebrated as an integral part of the nation's identity. In 1890, for example, the Karaghiozis shadow puppet theatre, which had hitherto been deemed an unacceptably subversive form of popular entertainment and a pernicious Ottoman legacy, was re-established in Athens after an absence of several decades.[51] There was similarly an interest in non-Western forms of music.[52] In art, painters such as Nikolaos Gyzis (1842–1901) and Nikiforos Lytras (1832–1904) drew upon rural and Oriental themes for their inspiration, while the popular melodrama *Golpho, the Lover of the Shepherdess* (1894), a rural romance by Spyros Peresiadis (1864–1918), was the first feature film to be made in Greece in 1914.

The "back to nature" movement in the final decades of the nineteenth century was closely bound up with a "turn to the people" among the urban elite which was articulated on a political level in socialism in the 1880s (although the Socialist Labour Party was not established until 1918), and in demoticism, the championing of the popular, spoken language.[53] As already stated, the movement was by no means unique to Greece. Within the Ottoman Empire, Tanzimat writers were increasingly interested in folklore and folk literature as expressions of a Turkish national identity, particularly between 1860 and 1900 when Ziya Gök Alp (1876–1924) coined the term *halkiyat* ("lore of the people").[54] In Russia, as in Greece, this populist movement, or *narodnishesvo*, gained increasing momentum from the 1870s. Communal principles which were believed to have survived in the village *mir* and were deemed a distinctively Russian way of life, were idealized. Alexander Herzen (1812–1870) encouraged the radical intelligentsia to go out from the city to the peasants. In both Russia and Greece, this emphasis on the people (*laos, narod*), a body which was reinscribed in its biblical sense as "the chosen people",[55] was also reflected in the subject of literature. In Greece, the *laos* were the uneducated masses and the purpose of folklore, or *laografia*, was to demonstrate how the masses belonged to the nation or *ethnos*.[56]

4.3   EDUCATED INTO UNBELIEF

Nikolaos Politis, the founder of the Folklore Society (1908), who coined
the term *laografia* for folklore in Greek some forty years after the anti-
quary William Thoms had introduced the word in the pages of *The
Athenaeum*, was the central figure in the Greek folklore movement.
Born in the southern Peloponnesian town of Kalamata in 1852, he
studied at the University of Athens and later at Munich before
returning to Greece. The circle of writers that gathered around the
journal, *Estia*, over which Politis presided, congregated in a beer house
on Homer Street in Plaka at the base of the Acropolis, of which
Drosinis left a memorable account in his autobiography.[57] The
common purpose of the group, as Drosinis asserted, was freedom
"from the enslavement to foreign models and the creativity of our own
national life in all its expressions".[58]

   Folklore celebrated the local. At the beginning of his *Study of the Life
of the Modern Greeks: Modern Greek Mythology*, published in two volumes
in 1871 and 1874, Politis noted that his intention was to record
"various local traditions".[59] His aim was to refute the theories of Jacob
von Fallmerayer, who, half a century earlier, had drawn attention to the
Slavic origin of place-names in Greece when arguing against the ethnic
purity of the modern Greeks.[60] In fact, Politis's *Modern Greek Mythology*
was produced as a response to the second competition instituted by
Pandora in 1871, which was sponsored by the wealthy Odessa philan-
thropist Th. P. Rodokanakis, and had as its theme "the collection from
as many locations as possible of the Greek manners, customs, and practices and their comparison with what is recorded in the surviving
authors, so that their similarities and differences may be made
known".[61] The concern for local traditions was also bound up with an
interest in dialects as survivals from the nation's uncorrupted pre-
history. The idea that local dialects represented an unadulterated
language, as opposed to the cosmopolitan centres, was articulated most
fully, perhaps, by Friedrich Max Müller in his influential theories of
dialectical regeneration, which were to have an important impact in
Greece.[62] "Literary language, the language of the cities", he argued,
"decays as it develops away from experience and must be reinvigorated
by input from the regional frontiers where the forms of speech should
still touch the forms of experience".[63] In Britain a clear connection was
sustained between the state of language and national health. Like
Müller, the English dialect poet and philologist William Barnes (1801–
1886) asserted that the purest English was spoken by those furthest
from the international centres, especially the Wessex folk. Such ideas
were also reflected in the importance of dialect in prose fiction which
was construed as a source of aesthetic and ideological renewal.[64]

However, the danger of linguistic subversion was also evoked. In Greece, for example, the popular drama known as *Komidillio* exposed the differences between regional dialects and affiliations, particularly between Zakynthiots and Roumeliots; linguistic variations provided a source of misunderstanding and potential conflict. In 1888, the staging of Vyzandios's play *Babel* further reminded Greeks of the dangers of linguistic fragmentation.[65] As Aristidis Kyprianos (1830–1869) had remarked in the pages of the journal *Filistor*, linguistic diversity was symptomatic of a wider political, social and moral instability.[66]

If folklore was concerned with the survival of local traditions, it was also, as Politis makes clear, concerned with demonstrating the continuity and unity of Greek culture; with illustrating the essential Greekness of the territory from which the customs had been collected. The very fact that folkloric material was anthologized thematically, as opposed to by region, suggests the extent to which folklore was an integrative practice aimed at obliterating regional differences. As Lawson declared in his *Modern Greek Folklore*, local customs "bear witness to the genuinely Hellenic nationality of the inhabitants of modern Greece".[67] The object of the folklorist was to identify "certain elements of modern Greek culture as fossilized relics of ancient Greek culture".[68] In this sense, too, there was a link with geography and geology, which strove to uncover interred histories. Folklorists, no less than geologists who delved into the physical substrata, strove to disinter the remnants of the nation's buried pre-history; what Politis termed "the continuation of a former life".[69] Folklore's aim was to affirm what Drosinis, employing a geological metaphor, called "the granite-like foundations of [Greek] moral and spiritual authority".[70] Just as fossils were employed as a means of reconstructing a geological history, so the study of folklore was conceived as a way of reconstructing an ancient cultural heritage: "European folklore was to the history of human civilization what the fossil record was to earth history".[71] Politis himself was to compare these cultural survivals – a term which he borrowed from Sir Edward Burnett Tylor, the founder of cultural anthropology (1832–1917) (*epiviosis, engatalimmata*) – to "sea shells of previous geological ages stuck to the rocks of the mountains".[72] As he also declared:

> The hope that the great figures of classical antiquity should not forever remain just empty shadows, but that they may be transformed into life, into a body with flesh and blood, this is the one truly interesting and truly enticing issue; to search out in modern Greece – and find – antiquity.[73]

There was urgency in this search for Greece's sedimented antiquity since folk culture, Politis maintained, was fast disappearing under the advancement of education. In the first issue of *Folklore*, the journal which he had founded in 1909, he wrote about "the psychic and social expressions of the life of the people (*laos*); the expressions, in other words, whose origins remain unknown" and added that these "do not originate from the influence of any exemplary person, furthermore they are not the result of breeding or education".[74] Elsewhere he remarked:

> For the ancient tales which for centuries the folk had retained passing them on in their ignorance, narrating them at their village festivals or around shepherds' hearths are now disappearing with the advance of education. Twenty years ago one could collect five or six times what one is capable of gathering of these same tales today. If another ten years are allowed to pass, and no one concentrates on this matter, then none of these tales will be saved. In this respect they are worthy of the complete attention of those who are educated.[75]

Ironically, Politis, as Professor of Mythology and later rector at the University of Athens, was deeply involved in the eradication of his own subject; in that process in which, as W.H.D. Rouse noted in his preface to Eftaliotis's collection *Island Stories*, the population was being "educated into unbelief".[76] From 1884 Politis had worked for the Ministry of Education and in 1887 had been appointed the Chief School Inspector, responsible for sending out a circular requesting teachers to record folklore.[77]

Folklore, as a practice, was characterized by a contradiction which has already been touched upon in the discussion of literature's performative and pedagogic functions in Chapter One. "Those who were educated" were safeguarding folklore from "the advance of education". It was a contradiction which Gustave Le Bon (1841–1931), the French social psychologist, diagnosed in his reflections on traditions which "represent the idea, the needs, and the sentiments of the past". Yet, as he added in his classic study *The Crowd* (1895), "civilization is impossible without traditions, and progress impossible without the destruction of those traditions".[78] As Homi Bhabha has argued, in nationalist discourse, the *Volk* are caught in a double-time. As objects of a nationalist pedagogy they are imagined as belonging to a space that is incorporated within a teleology of "progress" at the same time as it is characterized by the repetitive nature of the "timeless" national life:

> In the production of the nation as narration there is a split between the continuist, accumulative temporality of the pedagogical, and the repetitious, recursive strategy of the performative. It is through this

process of splitting that the conceptual ambivalence of modern society becomes the site of *writing the nation*.[79]

Folklore was bent on revealing *and* teaching. It sought to preserve the local. Yet as a practice promoted by the state, it was bound up in the eclipse of the local. As the German journalist and historian Wilhelm Heinrich Riehl (1823–1897) remarked, folklore was one way of revealing the road for right government and he repeatedly stressed its connection with geography. Riehl insisted on the need to study the "general characteristics of the German peasantry" and the context of regional variations. George Eliot, who reviewed two of his books in 1856 in her influential essay "The Natural History of German Life", was convinced that similar studies needed to be undertaken of English peasants since social questions could only be answered "with a real knowledge of the people, with a thorough study of their habits, their ideas, their motives."[80] In 1859, in an article on "Folklore as Science", Riehl noted:

> The study of folklore will be most beneficial to the whole sphere of administrative discipline. For if the policing of culture [*culturpolizei*] is merely conditioned by the practical needs of the population, then it can and must be able to organize itself according to the ethno-graphic laws on which these needs are based...the highest triumph of the internal art of administration would then consist of the assim-ilation of every police action to the inner life [*Natur*] of the folk such that the population would come to believe that even in troublesome and aggravating matters the police acted only in their own interest and on behalf of their sentiments.[81]

In this essentially Romantic formulation, folklore as a form of social knowledge was inextricably bound up with power and, more specifi-cally, with the political imperative to unify the nation-state: "knowledge of a territory and its people", or geography and folklore, was crucial for the act of governing.[82] As Uli Linke has observed of an earlier phase of German folklore:

> The many territorial and administrative divisions not only inhibited attempts to standardize commercial and religious practices but also hindered any efforts toward national unification. Under these circumstances, the study of folklore was perceived by the romantics as a means to forge a sense of unity among the German population and thereby supersede all existing (sociopolitical) boundaries.[83]

It was a view later articulated by Edwin Sidney Hartland (1848–1927) in his presidential address to the Folk-Lore Society in which he formulated his "empire theory", stressing the practical advantages of folklore in the British Empire for governors, district officers and judges: "No ruler who does not understand his subjects can govern them for the best advantage, either theirs or his."[84] Social knowledge was transformed into an agent of power and folklore was inexorably bound up with the domesticating endeavours of the state. Not only did folklore express the spirit of people, but it "became a pedagogical tool in a process of 'national' socialization".[85] It was impelled by a directive to know the people so that the government could be in tune with the population governed, and at the same time strove to shape the population into model national citizens, according to the state's requirements.[86] As the folklorist Stylpon Kyriakidis (1887–1964) expressed it, folklore was a means for the elite to understand the ways in which the less developed folk thought and acted, and thus made an indispensable contribution to effective government.[87]

On the one hand, the past recorded by folklore needed to be preserved as part of the national heritage. On the other hand, the compilation of folkloric collections represented a way of controlling and circumscribing these survivals. The peasant was reified; celebrated both as the essence of Greekness and as a bulwark against an encroaching modernity exemplified by the newspapers and a national education. Yet folklore was a practice that drew upon the taxonomic preoccupations of science, and in so doing, was implicated in the very progress that threatened the rural peasantry.[88] As Tylor asserted in his most famous work *Primitive Culture* (1871), which appeared in the same year as *Modern Greek Mythology*, anthropology was essentially a reformer's science whose goal was to aid progress by identifying these survivals and marking them out for destruction. Politis acknowledged Tylor as an influence and wrote an article entitled "On the Breaking of Vessels as a Funeral Rite in Modern Greece" which was delivered as a lecture before the Institute of Anthropology in March 1893 at Tylor's suggestion (Tylor himself spoke at the same session on the "Tasmanians as Representatives of Palaeolithic Man").[89] Folklore revealed the savage in the peasant so that there was "scarce a hand's breadth of difference between an English ploughman and a Negro of Central Africa".[90]

While the outlying regions were a measure by which national progress could be charted, that comparative perspective itself stimulated what Michael Hechter has called a process of "internal colonialism".[91] The inhabitants of the regions, no less than "women and children, the peasantry, the urban poor or the ethnically other", furnished an internal Otherness which required regulating by the state.[92] In his article "Border Crossings: Cornwall and the English (Imagi)Nation", James Vernon has noted the ways in which:

> The romantic rhetoric of a world that had been lost was offset by the realisation that loss was an essential element of modernity...Like the colonial 'primitive', the 'savage within' was a prisoner of nature and irrationality, a remnant from an earlier stage of civilization against which the civilized could measure their own modernity.[93]

The "realization" of this gulf between the modern and the primitive was translated into racial arguments in studies such as John Beddoe's *The Races of Britain* (1885), in which the author strove to measure the proportion of "nigrescence" within the British Isles. If exotic places were being translated in terms of the familiar, familiar places were being correspondingly mapped in terms of the exotic.[94] In France, overseas colonies provided an analogy for the undomesticated provinces and furnished a comparative framework for the description of rural French customs and idiosyncrasies.[95] The exotic was not only an extraneous, colonial Other, against which European authority was defined; it was also an internal category that marked out differences within Jebb's "organically composite nationality". As Richard Dorson has remarked: "In the folklore of the peasant, the observer could witness on the edge of his own enlightened culture the relics of barbaric rites".[96] Such a comparativist view of folklore, derived from Tylor, fed into Politis's approach. He sought to analyze the myths of the separation of the earth and the sky in modern Greek folklore with similar Polynesian and African mythologies,[97] just as he studies Greek funeral rites in comparison to similar customs among "Asiatic, African, American and Australian peoples".[98] This approach, however, sat uncomfortably with the avowed historical orientations of Greek folklore which was bent on asserting the ancient Greek origins of mythology. Indeed, the notion of primitive survivals and the tripartite periodization proposed by the American ethnologist Lewis Morgan in *Ancient Society* (1877) of the wild, the barbarian and the civilized was reworked through the prism of Greek nationalism into a theory of continuity through time.

Something of the contradictions of the Greek folklorist's activity are apparent in the statement of the folklorist Dimitrios Loukatos:

> Folklore thus becomes a truly national discipline, because it tells the Nation: 'Know Thyself'...In particular, Greek folklore helps our national philology and ethnography both ancient and modern, to demonstrate their continuity and their similarity over the ages and to strengthen in this manner the reputation of our people and our

Nation in the eyes of the international intellectual community. In difficult hours of attack on the ethnological character of the modern Greeks (Fallmerayer), Folklore (together with Linguistics) has risen to the defence with its arguments. And in more serious times, of slavery and of occupation (sometimes even of internal oppression), Folklore affirms the sound political convictions of its practitioner so that they can stand up against the dangers of anti-Hellenism and the deprivation of Freedom. And in times of national independence, Folklore marshals its arguments once again in order to help...prevent the detachment of territories from its ethnological corpus.[99]

For Loukatos, folklore was a patriotic enterprise bound up with the protection and integration of the Greek nation-state; the incorporation of ethnographic material into a corpus was inseparable in his mind from the incorporation of the national space. The folklorist was involved in a two-pronged offensive that looked both inwards at the potential for "internal oppression" and outwards ("standing up against the dangers of anti-Hellenism"). In short, the function of folklore was to represent internal differences and to abolish them. Like the frontier fictions discussed in Chapter Three, folklore evoked the border only to erase it and suppress the savage spaces within "so that the state could achieve Weber's 'monopoly of legitimate violence'".[100] Haunting the project was the threat of detachment, fragmentation and violence induced by the folk's untamed savagery.

Chapter Five

Local knowledge, national history

5.1 TOPOGRAPHICAL LITERATURE

During the 1880s and 1890s there was a pronounced focus on local knowledges in Greece, which was articulated in the emerging discipline of folklore, as we have seen in the previous chapter, but was also manifest in the publication of numerous local histories and geographies. In 1894 the geographer Konstantinos Papamichalopoulos asserted that geography should be taught to children in order to demonstrate how "every corner, every inch of territory is linked to an historical event worthy of being mentioned and celebrated".[1] The emphasis on an imperialist geography that underscored Greek irredentist ambitions of a reconstituted Byzantine Empire with its capital at Constantinople thus co-existed with a celebration of local, regional geographies. A key word in late nineteenth and early twentieth-century nationalist discourse was "place" (*topos*).

From the 1880s the "local" homeland or *patrida* was emphasized as an essential cultural and historical constituent of the national space. In part, this shift took place under the influence of the *heimatkunde* movement in Germany and was expressed in *patridografia*, the term – first used in 1883 – to describe the dissemination of local geographic and historical knowledges. The school curriculum increasingly focused on students' acquaintance with their localities before moving outwards to engage with other larger geographical categories. In much the same way, the geography syllabus established in France, in the wake of the reforms inaugurated by the Minister of Education Jules Simon (1870–1873), gave priority to the teaching of "geography which proceeded from the concrete and familiar to the abstract and unfamiliar, rather than *vice versa* as was characteristic of the existing programme".[2] Children were encouraged to fill in the names of places on maps, while exercises conceptualized the centrifugal trajectory from region to nation and world geography as a circular peregrination across space from the core locality and back.[3] Not surprisingly, perhaps, preoccupations with walking and circulations around the local *patrida* figure prominently in Greek fiction of the period, such as the island stories by Papadiamantis. The protagonists in these texts walk along paths and in the process activate a local, indigenous history so that the circuitous tracks reflect the meandering shape of the narrative. As the narrator poignantly remarks in Dragoumis's novel *The Blood of Heroes and Martyrs* (1907): "If only by walking over the ground I could make it [Macedonia] Greek".[4]

As Chapter Four has demonstrated, the state-controlled process of nation-building centred on the fostering of a national loyalty that was promoted against "local loyalties".[5] By the same token, the local was projected onto the national. In the words of the ethnographer and folklorist Charles-Arnold Van Gennep (1833–1957), nationhood is "the extension of real or symbolic love felt for the corner of land which belongs to the community, to an entire valley, an immense plain, the steppe and the great city like Paris or Vienna".[6] Finally, the nation-building process in Greece, as elsewhere, involved the celebration of places tied to collective memories.[7]

In late nineteenth- and early twentieth-century Greece the particularities of place were construed both as underpinning the state's territorial expansion and as a resistance to the homogenizing drive of a state-sponsored nationalism, in much the same way that folklore was marshalled both to resist *and* to promote regional incorporations into the state. This contradiction characterizes many of the regional histories and geographies. On the one hand, the particularities of place were mobilized as evidence of those "primordial attachments"[8] upon which the nation-state was predicated. Place was championed as part of an affirmation of Greece's "old traditions", in much the same way as they were in France after 1870 and in England where "Englishness" was reconstructed through a celebration of the rural.[9] It was during the 1880s and 1890s, as Weber has observed, that wall maps and prints representing the different regions of France were introduced into schools.[10] Drosinis, recalling his Athenian childhood in the 1860s, noted that in his school: "we learned geography without maps. It didn't consist of anything but a list of foreign names of mountains, rivers and cities."[11] By the 1880s, however, in Greece, as in France, maps had become increasingly central to the school curriculum and in an act promulgated in 1895, maps needed to be sanctioned by a special governmental committee.[12]

On the other hand, as in France, regionalism was used to provide a critique of the centralized state which had usurped deep-rooted local authorities. At the beginning of the twentieth century there were many commentators, such as Dragoumis, who were convinced that the nation-state had attenuated the ingrained local affiliations upon which Greek identity depended.

Local consciousness (*topikismos*) had been traditionally strong in Greece[13] – indeed, had arguably thwarted the development of a powerful centralized state – but the insistence on local histories and geographies was due, in part, to the economic expansion of provincial cities such as Patras, Kalamata and Piraeus after 1860; a development which served to encourage local cultural activities in competition with Athens. The erection of public buildings and theatres, copiously reported in local newspapers, together with cultural activities such as opera, theatre, orchestral concerts and local sports and literary clubs reflected local civil pride. Local patriotism was articulated in local geographies and histories, such as Panayiotis Komninos's geographical history of Laconia (1896),[14] E. Manolakakis's geographical history of Karpathos,[15] or Stephanos Thomopoulos's *History of the City of Patras* (1888), in which the author describes his task as a local historian in rousing patriotic terms: "Love for the homeland, that noble spring of every sensitive heart, dictates a person to research his homeland's diverse fate and adventures...".[16] Patras had acquired a theatre in 1870 and three philharmonic orchestras between 1870 and 1880. The town hall at Ermoupolis on the island of Syros, an important trading centre for much of the nineteenth century, was a similar manifestation of local pride. As one recent commentator has observed in a study of opera and melodrama in nineteenth-century Greece:

> ...through the cosmopolitanism of the melodrama the societies of Patras and Ermoupolis found the opportunity of expressing a local consciousness and declaring a spirit of antagonism against Athens. The structure of the cities' societies was different from that of Athens, but the capital as the national centre had the power to project models of behaviour.[17]

This spirit of local consciousness was similarly strong in Piraeus, characterized as the "Greek Manchester". Founded in 1835 on the site of the ancient port, the city had consolidated its importance as a commercial centre in the 1860s, initially through the import of cotton and cereals, but later with the growth of industry.[18]

The proliferation of local geographies, however, was not limited to the Greek state. Numerous geographies were published of Greek-speaking localities within the Ottoman Empire, such as Archimandrite Melissinos Christodoulou's *Historical Description of the District of Saranda Ekklisies* (1881), which the author dedicated to his homeland, or Savvas Ioannidou's *History and Statistics of Trapezon and the Surrounding Area* (1870).[19]

The intention of such works was to inculcate a sense of local pride, but the wider ideological purpose was to preserve a Greek identity in the increasingly tense political climate of the Ottoman Empire at the close of the nineteenth century. In the late Tanzimat period in Abdulhamit II's reign (1876–1909) Turkish nationalism and Islamism were the ascendant ideological forces within the Ottoman Empire.[20]

During the 1880s and 1890s the Athenian historian and geographer Antonios Miliarakis wrote numerous local geographies of Greek provinces, towns and islands including tomes on the Cycladic Islands (1874, 1880), on the island of Amorgos (1884), an ancient and modern political geography of the Argolid and Corinth (1886), and a study of Kefalonia (1890). As we have already seen in Chapter One, he was also responsible for rediscovering and promoting Philippidis and Konstantas's *Modern Geography* (1885). In 1889 he produced a comprehensive bibliography of Greek geographical writing from 1800 which was arranged by region. Throughout his work Miliarakis emphasized the importance of topographical research and dealt explicitly with the reciprocal relationship between physical and cultural histories which were inscribed in Greek places. In his *Guide to Simple Topographic Descriptions* (1882), for example, he reflected on the meanings of *topos* and of *topography* as an activity:

> Every topographical treatise contains two essential sections: a) the physical b) the political description of the place. In the physical description the place is described as a natural body, in the political as man's habitat.[21]

The range of interests which Miliarakis assigned to topographic research, such as local idioms, customs, traditions, buildings and ruins, are virtually indistinguishable from those of the folklorist and conforms to the prescription for folkloric studies laid out by Politis in the first issues of the journal *Folklore* (1909).[22] These were preoccupations reflected in folklore and ethographic literature. Miliarakis's summary of the aim and scope of the topographical treatise could serve as a fitting description of the folkloric orientations of prose fiction, the purpose of which was both to celebrate local particularities and to demonstrate the "essential unity" of Greek culture in time and space. Indeed, this "unity" was progressively stressed in the diasporic Greek communities of the Ottoman Empire, over which the institutions of the Greek state were exerting pressure for linguistic and cultural conformity:

> ...although the number of newspapers and printed works multiplied in the major centres of Greek population throughout the empire,

these were in turn overtaken by the printed matter emanating from Greece. Books, journals, papers, and pamphlets published in the kingdom and distributed abroad to the communities increasingly overshadow the regional significance of Greek centres in the empire after 1870. Their emphasis was on secular rather than religious matters, national rather than community concerns, and reflected an overarching, standardized culture instead of regional variations.[23]

5.2 ENVIRONMENTAL DETERMINISM

Topographic literature, of which Miliarkis's work is perhaps the most representative, needs to be seen within the context of a geographical determinism which became increasingly influential in Greece and which stressed the biological and geo-climatic factors that determined cultural identities. While Miliarakis saw himself working in a tradition of geographical writing that could be traced from *Modern Geography* at the end of the eighteenth century, much of his geographical work bears the stamp of a determinist thinking formed by the impact of post-Darwinian racial and biological theories of culture from Europe. Darwin's work had first appeared in translation in *Estia* and had been promoted by Miliarakis's younger brother, the botanist and zoologist Spyridon Miliarakis (1852–1919). Trained originally as a doctor, Spyridon was later to become Professor of Botany at the University of Athens (1892) and a promoter both of Darwin and of German environmental determinism. These views were supported by several prominent Greek geographers such as the German-educated Stavros Statho-poulos, even while they drew upon a tradition of eighteenth-century writing that sought to explain the impoverishment of modern Greek culture on climatic grounds.[24] C. Fraas, for example, the first Professor of Botany at the University of Athens, had argued in his *Klima und Pflanzenwelt in der Zeit* (1847) that Greece's cultural state was attributable to environmental factors. Similarly, the economist Ioannis Soutsos, Professor of Political Economy at the University of Athens from 1837 until his death in 1890, argued in an article in the journal *Pandora* in 1867 on the importance of the physical environment on culture. Drawing broad comparisons between relative levels of civilization in Africa, South America, India, America and Europe, Soutsos maintained that the different moral and political outlooks were in large measure environmentally determined.[25]

Champions of the demotic language, like Psycharis for example, seized upon the implications of such environmentalist theories in arguing for an indigenous language and literature organically tied to the Greek earth:

Instead of reading foreign books and writing foreign books, go to the islands, go to the mainland. We expect Greek novels from you, we expect novels which smell of [the] Greek earth. [26]

Biological and climatic factors were construed as determinants of culture and emphasis was placed on the particularities of Greek art. Eftaliotis, for example, identified the short story as a native Greek form which thrived "unwatered, untended, like a wild herb", as opposed to the novel which had been imported from the West and languished on Greek soil.[27] And amongst other voices, the educationalist Alekos Delmouzos declared that "only by studying and knowing the Greek earth...will we be able to be territorial (edafiki) and create...truly our own modern Greek culture".[28] Similarly, Dragoumis announced that Greek artists should study and represent Greek nature, instead of imitating artificial, foreign models:

From the great, varied nature of Greek places, cherishing it, we must take colours and lines, lights and shadows, tones and depths, in order to throw them on wood, paper, canvas, walls.[29]

In the same vein, Dragoumis also lamented the "degeneration" (ekfil-ismos) of Greek culture which had come about through excessive exposure to European civilization.

The influences of the geographer Ritter, and later of Ratzel, were also strong. Ritter's emphasis on a primarily human, regional geog-raphy, together with his teleological conception of geography, fitted in with a messianic Greek irredentist vision that sought to display the natural coherence of the nation by underlining the intrinsic Greekness of the regions – redeemed or unredeemed – which were claimed. While he was intensely concerned with localities, Miliarakis – who repre-sented Greece at the International Geographical Conference at Venice – sought to place his topographical studies within an encompassing national geography. In his article "Concerning the Benefit of Geographical Knowledge" (1877) he stressed the ideological role of geographical studies devoted to Greek lands still under Ottoman rule. The political import of local studies was manifest in the work of Anas-tasios Hourmouziadis, a professor at the famous Megali tou Yenous Scholi in Constantinople, who had sought to demonstrate, in his detailed study on the Anastenaria in Eastern Thrace (1873), the manner in which the investigation of local customs could become an important way of connecting contemporary Greek practices to antiquity, and hence of legitimating them. The Greek fire-walkers were a direct link, in Hourmouziadis's mind, to Euripides's Bacchae.[30] Other historical geographies, notably of Macedonia published in the 1880s and 1890s (such the one produced by the nationalist society, *Ellinismos*), had more explicit political agendas. The preface of this last geography was addressed "to the Youth of Greece" and spoke in rousing terms of the imperative to liberate the province:

> O children of Greece, do not forget Macedonia, that sacred land which is the gateway towards national glory. Who will open this gate to Greek hopes? The magnanimity of Greek youth and the justice of God.[31]

Significantly, too, Miliarakis was employed by the state as a member of the delegation sent to Preveza in 1879 by the Greek government to review Greece's frontiers and was appointed to the commission in charge of reviewing the names of regional municipalities in 1897. Together with Politis, he was a founding member of the Historical and Ethnological Society of Greece in 1882 and served as its Secretary.

Thus, it could be argued that local geographies were implicated in the celebration of the local and its concomitant eradication within a homogenized national space since they sought ultimately to assemble local "facts" within the continuous, logical space of the nation. Local knowledge was forced open by state-sponsored institutions to become, in Gellner's words, components of "a common or single conceptual currency":

> By the common or single conceptual currency I mean that all facts are located within a single continuous logical space, that statements reporting them can be conjoined and generally related to each other, and so that in principle one single language describes the world and is internally unitary; or on the negative side, that there are no special, privileged, insulated facts or realms, protected from contamination or contradiction by others, and living in insulated independent logical space of their own. Just this was, of course, the most striking trait of pre-modern, pre-rational visions: the co-existence within them of multiple, not properly untied, but hierarchically related sub-worlds, and the existence of special privileged facts, sacralized and exempt from ordinary treatment.[32]

The production of what Miliarakis termed "topographical treatises", local histories, and anthologies of folklore, while ostensibly affirming and celebrating local particularities, were involved in the process of their eradication, since the avowed aim of such endeavours was to demonstrate the integrity of the nation. As Gellner has noted, while nationalist ideologies claim to safeguard traditional folk cultures, they are, in actual fact, intent on amalgamating them within a monolithic national culture.[33] Correspondingly, the economic development of provincial cities in Greece, such as Patras, brought about their consolidation within the centralized apparatuses of the state and led, ultimately, to their eclipse by Athens. A marked decline is evident at the turn of the century, when cities such as Patras were overtaken by Athens.[34] The establishment of the railways in Greece reflected an intensification of state control and contributed to the diminution of regional diversity:

> a developed railway network increased and stabilized state control over the provinces...in this way a population with uncertain ideas about state authority and nationhood which, in many cases, spoke various languages or dialects and supported different regions were more likely to be brought together and transformed into loyal citizens.[35]

In short, the process of integration was predicated upon the disintegration of the region.[36] As Chapter Four sought to demonstrate, this tension between regionalism and centralism lies at the heart of nationalism itself as an ideology that is embodied in state institutions, but which manipulates popularly emergent sentiments and local affiliations.

5.3 CRITICS OF THE STATE

The tension between a local consciousness, or *topikismos*, and larger administrative structures promoted by the nation-state, can be traced back to von Maurer's introduction of a new, state-imposed system of government in Greece (1834). This undermined traditional allegiances and established a three-tiered system of *nomarhies* (or provinces), *eparhies* and *dimarhies* (or communes). At the beginning of the twentieth century there were many writers, such as Dragoumis, who were convinced that the nation-state had attenuated the deep-rooted local affiliations upon which Greek identity depended. For Dragoumis, the state's efforts to unify the country's rural populations amounted to a form of cultural, political and economic colonization. He held that it was outside Greece, in the diasporic communities within the Ottoman Empire which had remained unaffected by the state, that a genuine national consciousness had been preserved. The borders of the state and the nation were not coterminous and an unresolved tension existed between the idea of the state as an apparatus which expressed the spirit of the people and, conversely, a conception of the state as a foreign imposition which thwarted national expression and homogenized difference.[37] Such tensions characterized topographical literature, which both undertook to preserve local customs and traditions from the encroaching activities of the state, but simultaneously claimed them as part of a national, state-promoted culture.[38]

The Cretan uprising of 1896 and the defeat of the Greeks by the Ottomans in 1897, in which Dragoumis himself, like other writers, took part as a volunteer, had "intensified a long and continuous debate over what the nation's foreign policy ought to be and what were its legitimate national interests".[39] The defeat brought latent anxieties into the open. It made the Greeks aware of the debilitated condition of the state's institutions which was concealed beneath the sabre-rattling rhetoric of the "Great Idea". As Neoklis Kazazis, a university professor and President of *Ellinismos*, declared:

> The state had been defeated and not the nation, and this because of its defective organization and functioning; as for the nation, its forces emerged sound and undamaged.[40]

Growing exasperation with the Greek state after 1897 was to lead to the 1909 officers' coup at Goudi; an event which brought about the rise of the reforming politician Eleftherios Venizelos. It was not until after the two Balkan Wars of 1912 and 1913 that "Greater Macedonia", which had formed part of the Ottoman Empire, was divided up between Greece, Serbia and Bulgaria, a subject examined in Chapter Eight of this book.

Dragoumis was one of the most outspoken critics of the state's policies and in his writings he sought to explore the historical relations between the nation and state. Had the state brought about the nation or, conversely, had the nation given rise to the state? How did state and nation relate in the process of nation-building? Other figures, such as Perikles Yannopoulos (1869–1910), A. Souliotis-Nikolaidis (1878–1945), and the lawyer Konstantinos S. Sokolis (1872–1920), were to pose similar questions. In a remarkable pamphlet entitled *Empire* (1916) Sokolis had condemned nationalism as an importation from the West which had destroyed the traditions of the East. Instead, he explicitly looked back to the republican multi-ethnic state envisaged by Rigas Velestinlis in the late eighteenth century.[41] "The Greek fatherland" (*patrida*), had, he maintained, "buried the Empire".[42] In a discursive historical survey, Sokolis attempted to demonstrate how, in contrast to the Roman and British Empires, the Byzantine Empire fostered an ideal religion based on notions of brotherhood and socialism. This religion, for Sokolis, was inseparable from Hellenism; the heroes of the War of Independence had not fought to erect narrow national frontiers, but to reclaim Byzantine ideals. The Greek state had betrayed the ideals of the "Great Idea" by recasting older notions for political expediency. In so doing, the state was seeking "to contain the uncontainable".[43]

In Dragoumis's writings a geographical determinism went hand in hand with an anti-Occidentalism, articulated most uncompromisingly at the beginning of the century by Yannopoulos. Like Dragoumis, Yannopoulos sought to resist what he perceived as the adulteration of Greek authenticity emanating from Western Europe. Since the political establishment was westernized, inevitably the process of national recovery had been hijacked from within. In 1903, Yannopoulos published his *New Spirit*, a fierce attack against Europe, in which he argued for the need to create a new and pure Hellenic civilization. Yannopoulos stressed the organic connection between the Attic landscape and cultural productions. "The basis of Greek Aesthetics", he asserted, "is the GREEK EARTH. Every land creates a person in its own image and likeness".[44] Greek art was thus the product of an interaction between environment and people and a new Hellenic culture could arise only if the nation's artists had an intimate understanding of their country's landscape. This unity of the landscape Yannopoulos called "the Greek line" (*i elliniki grammi*).[45]

Words such as "local", "native" (*dopios, enhorios*) and other synonyms for the indigenous pervade the literature of the late nineteenth and twentieth centuries, as do organicist analogies of rootedness and uprootedness. Such organicist metaphors underline the influence of geographical and racial determinist thinking from Europe and, in Dragoumis's case, that of the French writer and politician Maurice Barrès (1862–1923). Barrès, in his novel *Les Déracinés* (1897), had argued for the value of "rootedness" as opposed to "uprootedness".[46] Rootedness signified an awareness of one's cultural heritage and a rejection of pernicious foreign influence which led, Barrès maintained, to a weakening of the national French character. At the same time, however, Barrès was a champion of regionalism which he sought to reconcile with his nationalism by insisting on the dangers of submitting people to a rigid, unified system. Born in Lorraine, which had been annexed by Germany following the French defeat in the 1870 Franco-Prussian War, Barrès's writing came out of a specific experience of a contested place and threatened cultural identity. This was not dissimilar to the Greek experience of 1897 which shaped the outlook of Dragoumis's generation. Analogies between Alsace-Lorraine and Greece were drawn, in fact, by contemporaries. In the dedication of her novel *Grecque* (1879) to the Alsatian painter Jean-Jacques Henner (1829–1905), Juliette Lamber (later Adam) declared:

Vous aussi, vous avez deux religions, que vous pratiquez tour à tour dans vos œuvres, et que vous confondez dans votre cœur:

vous avez, comme moi, le culte de l'Alsace et celui de la Grèce.

J'ai mis dans l'âme d'une Grecque la tristesse et la passion alsacienne, essayant de décrire ce que vous avez peint. [47]

The cultivation of the region (le régionalisme) in France, as in Greece, provided a critique of the centralized state by people with widely differing political convictions. On the one hand, the region was linked to the family, the Church and local institutions which were being steadily undermined by the encroachment of the state. At the same time, however, it was argued that the region was used as a defence against a radical individualism that threatened to dismantle the cohesive role of society.[48] In this sense, the particularities of place celebrated in novels and in histories cannot be separated from wider political debates, just as the new geographical curriculum designed after the Franco-Prussian War focused on the local regions and stressed "the immediate vicinity of the child's home, school and commune".[49]

Ironically, then, in making their case for a distinctive Greek tradition, Greek writers like Dragoumis drew deeply upon European determinist thinkers such as Barrès, on the determinist racial theories of Joseph-Arthur Gobineau (1816–1882), as well as upon the celebration of the region. Many of the fiercest critics of the infiltration of European culture in Greece, like Eftaliotis and Psycharis, resided for most of their life in Europe, while Yannopoulos himself had studied in Paris. Writing in the periodical Panathinea in 1907, in an article entitled "Ourselves and Foreigners", Pavlos Nirvanas (1866–1937) pointed to what he saw as a blatant contradiction in the relationship of Greek writers to Europe: even while they purported to reject European culture, their work was manifestly and slavishly imitative of it.[50]

5.4   CULTURE, RACE, ENVIRONMENT

The most conspicuous tension or ambivalence in Dragoumis's work emerges from his definition of the nation. At times, the nation is conceived as an essentially cultural construct, but it is also frequently evoked in racial terms. To a certain extent this is one aspect of a tension already touched upon: namely, that Greekness was expressed at the turn of the century, alternatively as a choice and as an inevitability. It is an ambivalence that informs the irredentist vision of the "Great Idea", as articulated by Kolettis in 1844, where a native of the new Greek Kingdom was defined as the inhabitant of any "land associated with Greek history or the Greek race". Countering the view of the nation as a racial concept, Dragoumis argued:

If only one Greek remained alive and all the others had died and Swedes and Irish and Egyptians came to live in Greece, on the islands and in the Aegean basin, they would become Greek. The one living Greek would teach them the language and his Greekness would be divided amongst all of them and would flow over them and they would absorb it slowly as the earth drinks up water or blotting paper ink. And the earth and the stones give birth to spirits and as soon as you sit in a Greek place you can't live at peace, unless you become Greek.[51]

Place here is construed as a repository of social and cultural values which act determinately upon the character of the inhabitants. Dragoumis's emphasis on Greek culture's formative power and his corresponding acknowledgement of Greece's hybridity is reminiscent of Paparrigopoulos's essay of 1843 on Slavic settlements in the Peloponnese. In this work, the historian had sought to refute Fallmerayer's thesis by expostulating that the Slavs had not arrived in Greece as despoiling marauders but, on the contrary, had been amicably assimilated into the indigenous Hellenic culture.

At the same time, however, Dragoumis could maintain that Greekness was racially determined, exclaiming, for example, that: "Greek lands are those which for thousands of years now are settled and worked by Greeks; those in which are buried the bones of thousands of Greek generations". It was beyond the bounds of possibility to change one's national identity: "the nation is a bond and we can't break it". In short, Dragoumis maintained contradictory positions: an individual's national identity was simultaneously contingent and pre-determined. The landscape was both a reflection of a national identity and constitutive of that identity.

Nations, according to Dragoumis, like individuals, are defined in relation to, and against, other nations and individuals. Yet the borders of the Greek state posed problems here, since many Greeks continued to reside on the other side – and ironically it was these other Greeks who, in Dragoumis's view, had been most resourceful in keeping alive their national identity. Thus, antithetical stereotypes no longer worked and the absolute difference between the Self and the Other was troubled. As a response to this dilemma Dragoumis sought to dislodge the hyphen between state and nation,[52] to transpose the spatial model promoted by the state and turn it inside-out. The centre (Athens) became the margin ("a narrow-minded provincial city" was how he described it) and the margins, or borderlands, were transformed into the centre.

In 1906, having successfully completed his law degree at the University of Athens and before setting off for Paris to pursue his studies, the novelist, poet and dramatist Nikos Kazantzakis (1883–1957), a friend and one time "disciple" of Dragoumis, made what he called in his fictional autobiography *Report to Greco* a three-month pilgrimage though Greece. "How pleasant", he observed:

> if the Greek could stroll through his country and not hear stern, angry voices beneath the soil! For the Greek, however, a journey through Greece degenerates into a fascinating and exhausting torture. You stand on a spot of Greek land and find yourself over-come with anguish. It is a deep tomb with layer upon layer of corpses whose varied voices rise and call you – for the voice is the one part of the corpse which remains immortal. Which among all these voices should you choose?[53]

And later in the same passage Kazantzakis added:

> When a Greek travels through Greece, his journey becomes converted in this fatal way into a laborious search to find his duty...How can he continue his national tradition without disgracing it?... In the modern Greek no region of his homeland calls forth a disinterested quiver of aesthetic appreciation. The region has a name...and it is bound up with a memory... All at once the region is transformed into much-swept, wide-roving history... Each Greek region is so soaked with successes and failures possessing world-wide echoes, so filled with human struggle, that it is elevated into an austere lesson which we cannot escape... It becomes a cry, and our duty is to hear this cry...
>
> New forces are rising from the East, new forces are rising from the West, and Greece, caught as always between the two colliding impulses, once more becomes a whirlpool... Once more its duty is to reconcile these two monstrous impulses by finding a synthesis. Will it succeed?[54]

Landscape, memory, duty, the traveller who activates places by revealing their inseparability from history: these concepts are central to the nationalist creed and the extracts from Kazantzakis stand as a fitting epigraph to this book which seeks to explore the shifting and often contradictory relationship of these concepts across diverse prac-tices from folklore, geography to fiction and archaeology in the intellectual and political "whirlpool" of the nineteenth and early twen-tieth centuries.

Chapter Six

Islands apart: rural fictions

6.1   FIGHTING AND WRITING

Travelling to Piraeus in the 1880s from the small port of Preveza on the western coast of mainland Greece, the poet and writer Yeoryios Drosinis found himself in the company of a Turkish family bound for Constantinople. In the course of a genial conversation Drosinis was startled by the vehemence with which the Turkish father expressed his aversion to journalism as a profession. Surely, Drosinis retorted, the Turk was exaggerating the influence that writers exerted on the outcome of historical events:

> "What can anyone do without the power of weapons, with nothing
>   but pen and ink?"
> His face suddenly took on an ironic expression:
> "What can he do? He can make Thessaly Greek, just as you have
>   done."[1]

Published in 1885, five years after the annexation by Greece of the agriculturally rich Thessaly and the Arta region of Epirus from the Ottoman Empire, following the Treaty of Berlin (1878), Drosinis's account of his fortuitous encounter with a Turk took place at the very moment when the issue of a national literature was being vigorously debated in Greece. In the same year, Ioannis Pantazidis (1827–1900), in an article that appeared in *Estia*, a publication which characterized itself as a national family journal, had argued in favour of *logotehnia* as a generic term to be used in Greek for literature, since, in his view, it corresponded more faithfully than the commonplace *filoloyia* to the German *Nationalliteratur*.[2]

As Pantazidis himself acknowledged, the word *logotehnia* had been mooted some two decades earlier. Aristidis Kyprianos, in the preface to his translation of a history of Greek literature (1867), had evoked the term only to dismiss it out of a fear of alienating his readers with a ponderous neologism. In the 1880s, however, the increasingly exhortative debates about literature's national scope required a befitting word to describe the institution as a discrete discourse with specific aims and conceived for an explicit readership. It was no coincidence that Pantazidis's article had appeared in the pages of *Estia*, a non-subscription weekly journal that was closely linked to a conscious endeavour to nurture a new, more encompassing, national forum.[3] Ten years previously, in the journal's first issue, in an article entitled "National Catechism", for example, the journalist Anastasios Vyzandios had elucidated terms such as "homeland" and "Greece", while emphasizing the journal's promotion of national, moral values.[4]

Set against this background, Drosinis's sketch raises issues about the power of the pen as a tool in a national armoury; about the relationship between authorship and authority. More specifically, it underscores the ideological role of writing in claiming and consolidating national territory and draws attention to the relationship between modes of literary production and nationalism as a territorial ideology. As we have already seen in earlier chapters, a close relationship was sustained between fictive narratives and the process of mapping. Significantly, in the course of Drosinis's sketch, the narrator remarks that whenever he travels he brings with him a map to identify the places he is travelling through. However, when he displays the map to his Muslim travelling companion, who is unfamiliar with maps, the chart appears to the Turk as a painting; in other words, as an aesthetic whole rather than as a graphic representation of national differences. The Greek's sensitivity to national frontiers, which are depicted on the chart, are thus undermined by the Muslim's enthusiasm for the map as an artistic composition. By the same token, in his autobiography, Drosinis notes that the room in which he worked was adorned with a school map of Greece.[5] He recalls his impressions on looking at a map for the first time, acknowledging that:

> even now, the name of every country (especially those in Europe with which I was more familiar) conjures up before my eyes its colour – the colour on that geographic map.[6]

The convergence of fighting and writing as an adversarial discourse intimated by Drosinis's Turk was explored by Grigorios Xenopoulos (1867–1951) in his *Military Tales* (1892),[7] but was perhaps most vividly dramatized in the two volumes of short stories published in 1900 by Yeoryios Aspreas, the war correspondent of the *Acropolis* newspaper in Thessaly during the 1897 conflict, who was later to write a political history of modern Greece.[8] In Aspreas's self-professed documentary fiction, the regional folkloric preoccupations of Greek prose fiction conjoin with the military contestation over the possession of territory.[9] What Aspreas's text highlights is the extent to which, in the case of Greece, nationalism as a movement of political liberation overlapped with nationalism as an intellectual movement that proclaimed the self-sufficiency of culture. For this reason it becomes impossible in Greece to distinguish between nationalism as a political struggle and as a system of thought.[10] Aspreas's texts also underline the extent to which this adversarial writing and the heroic model of the writer as soldier, discussed in Chapter Three, promoted specific ideas of male author-ship and masculinity.[11]

6.2   FICTIONS OF FOLKLORE

The ideological dimension of literary production is evident in the political roles assumed by writers within state-sponsored institutions, as well as in the close connections between the practices of folklore and literature, both of which were central in envisioning a national geog-raphy. Drosinis, for example, was one of Greece's most eminent journalists and the Editor of *Estia*, initially with Nikolaos Politis, before taking over as Editor-in-Chief himself and supervising the weekly peri-odical's transformation into a newspaper in March 1894. Drosinis served, too, as Secretary of the Society for the Dissemination of Useful Books, an organization founded in 1899 by the writer Dimitrios Vikelas under the auspices of Princess Sofia, which produced inexpensive and accessible illustrated booklets on topical and patriotic themes. The Society's distinctive red booklets, which were dispatched post-free throughout the Greek provinces, were also acquired in bulk by the Admiralty and the War Office. As Drosinis was later to observe point-edly in his autobiography, quoting from a Greek commentator: "all those who hold this small weapon of the spirit, the pen, are soldiers".[12]

The term *ithografia*, used of the fiction produced by the 1880s gener-ation, refers to a current of folkloric realism which drew its inspiration from similar tendencies in Europe and Russia, where "the urge to give solidity to [a] particular and differentiating 'spirit' of the people" led not only to the collecting of folklore, but to the affirmation of distinct national literatures.[13] Combining naturalism's penchant for documen-tation with the folklorist's mission to preserve rural traditions, the movement's nationalist aims were never far from the surface. The folk-lorist Politis was involved in establishing and running the journal *Estia*, which was appropriately named (*estia* signifies "hearth" in Greek)[14] since it conjured up both ideas of domesticity, social order, and those rural shepherds' hearths around which local customs and traditions, or in Politis's words, "ancient tales", were recounted. It was in the pages of *Estia* that many writers of the 1880s generation first appeared. A writing competition held in *Estia* in 1883 invited submissions of a short story, a fact that was significant, since this was a form construed as being close to orality, the Greek word itself (*diiyima*) deriving from the verb to narrate. The oral was privileged over the written since speech was "considered as the only point of access to an essential unity" of the community.[15] The preferred genre of ethographic writing was the short story which centred, through oral histories, on descriptions of local, contemporary life, with particular attention paid to rustic manners and customs. As the announcement of the 1883 competition expressed it: "The theme of the short story is to be Greek, in other words to consist of the description of scenes from the life of the Greek nation in whatever period of its history, or of episodes of Greek history".[16]

Drosinis's *Rural Letters* (1882) are an example of such ethographic fiction in which the narrator, who is also a landowner, dispatches his reports on the life of the village of Gouves in Euboia back to the city for an urban readership. Such writing was clearly bound up in an organicist discourse that extolled an indigenous national culture, which was conceived as being deeply rooted in local traditions, as opposed to a shallow, but encroaching, cosmopolitan modernity. The *Rural Letters*, in particular, were undoubtedly inspired by Alphonse Daudet's (1840–1897) *Lettres de Mon Moulin* (1869), sketches of Provençal life, which had appeared in the pages of *Le Figaro* in 1866 and sections of which had already appeared translated into Greek in the Constantinopolitan Greek journal *Mi Hanesai* in 1880.[17] Daudet's novel *Le Roi en Exil* (1879) had been published in Greek in 1880, while Papadiamantis's translation of Daudet's burlesque novel *Tartarin de Tarascon* (1872) appeared in 1894.[18] The French writer's earlier collection of tales, many of them purportedly told by peasants around the narrator's hearth, exemplifies a widespread interest in regional folk culture throughout Europe and Russia, which was being produced for a city reading public in the second half of the nineteenth century and was closely bound up with anxieties attendant upon the process of modernization. As populations were compelled to migrate to the cities for employment, the need to establish roots became more urgent. Likewise, the impetus to unify the state provoked fears about the eradication of local identities in the outlying regions. While there had been a tradition of regional writing in France that extended from George Sand's idealized romances of country life to Guy de Maupassant's tales of his Normandy childhood, Daudet was himself associated with the poet Frédéric Mistral (1830–1914). Mistral, winner of the Nobel Prize in 1904, was the leader of the Félibrige movement for the revival of the Occitan (Provençal) language and literature, which was to act as a spur to the revival of Catalan literature. The preoccupation with the countryside was reflected, too, in the rural paintings produced by the artists of the so-called Barbizon school, which centred on the village of Barbizon and its surroundings on the edge of the Forest of Fontainebleau, some fifty kilometres outside Paris. Increasingly the country was being evoked as a refuge from the city, as a place of "retreat and recreation".[19] At the same time, depictions of rural France, whether in literature or in painting, gave expression to an immemorial "nation" culture – "la France profonde" – rooted in the soil and strikingly opposed to the corrosive infringements of modernity.[20]

The concentration on country themes was manifest in many different "national" literatures. In Russia, for example, it found expression in the sketches of Ivan Turgenev (again translated by Papadiamantis), and in the short stories of Nikolai Leskov. In Britain, too, the writers Thomas Hardy, Rider Haggard, W.H. Hudson and Hall Caine – whose numerous novels, such as *The Manxman* (1894), are set on his native Isle of Man and enjoyed wide popularity as far afield as Greece – commemorated local, rural identities as expressed in dialects, folklore, and the historical memories and beliefs that were embedded in the texture of regional landscapes. Regional studies transcribed local customs, legends and dialects, in the same way that different flora, fauna and landscape morphologies were assiduously documented. In Germany, Austria and Switzerland the preoccupation with rural village life was articulated in the *dorfgeschichte* movement and, towards the end of the century, in the *heimaliteratur* movement, where the celebration of the regions was closely bound up with German nationalism. Thus, Berthold Auerbach published his Black Forest stories in the 1840s and early 1850s,[21] while the novels and sketches by Clara Viebig, Wilhelm von Polenz and Hermann Löns celebrated the villages of Eifel, West Prussia, Saxony, and the Lüneberg Heath. Similarly, in Spain interest in rural village life found expression in *costumbrismo*,[22] in the writings of Fernán, Caballero, and Alarcón; in Italy with authors such as Verga, Capuana, Deledda, Serao and d'Annunzio. Verga's *Novelle Rusticane* (1883), for example, focuses on a fishing community, while Deledda's *Fior di Sardegna* (1892) celebrates the writer's native Sardinia and *Il Vecchio della Montagna* (1900) describes the life of mountain shepherds. Other texts include d'Annunzio's *Novelle della Pescara* (1902).

There was a close institutional connection between writers and folklorists in Greece. It was Nikolaos Politis who masterminded the celebrated *Estia* competition in 1883 for the best short story with a national theme. The winner of the competition, which was adjudicated by a nine-member jury that included Politis, was none other than

Drosinis, whose entry, characterized as "a charming idyll", was entitled "Chrysoula".[23] The plot line of Drosinis's tale, which, like much fiction of the 1880s is set back several decades to the early 1850s, is simple enough: a young heroine, persecuted by her cantankerous mother-in-law, leaves her village for employment as a domestic in the island's capital. There she falls in love with the son of the family who employs her. In an act of altruism, however, the young man sends Chrysoula back to the village lest she be spoiled by the insidious influence of the town. In the village the heroine settles down to a contented family life. "Chrysoula" is exemplary of much prose fiction of the time, while the poeticization of rural life is characteristic of the writing that appeared in the pages of *Estia* in the 1880s. The title of another story short-listed for the prize was "Scenes of Greek Life", while two others were inspired by folk songs.[24]

Drosinis was a prominent figure in the group that had formed around the folklorist Politis, and he acknowledged Politis as the inspiration for his work, just as Politis conceded Drosinis's collaboration. Following Politis's prescription, in "Chrysoula" Drosinis manifestly draws on folklore so that the figure of the stepmother, for example, is a staple character in folk songs. In like manner, the tale is pervaded with details of country lores and customs. Drosinis, like many other contemporaries of his, such as Karkavitsas, collected folkloric material for *Estia* which he later reworked into his fiction, while his *Fairytales* were translated into English in 1892.[25] He was instrumental in founding the Museum of Folklore in Athens. Writing in the preface to his collection of short stories in 1892, Karkavitsas likened the writer to a photographer whose task it was to record the customs of rural Greek life before they became extinct: "take us, photograph us before we become extinct; the next generation won't be able to find us".[26] Just as prose fiction was preoccupied with ideas of orality, so was folklore conceived as a textual affair focusing on the "monument of the word"; on transcribing and anthologizing folk poetry and furnishing etymological explications.[27]

While Politis drew on folkloric material embedded in works of prose fiction as evidence to ground his own research, many of the writers were themselves amateur folklorists. Karkavitsas, Drosinis, and Vizyinos, for example, re-worked material into their fiction, while Eftaliotis called his short stories "fairytales" (*paramythia*). Karkavitsas published his fiction initially in the form of folkloric fieldwork. As a doctor in the army, his postings around Greece provided him with opportunities for collecting rural folklore. Thus, much of the details worked into his novel *The Beggar* appeared initially as folkloric material in *Estia* in 1890, while he had also contributed to the newsletter of the Historical and Ethnological Society in the mid 1880s. Following the success of his

Rural Letters, Drosinis was dispatched to the island of Tinos and mainland Greece by the Editor, Yorgos Kasdonis, to write a series of folkloric travel pieces with an injunction to focus on the "manners, customs, traditions and every aspect of the social life and characters of the population and the physical situation of the place".[28]

Greek prose fiction in the 1880s and 1890s concentrated largely on evocations of Greek rural landscapes. The titles of Greek short story collections, such as those by Christos Christovasilis, for example, read like anthologies of folk tales: *Tales of the Fold* (1898), *Thessalian Tales* (1900) and *Tales of the Mountain and the Valley* (1902). As Roderick Beaton has noted: "The common denominator of almost all the fiction published during the last two decades of the nineteenth century is the detailed depiction of a small, more or less contemporary traditional community in its *physical setting*".[29] In particular, villages served as bounded sites and as "mapable centres for the community and, by extension, the culture". The village in much ethographic writing functioned as a way of localizing and centralizing culture; indeed, as a synecdoche of culture.[30]

The emphasis on the rural community in Greek fiction closely paralleled the preoccupation with the *mir* as a repository of traditional communal values in Russia at the same time. In the United States of America the village, and particularly the New England village, became a symbol of "covenanted community, cultural enlightenment and democratic self-government". The village thus served as a geographical metaphor "for inherited pastoral ideals" and stood "in stark contrast with the actual landscape".[31] In Greece many writers of the 1880s generation wrote about the village communities where they were born and grew up, which were construed as an ideal image of communion, embodying "organic" social relations of what Raymond Williams calls the "knowable community".[32] Finally, the village was an important topos in British folklore, championed by George Laurence Gomme (1853–1916), for example, in his research into the prehistory of English village institutions and documented in such publications as *The Village Community, with Special Reference to the Origin and Form of its Survivals in Britain* (1890).[33]

A central role was assigned to setting in ethographic literature, since the Greek landscape was conceived as a repository of Greek culture and an arsenal of national heirlooms. In a letter to the Minister of Foreign Affairs, written in 1885, Vizyinos stressed the role of literature in keeping the Greek national identity alive in areas outside the Greek state. He also emphasized the link between landscape and folklore when he requested information from the relevant Greek consulates about the geographical location of sites around which popular stories had accrued:

...are there any mountains, springs, streams, rivers, ravines and locations in general, or any natural phenomena such as strangely shaped rocks, vases, ancient trees etc., the names of which are referred to by the local population in their folk-songs, folk-stories and legends? Are there any constructions such as castles, large bridges, ruined churches, ancient aqueducts, abandoned villages – remembered only by name – deserted cemeteries, and such things, which occupy a place in the popular belief of the local population?[34]

The list of natural phenomena singled out by Vizyinos reads like a thematic concordance to the work of many of the ethographic writers which focus on precisely such sites: ruined churches, springs, streams, strangely shaped rocks, the abandoned village, ravines, ancient trees and deserted cemeteries. It also echoes the field of research charted for folklore by Gomme in his first annual report as secretary of the Folk-Lore Society in Britain in 1879 in which he singled out the superstitions associated with "topographical objects...traditional ballads and proverbial sayings incident to particular localities; the retention of popular names for hills, streams, caverns, springs, tumuli; foundations, fields, trees, etc."[35] The political and determinist implications of this ethographic concern for landscape, which was value-laden and moralized, were noted, as we have seen, by Dragoumis. National traditions were environment-bound; the nation was an organic unit and Greek cultural identity could only be defined in the context of the Hellenic landscape in which it was rooted.

In summary, the implicit project of ethographic writing was to demonstrate the historicity of the national territory, just as it reflected the territorialization of the nation's history.[36] The acquisition by Greece of Thessaly and the Arta region of Epirus in 1881 was another spur to folkloric literature which, as in Macedonia after 1913, was deployed to consolidate Greek national identity in the newly acquired territories by displaying the continuity of Hellenism over time and space.

6.3 CIVILIZATION IN THE VILLAGE

Such ethographic literature promoted a view of the countryside predominantly for urban consumption.[37] On the face of it a celebration of the rural, it nonetheless reproduced and reinforced the differences dividing the city from the country. As previous chapters have sought to show, this writing was bound up in an organicist discourse that extolled an indigenous national culture which was conceived as being deeply rooted in local traditions in antithesis to an extraneous cosmopolitanism. Accordingly, the roots of the nation were construed as being in the country, far from the degenerative effects of the city.

While much of the writing, including Drosinis's story "Chrysoula", evoked the possibility of change, of oppositions being overcome, most narratives ended up, more often than not, reasserting these unbridgeable differences. In the final analysis, the differences between city and country were maintained. Thus, in Drosinis's short story "The Rivals", the well-travelled Athenian protagonist, Yeoryios, abandons the island of Syros and the two local women who are rivals for his affections in order to return to the city. In Eftaliotis's story "Angeliki", a schoolteacher, arrives in the remote rural community bent on introducing changes, although these come to nothing in the end. In Papadiamantis's "Civilization in the Village" (1891), as the title itself intimates, the focus is precisely on the interaction between the local community or village, and the wider entity of the state which is associated with the city, the noun *politismos* being a cognate with the noun for city.[38] The indigenous population is juxtaposed against the state-appointed functionaries and a local identity pitted again notions of national citizenship. Throughout the text the narrator also stresses the hazardous weather conditions and the clogged channels of communication intimated by descriptions of the snow and the shuttered village houses. Visibility is poor and in contrast to the relative ease with which the state employees circulate within the formal peripheries of the state, movement in the village is obstructed. It is more effortless to pass from one end of the Kingdom to the other, than to traverse the village.

In Drosinis's novella *Amaryllis* (1886), the protagonist is a young Athenian lawyer, Stefanos, who is sent off by his uncle to a family estate on a remote island. There he falls in love with the beautiful Amaryllis, who lives with her father on a neighbouring estate. On one level, city and rural community are consistently juxtaposed. The literate Stefanos composes his letters on a thick wooden table resembling a butcher's table[39] and complains about the difficulty of sending mail to the city from the island.[40] He arrives on the island with books to while away his time and complains bitterly about the dirty, uncouth local peasants.[41]

These differences are simultaneously undermined, however, by the very terms in which Drosinis's rural landscape is described. The natural world of the island is described as a "book" written by God in such bold letters that only the blind are unable to read it. Even the name "Amaryllis" is culled from a text: Theocrius's *Idylls*.[42] The subject of Stefanos's adventure, his friend observes, is perfect material for a novel.[43] In *Amaryllis*, the estate belonging to the heroine's father is described through analogies with familiar urban spaces. As the narrator declares: "imagine the most beautiful garden in Patissia [an area on the outskirts of Athens] transported to the edge of Greece".[44] The garden metaphor here renders the unfamiliar in terms of the familiar and eradicates difference, so that the island is imagined in conventional terms. Thus, the narrator remarks that he loves the shepherdess as a wild flower of the mountains, just as he does the princess, or cultivated flower of the garden.[45] And Amaryllis represents their convergence: she is both "a village girl in the mountain and a queen in the city".[46] When Amaryllis first appears she does so as the presiding spirit of the garden, decked out in garlands of flowers.[47] Her father, we learn, is a keen gardener, reading gardening manuals and planting his garden with roses transplanted from all across Europe.[48]

Much ethographic fiction highlights the predicament of how the unfamiliar can be made comprehensible by employing conventional metaphors.[49] In *Amaryllis*, it transpires that the peasant is none other than the city dweller who continually asserts the difference between the rural and the urban.[50] Drosinis's literary island is defined by its legibility as a space in which codes are deciphered and, through their decipherment, ultimately arrogated by the city. In *Amaryllis* the father's estate becomes the consummate locale for the imaginative retreat of the city dweller.[51] The countryside is represented through allusions to universal values of domesticity and social harmony. Unknown to Stefanos, Amaryllis, the genus loci of the island who initiates the protagonist in his lessons of the country, turns out, in fact, to be a city dweller too. She is the daughter of a rich merchant from Marseilles who has settled on the island after his wife's premature death for consolation, and in order to bring up his daughter in innocence, far from the madding crowd.

The country thus becomes a setting or staging for urban desires and, appropriately, allusions to the theatre pervade the novel. The narrator reminds the reader that the fairytale of the prince and the shepherdess is just that: only a fairytale. Suggestively, Stefanos hands the narrator his letters, which make up the bulk of the novel, while the sighs of an audience can be heard from a theatre nearby.[52] The heroine plays a part, weaving her own peasant clothes with a dexterity and aplomb that make her the most accomplished weaver in the village. "Everything is magical here", Stefanos declares as he catches sight of Amaryllis in her father's garden[53] and he later recalls his experience as a "fairytale" – the generic term which Eftaliotis gave to his rural short stories. The implication of such ethographic writing is that the urban protagonist cannot elude metropolitan values. When he appears to do so and communes with the rural inhabitants, it transpires that the accommodation is a deception; the magic of the theatre. Just as one of the peasants in the novella pictures himself on stage, in the capital's theatres, so does the city dweller picture the city reflected in – what

Nicholas Green has called – "the spectacle of nature".[54] Not surprisingly, perhaps, the mirror figures prominently in ethographic fiction. Writing in a foreword to a collection of short stories in 1907, Eftaliotis described the stories as "mirrors" which reflected the nation's life:

> Mirrors, all of them are mirrors. Sparkling, well fashioned, crystal clean. Such mirrors as these of yours, which you've brought out for us, the country needs. The nation begins to stir, to feel itself. It longs to peer into the mirror, to see how it looks.[55]

6.4   ISLANDS

The focus in much rural fiction, as we have seen, was on the village community as a defined sphere, a discrete, bounded space that was at once knowable and because of its consolidated form, readily defensible. In this way, the village provided a figurative model of the space of the nation-state as a finite political community; a primordial community of "face-to-face contact" that is "imagined as both inherently limited and sovereign".[56] Given Greece's fragmented geography, the village was projected as an ideal and merged with another striking emblem of the nation-state: the island.

For writers, as much as for folklorists, the island represented the last bastion of uncontaminated national culture. As Victor Hugo declared in his book *Les Travailleurs de la Mer* (1866), islands are places where "traditions are never-ending".[57] The idea of the island as a repository of memory found its equivalence in the construction of reservations or "island" conservation sites where particular physical and cultural habitats could be preserved. In Fredric Jameson's words, "island" literature was invested with "the function of inventing imaginary or formal 'solutions' to unresolved social and [political] contradictions".[58] The island was central to this national imaginary, and functioned as a *topos* for resolving the problematic relations between nation and state, and between local knowledge and national unity.[59] It furnished a setting for the convergence of nationalism, as a totalizing system, with local knowledge.[60]

During the nineteenth century, national cultures were increasingly construed as discrete island spaces set apart from other communities beyond. From the second half of the century, attention was also paid to those authentic "island" spaces within the nation-state. In this expanded topographical definition, the "island" came to signify an identifiably different and contained habitat. A relationship was sustained between these distinct spaces within the nation-state and the island as it was represented in evolutionary writings – notably in

Charles Darwin's (1809–1882) *The Origin of the Species* (1859) – as a site for observing preserved life forms and diversification. The naturalist, geographer and social critic Alfred Russel Wallace (1823–1913) had hit upon the idea of natural selection as the solution to the problem of evolution on the Maluku Islands of Indonesia in 1858 and in *Island Life* (1880), he expanded upon Darwin's study of oceanic islands, arguing for the importance of islands in highlighting generalizable problems and solutions:

> Islands possess many advantages for the study of the laws and phenomena of distribution. As compared with continents they have a restricted area and definite boundaries. And in most cases their geographical and biological limits coincide. The number of species and of genera they contain is always much smaller than in the case of continents, and their peculiar species and groups are usually well defined and strictly limited in range. Again, their relations with other lands are often distinct and simple and even when complex, are far easier to comprehend than those of continents...[61]

The island represented a framed perspective of the world; it marked out a bounded site that in turn legitimated the imposition of taxonomic categories upon that world.[62] Accordingly, the island served as a metaphor for the parameters that defined distinct disciplinary enclaves (botany, biology, anthropology, geology and zoology). A connection was established between the emergence of disciplinary "islands" and the promotion of the "island" in nationalist discourse, just as a relationship can be traced between the island as a site that encourages classifying activities and nationalism as a "classifying discourse".[63]

This evolutionary discourse of the island was to have an important impact on emerging disciplines such as folklore and regional literature. Wallace's emphasis on the island as a site that threw into relief the isolation of life forms and its "intermixture" provided a readily usable model that was applicable to cultural phenomena. "Isolation" and "intermixture" were politicized and translated into concepts of cultural purity and hybridity. As "islands", the state's far-flung regions were construed both as repositories of an indigenous and unadulterated national culture and, at the same time, as potentially recalcitrant pockets of backwardness that needed circumscribing and, ultimately, domesticating. Often they were mapped through comparison with exotic island cultures, just as those "foreign" places were evoked through reference to the traveller's distant home provinces. Just as colonized populations became the object of a discourse which sanctioned European ascendancy, so European ethographic writers were involved in a project to isolate those internal survivals they identified.

The island, in this sense, was both a space where "native" customs might be preserved and, simultaneously, a space in which potentially destructive, atavistic forces might be supervised and regulated. It is here that the island emerges as an ambivalent, problematic place: at once a refuge and a place of incarceration and ex-isle; the scene of innocent childhood adventure and of beastly aggression. In short, the island served as a space for externalizing a collective national identity, even while the island was internalized in a process of self-definition that involved equally violent exclusions; it figures as a "site of double identity".[64]

Precisely because the island held out the possibility of absolute control and dominion, it became the site for the struggle between freedom and authority. Even while it was evoked as prison, the island betokened an organic unity; it was imagined as a place of authenticity, a protected zone where the individual's resourcefulness was tested and, in the process of being tested, was heroically reconstructed. Indeed, the island's ambiguous "double identity" – its "problematic shores"[65] – are explored in Daniel Defoe's *Robinson Crusoe* (1719), which remained the most influential island narrative throughout the nineteenth century. The island, in this text, becomes a site where the eponymous hero both longs for and evades communal integration; and in the process, embodies a "double relationship to society". The island is identified with Crusoe's ingenuity and self-reliance; it comes to represent a model of happy communion. As John Richetti has recently argued: "*Robinson Crusoe* is an allegory of modern individualism that sketches its achievements and its accompanying deep anxieties".[66] Defoe's narrative can be read on one level as a collective history that is iconized into an individual life.

The island was central to British identity as a maritime power, but it functioned, too, as an important model for thinking though the relationship between region and nation-state elsewhere in Europe. This contradiction between the island as a repository of national memory and a place of potential threat was evident in the Kingdom of Greece, where folklorists, writers and ethnographers became increasingly interested in the Aegean islands which became central to a Greek national imaginary. Given the contested nature of Greek identity,[67] the island functioned as a space for resolving contradictions. In Greece, geology was used as a way of demonstrating that the islands of the Aegean were indisputably Greek.[68] Since the German meteorologist and geophysicist Alfred Lothar Wegener (1880–1930) set out the theory of continental drift in his monumental study, *The Origins of Continents and Oceans* (1915), the notion of islands as "submarine elevations", or continuations of landmasses, had been increasingly mobilized for nationalist ends.[69]

To a large extent, the island as an imagined community was borrowed by Greek writers from British and French writing. Indeed, Greek islands also featured in English fiction, such as the novel *Phroso* (1897), by Anthony Hope, (the author of the best-seller *The Prisoner of Zenda* (1894)), in which an English aristocrat, Lord Wheatley, buys a Greek island from the Ottoman government for £7,550 and a yearly tribute of £100.[70] Similarly, the volume by the children's writer, Julia Dragoumis, *Tales of a Greek Island*, was set on the island of Poros in the Saronic Gulf and published in English in 1912 before it appeared in Greek.

In the late nineteenth century, generally, the island was a motif that recurred in popular texts such as Jules Verne's *The Mysterious Island* (1875), Robert Louis Stevenson's *Treasure Island* (1883) and H.G. Wells's *The Island of Doctor Moreau* (1896). Particularly in Britain, such island literature, much of which falls into the category of "Robinson-nades",[71] or rewritings of Defoe's romance *Robinson Crusoe*, was appropriated within colonial discourse where the New World was conceived of in island terms[72] and became deeply embedded in the educational apparatus: specifically in children's books such as Johann Wyss's *Swiss Family Robinson* (1814), Frederick Marryat's *Masterman Ready* (1841) and Robert Ballantyne's *The Coral Island* (1857). In this literature the island functioned as an ideal model for Britain's engagement with its imperial dominions. The island connoted both retreat and discovery; a place where home anxieties could be worked out.[73] As a topos, the island provided a powerful context for the "assimilation of the language of conquest, masculinity, supremacy and authority and also for the supposedly inherent, eternal values of that language".[74] As such, the island signifies "the ultimate gesture of simplification", while it "draws a line around a set of relationships which do not possess the normal political, social and cultural interference".[75] Thus, in Dragoumis's novel *Samothraki*, the island becomes a mirror of Greece as a whole and an emblem of organic community with incontestable boundaries:

Those who dwelt on the mainland were forced to take mountains as their frontiers and to build castles on the narrow passes and lookout ridges. And their state was as contained as an island and from a small mountain in the middle of the plain all the surrounding castles were visible as were the mountains, which encircled them like a necklace, as frontiers.

Others made their land so extensive that the frontiers could not be seen. Not even they knew where their land ended.

But expansive frontiers do not always reflect an open minded and accommodating people; they reflect only a great collective. And the mass of people stretches out further and further, until it disappears into the distance, and loses its shape, and the soul of each individual diminishes as a consequence.

And still others, who have narrow boundaries which they see all around them, gather themselves up. They are more on their guard, their souls are furled up, they cannot forget themselves easily and they climb upwards. They become twisted and taller.

This is the case with the island which is tightly circumscribed by frontiers...

The Greeks are almost all island dwellers. Their frontier – the sea – is visible from almost everywhere. But the sea which divides people, also provides opportunities to journey to different places.

The island is always something separate and complete. That is how it appears from the outside. And from the height of its summit that is how it also looks – solitary in the midst of the sea.[76]

If, for Dragoumis, the personal is iconized in terms of the national and the national in terms of the personal, so the island stands in a symbolic relationship to the national space; it is characterized by its legibility and dramatizes the world as a text with a specific set of circumscribed meanings. *Samothraki* is, in this sense, a culmination of Greek island literature where the island serves as the mirror of Greece and as an emblem of organic community with incontestable boundaries.

In Greece, *Robinson Crusoe* was a popular book and enjoyed an important status as an educational text. First translated into Greek by Perikles A. Raftopoulos in 1840, a second translation was published two years later by C. Christopoulos which became a standard school text until 1880. Rangavis translated a German Robinsonnade which saw five editions between 1851 and 1880. Finally, Wyss's *Swiss Family Robinson* was translated in 1854. Defoe's narrative also gave rise to numerous Greek Robinsonnades in the 1880s: *The Greek Robinson* by Vlasios Skordelis (1882), *Telemachos or New Robinson: Being the First Steps Towards Civilization* by P.G. Kourtidis and G. Konstantinidis (1883), *Will Robinson* by Ioannis Papathanasiou, *Apostolis the Sailor* by Miltiadis Vratsanos (1884), *The Greek Robinson* by Yeorgios Konidaris (1887) and *Robinson and his Lessons* by Nikolaos Metaxas (1893).[77] Psycharis also published a version of the Crusoe story, entitled *Life and Love in Solitude: The History of a New Robinson* (1904) which contained a lengthy epilogue in which the author sought to define, amongst other things, the different meanings assigned in Greek to the word "place" (*topos*).[78] Two years earlier, in October 1902, Psycharis had published an article on *Robinson Crusoe* in the French newspaper *L'Aurore*.

Not surprisingly, allusions to *Robinson Crusoe* pervade nineteenth-century Greek narratives. One of the protagonists in a short story by

Mitsakis (1890), for example, dresses like an English rambler and looks the "perfect picture of Robinson".[79] Drosinis acknowledged *Robinson Crusoe* as an influence[80] and in his novella, *Amaryllis*, the city protagonist, when he has disembarked on the island, likens himself to "another Robinson".[81] By implication, Stefanos's attempts to make a tolerable existence in the solitude of the Aegean island are akin to Alexander Selkirk's ingenuities on the uninhabited island of Juan Fernandez. Like many other Robinsonnades, in Drosinis's novella, as we have seen, historical and political contradictions are effaced by the idyllic setting, even though that setting is haunted by their displacement.

The similarity of Daudet's fiction with that of Drosinis and his Greek contemporaries is evident. Like Drosinis, Daudet dispatches "impressions, turns of phrase, local traditions" which have been gathered around the ashes of an "ancient hearth" back to the city from his "spiritual retreats" in the country, "a thousand leagues from newspapers, cabs, fogs".[82] And while Daudet celebrates rural Provençe, disparaging the iniquities of a "noisy, dirty Paris", visions of the metropolis nevertheless "haunt" the narrator. The book ends with the paradox that:

> Up there, in the barrack-rooms of Paris, we sigh for the blue of our Little Alps and the wild scent of their lavender; and now, here, in the very heart of Provençe, we miss our barrack-rooms, and everything that reminds us of them is dear to us!...Oh, Paris!...Paris!...Always Paris![83]

There are twenty-four tales in Daudet's collection of *Letters*, the same number of books that make up the Homeric *Odyssey*, and in his windmill the narrator imagines himself to be in a boat embarking for exotic journeys to "far-off islands". One of the stories is set in Algeria, while two take place in Corsica, so that Provençe becomes a space for imagining other foreign lands – "deserted and savage places", as the narrator expresses it – further afield:

> And when the mill's ramshackle walls creaked under the force of the *tramontane*, the noise of the rigging of its tattered sails stirred memories in my tired and anxious mind of sea-voyages, of halts at lighthouses, of far-off islands; and the sighing surge of the encircling pines completed the illusion. I do not know from where I have derived this liking for deserted and savage places.[84]

Islands in Greek literature of the period, as elsewhere, are simultaneously featured as "deserted and savage places" and as ideals of community. Many of the stories by Papadiamantis, Alexandros Moraitidis (1850–1929) and Eftaliotis are set on Skiathos and

Lesvos, respectively, while Panayiotis Axiotis's (1840–1918) fiction is set on his native island of Mykonos. The island functions as a symbol of close community and as a synecdoche of society as a whole, while the island's insularity is also a sign of its antiquity and stands for notions of a rooted, unadulterated, original culture, in contrast to those other detached "island" communities which urbanism itself gives rise to. As Peter Mackridge has observed: "islands such as Sicily and Sardinia lent themselves even more readily to this kind of treatment, since their culture could easily be seen as separate to that of the mainland."[85] This was a view shared by folklorists and ethnographers in the nineteenth century. W.H.D. Rouse noted in his introduction to the English translation of Eftaliotis's fiction (1897): "there is something Homeric still lingering about rural Greece, and especially about those isles of the Aegean where few travellers come".[86] James Theodore Bent, who wrote about the islands of Karpathos, Samos, and Thasos between 1885–1887, observed in his travel book *The Cyclades or Life Among the Insular Greeks* (1885) that the Aegean islands, as opposed to the mainland, "are more particularly rich in the preservation of manners and customs which have survived the lapse of years". According to Bent, the islands were especially favourable for folkloric study because unlike the mainland, they were never "subject to barbarous tribes". He concluded that "from these facts it will be obvious that these islands, especially the smaller ones, offer unusual facilities for the study of the manners and customs of the Greeks as they are, with a view to comparing them with those of the Greeks as they were".[87] Or as Bent expressed it in an article on Karpathos: "no happier hunting ground could exist for the study of unadulterated Greek peasant life".[88] The journalist H.N. Brailsford, who travelled through Macedonia shortly after the Ilinden Uprising of 1903, observed that "the true Greece is to be sought in the Highlands and the Isles". "Where Hellenism is still married to its barren rocks and the waves that cradle it", he added, "it lives triumphant and unspoiled".[89] Lawson noted in his *Modern Greek Folklore* that it was on the islands that "the grand and impassive beauty of the earlier Greek sculpture may still be seen in the living figures and faces of men and women", whereas "the ordinary Greek of the mainland, on the other hand, is usually of a mongrel and unattractive appearance".[90]

In a similar spirit, Eftaliotis, in the short story "Stravokostaina" (1890), exhorts Greeks who live in Athens or even abroad to visit the islands, prophesying that Europeans will soon be coming to see the grace and beauty of Odysseus's age still alive, after which the Greeks themselves will become interested by imitation:

And now, I would ask you the young generation of our ancient race, who spend your last farthing in travelling to Europe, why not make a trip each year amongst our islands, to see all these things, and much else that is even more strange and beautiful...[91]

This idea of the island as a museum, where the culture's historic roots were preserved, is expressed in numerous texts and relates to the assertion of an original, essential Greekness. The island heroine in Drosinis's tale "The Rivals", for example, is described as "a typical Greek girl, a worthy sister of the marble Kores of the Erectheion on the Parthenon".[92] This comparison, of an islander with a national monument at the heart of the Greek capital, represents the poignant transposition of the centre to the periphery: the island becomes a symbol of organic self-sufficiency, a place free from the tyranny of foreign influences. As such, the island represents the ideal locale from which the writer is able to survey and defend his national culture, circumscribing local traditions and dialects with a defensive sea of *katharevousa*, or purist Greek, in the main narrative.

6.5   THE WRITER AS TOURIST

Although many Greek writers in the 1880s and 1890s were writing about their birth-places, they were doing so from outside, offering an outsider's perspective on Greek rural culture for an urban reading public. Like many Greeks, both Drosinis and Vizyinos studied in Germany, and produced some of their first works of fiction while living abroad.[93] A gloss at the beginning of *Amaryllis* announces that a translation of the work has been published previously in the German magazine, *Der Tourist*. The Greek publisher resolved to bring the novella out in book form, the reader learns, since he anticipated it would elicit curiosity in "the nature and rural mores of Mother Greece".[94] In his autobiography Drosinis recounts a visit to the Harz Mountains when he was studying in Germany. On his trip he reads stories about his native Greece to two German girls, explaining the local traditions and customs to the foreigners.[95] Similarly, Vikelas spent most of his adult life in France and Britain, while Eftaliotis, who left his native Lesvos at the age of seventeen, lived in Liverpool and Manchester, spending more than a decade at Hessle in the north of England. In 1889 he had discarded his real name, Kleanthis Michaelidis, in favour of the pen name, Eftaliotis, that would identify him with Eftalou, a place near his native village of Molyvos. His collection *Island Stories* was actually written in Bombay where there was a sizeable Greek community and is dedicated "to my beloved Eftalou, that charming rural spot in my home".[96] The rural island community is described by Eftaliotis as a "survival" in a manner that recalls the factual preoccupations of a touristic guidebook. Thus, he prefaces a lengthy architectural description of the local houses by announcing:

> it may not be out of place to say something, as they are gradually becoming a thing of the past. They have not built one these last fifty years.[97]

Although Papadiamantis, Moraitis and Xenopoulos never travelled abroad, they spent much of their lives making a living in Athens from where they wrote about their native islands. This outsider's engagement with Greek culture is reminiscent of that situation described by Declan Kiberd in postcolonial Ireland where "the cultural life of the nation seemed less often geared to meet the people's own needs and more often addressed to the whims of foreigners. Eventually many Irish people learned how to act like foreign tourists in their own country".[98]

If Greek writers approached the Greek countryside from an outsider's perspective, European landscapes were also mapped onto Greece. In the preface of Xenopoulos's novel *Margarita Stefa* (1893), subtitled "Country Manners", the author notes the ways in which the Greek island is reminiscent of Andalusia.[99] Likewise, Drosinis's collection *Rural Letters* is set in an old tower in Gouves in Euboia, which the writer had inherited from his maternal grandmother,[100] and which is reminiscent of the windmill from where Daudet dispatched his letters. The connection is also made explicit in *Amaryllis* where the protagonist, Stefanos, writes letters to a city friend from a remote tower which, again, resembles a windmill.[101] Drosinis's landowner/narrator in *Rural Letters* was, in fact, modelled on a Swiss neighbour, while the epistolary form of both texts underlines the distance between the author, the subjects of his letters and the recipient. Not only did much prose fiction promote an outsider's view of Greek culture, but Greek fiction itself enjoyed considerable popularity abroad. Indeed, the final decade of the nineteenth century witnessed a spate of popular translations from Greek into English.

Two decades earlier in 1883, the same year as the first *Estia* short story competition, Vizyinos's tale "Who was my Brother's Killer?" had been published. In Vizyinos's text the narrator exposes the native Greek writer's displacement as a foreigner when his mother questions a stranger who has arrived in Eastern Thrace from Europe about her son's whereabouts. When asked by the traveller what her son is called, the mother replies:

"Do you think I know, myself? His godfather baptized him Yoryis, and his father, my husband, was Mihalios, the tradesman. But you see he's got ahead in the world and taken a name from learned circles; and now, you see, when they write about him in the newspapers, I don't know myself if it's my boy they mean or some European!"[102]

Not only did Greek writers promote a foreigner's view of rural Greece, peppering their texts with italicized words and asides to the urban reader, but in numerous short stories village life is represented from the perspective of an outsider. Sometimes the protagonists are outlanders, or natives who have been abroad for many years, and have become estranged from their homeland; sometimes they are disaffiliated, alienated members of the rural community who dwell in the wild, outside the precincts of the domesticated circle.

6.6   INTERNAL DISSENSION: THE SAVAGES WITHIN

Daudet's "liking for deserted and savage places" and their association with "far-off islands" intimates the possibility of threat. By the same token, the rise of ethographic fiction, folklore and regional studies in Greece is marked by a series of contradictions which we have already identified in previous chapters. The rise of the region was a spur to modernization, which had the effect of curtailing the autonomy of the region. In much the same way, the celebration of different local customs and traditions in folklore and literature entailed their sublimation within a homogenized national culture.[103] On the one hand, the differences represented by the regions, where venerable customs remained alive, were exalted. On the other hand, the evidence of barbarity within the national space was a cause for discomfiture and, more ominously, a source of possible dissension.[104] In much the same way as colonized peoples became the object of a discourse which legitimized European domination, so Greek folklorists and ethographic writers were involved in a project to isolate the internal Other. As the habitat of the native savage, the island had to be subjugated.

As Daniel Pick has observed, the relative ease with which it was possible to move within the state from the 1880s onwards increasingly drew attention to the "socially alien" within the populations in the country's hinterland and in outlying regions. "Travel afforded not only romantic delight"[105] at the contemplation of pastoral Greece, but also presented the prospect of future divisions. As Weber has shown in France, which was fragmented geographically and linguistically, a modernizing effort was made to unify the rural populations through cultural, educational, political, and economic self-colonization. In his *Études sur la Sélection chez l'Homme* (1881), Paul Jacoby intimated that the presence of an internal Other threatened the coherence and stability of the national order. After 1861 the priority of converting peasants into citizens began to preoccupy Piedmontese officials and intellectuals. Thus, the criminologist Cesare Lombroso's (1835–1909) theory of atavism owed much to the problem of Italy's fragmentation:

> The white races represented the triumph of the human species, its hitherto most perfect advancement. But then inside the triumphant whiteness, there remained a certain blackness. The danger was not simply external…indeed the problem was that it could not be held to an outside. It could not even be held to the south of Italy. Each region had its cultural, economic and political forces threatening the state.[106]

These threats are evident on Drosinis's remote island in *Amaryllis*, which is evoked through far-fetched comparisons with exotic travel and with colonial expeditions which were then being reported in the Greek press. Thus, when the narrator finally arranges to meet Stefanos at the railway station, he observes that his friend is as ruddy and sunburnt as if he had been travelling in Africa:

> The truth is that from the point of view of your health, you are glowing: ruddy and sunburnt as a traveller in Africa.[107]

In Drosinis's late novel *Ersi* (1922) a similar description is made of an official:

> The tropical cap gave his sunburnt face, with the white moustache and goatee, the style of a French general who had returned from distant expeditions in the heart of Asia and Africa.[108]

Drosinis's city protagonists are conceived as explorers, penetrating repetitive but mysterious rural rituals, while the country is envisaged as dirty and bestial, but innocent. The ethographer's journey to remote places involves a commensurate temporal journey, so that spatial and temporal distances are inextricably bound up. The peasants who are observed are removed from the time of the observer in a process that amounts to "a persistent and systematic tendency to place the referent(s) of anthropology in a Time other than the present of the producer of anthropological discourse".[109] These representations of unsanitary, outlandish, but guileless natives are only one step from the full-blown Orientalism of Konstantinos Metaxas-Vosporitis's tales set in the Middle East.

The mapping of exotic landscapes onto the familiar landscape of Greece is noticeable in the writing of many foreign travellers of the period.[110] Similarly, the vocabulary of ethographic writing owes much to depictions of distant and exotic peoples. The periodical *Pandora* contained a section entitled "Places and Descriptions" devoted to descriptions of foreign regions of the globe. The journal *Estia* took an interest in British colonial operations in Africa and followed Stanley's heroic exploits in the Congo.[111] Eftaliotis, who spent a part of his life working in India, published an article on Ceylon, which was accompanied by pictures of bare-breasted native women, in *Estia* (1890), while the journal was publishing his Greek island stories set on Mytilini. As one contemporary declared in 1885: "Any defeat of the English fighting in Sudan against barbarisms is a defeat of freedom and civilization".[112]

6.7   NARRATIVES OF EXCOMMUNICATION AND INTEGRATION

Many of the stories and novels produced in the 1880s and 1890s treat the theme of social integration and the threatened disruption of the community. The momentum of many narratives, though by no means all, is towards the incorporation of the outsider back into the collective life; of the alienated city dweller, for example, back into the village existence from which he has been uprooted. As such, these texts can be read as allegories of national integration. An example of such an integrative narrative is Kondylakis's novel *The Big-Foot,* which was serialized in 1892.[113] In this text the protagonist, Manolis, is a young goatherd who has grown up in the wilds of the Cretan mountains and decides to come back down to the village in order to find a wife. Like his compatriot Ioannis Dambergis (1862–1938),[114] much of Kondylakis's fiction is set in his native Crete, which formed part of the Ottoman Empire until 1912, though with autonomous status from 1897. The narrative of *The Big-Foot* focuses on the problems of the young goatherd's assimilation back into social life and the title alludes to the nickname which the villagers bestowed upon him, on account of his clumsiness and awkward physical appearance. Manolis's unfamiliarity with village codes and traditions soon brings him into conflict with the local population, while the goatherd's ignorance provides an alibi for the narrator's lengthy descriptions of those same customs which the protagonist transgresses.

In the course of the novella, Manolis is likened to a Turk, a ghost and a wild man, while the narrative charts the painful process of his

education back into the ways of communal village life. Far from desta-
bilizing, or undermining the customs which are transgressed, the
narrative ends by fully endorsing them. Significantly, the main action is
set in 1863, the year in which George of Holstein-Sonderborg-Glücks-
burg succeeded the ousted Otto as King George I of the Hellenes, an
event alluded to in the beginning of Kondylakis's book. The tension
between Greeks and Turks also forms a background to the main plot,
as well as the Cretans' desire for union, or *enosis*, with mainland
Greece. A revolt in 1858 was to give rise to the renewed Cretan crisis of
1866–1869 and the crisis was to flare up again in the late 1880s and
early 1890s when Kondylakis's novel was being serialized. Through
these historical allusions, Manolis's integration back into the village
community is given an allegorical dimension and made to intimate
larger patterns of incorporation: of Crete with Greece, for example.
Manolis's final acceptance by the villagers follows a confrontation with
hostile Turks at a village dance, in which the courageous goatherd
proves the mettle of his manhood and validates the community's
honour. The goatherd's adventures and his peripheral existence
acquire an added meaning in the context of the pervasive metaphors
of exclusion and inclusion which the nation-state, as an interpretative
community, both perpetuates and controls. The protagonist in Kondylakis's *The Big-Foot* exemplifies the other numerous deviant
protagonists in Greek prose fiction of the late nineteenth century who
remain ostracized from the community, sustaining what Jean Baudrillard has called, albeit in a different context, "a folklore of
excommunication".[115] In Kondylakis's later, more ambitious novel entitled *Les Misérables of Athens* (1894), clearly inspired by Victor Hugo's
novel (1862) which had been translated into Greek as early as 1863,
the heroine is a young girl from Tinos who arrives in the capital for
work as a domestic but encounters all the difficulties of being an
outsider, ignorant of city ways. The problems of the country woman's
incorporation into the life of the city are reminiscent of *The Big-Foot*
which deals precisely with the eponymous hero's inclusion into the
village community.

The theme of excommunication, and reciprocally, of assimilation, is
explored by Karkavitsas in his short story "The Outsider" (1888).[116]
The story is set in the writer's native Lehaina in the western
Peloponnese and the protagonist, Dimitris Noulas, is a hard working
and god fearing "foreign peasant who had settled in the town many
years before".[117] Unjustly accused of stealing 300 drachmas from a
cattle-dealer, and hunted from Lehaina by the enraged townspeople,
Noulas is anathemized and retreats into the mountains where he seeks
refuge with the Vlach shepherds. The poor but hospitable communal
life of the Vlachs provides a striking contrast to the peasants' vindictive

and hypocritical treatment of Noulas in the town, and the fraternity of the rural community is reminiscent of much ethographic writing of the early 1880s. Yet, even in the mountains, rumours of Noulas's reputed crime reach his hosts and the peasant retreats in shame into the remotest rural regions haunted only by *exotika*, or demons. Dangerously ill, the peasant fortuitously meets up with the cattle-dealer who, on hearing his story, forgives him and is about to take the sick man down to the town when Noulas dies.

The final chapter of Karkavitsas's novel *The Fair Maid* (1890) is poignantly entitled "Assimilation". The book describes a young girl's marriage against her will to a middle-aged grocer. As one recent study has suggested, *The Fair Maid* can be read allegorically as a tale about the eclipse of traditional ways by the spread of commerce and the railways. From this perspective, the assimilation becomes an ironic reflection of the process of eradication of traditional ways being wrought by social and economic change.[118]

Karkavitsas's concerns in "The Outsider" with alienation and the concomitant desire for incorporation in a communal life, with all the compromises that these entail, are recurring preoccupations not only in his own work, but also in the writing of his contemporaries. Disaffiliated protagonists pervade the fiction of the 1880s and 1890s. Often they inhabit the empty tracts of land or *terrains vagues* beyond settlement and are closely associated with ruins and other locations which convey concepts of liminality. Such outsiders are linked with ghosts and demons (*exotika*), which "cluster around marginal areas of the physical environment"; the Greek word itself reflecting ideas of spatial exclusion.[119] Frequently such outsiders as Manolis represent a social threat: waylaying, thieving and abducting villagers in the manner of devilish hobgoblins (*kalikantzari*). Manolis is teased for being a wild man and is repeatedly likened to a billy-goat. Similarly, the numerous outsiders in Papadiamantis's short stories are goatherds who dwell in remote huts on the mountainside. When Frangoyannou, the protagonist of Papadiamantis's novella *The Murderess* (1903), has been flushed out of her town house by the law, she makes for the wilderness where she seeks shelter among the goatherds. Like many other outcasts, Papadiamantis's murderess is associated with ghosts and haunted places. Moreover, Frangoyannou's speech, like that of the mountain-dwellers, is idiosyncratic and indeed, in Papadiamantis's texts, physical exteriority extends to linguistic alienation. Outsiders are often characterized by their inarticulateness and pronounced idiolects. In fact, many of Papadiamantis's tales explore reciprocal ideas of integration and disintegration, of identification and foreignness. In "Harvest Love", for example, published a year before Kondylakis's novel was serialized, a mountain-dweller is described as a "wolf man"; the wolf being a traditional symbol of voracity and evil. The popular nickname for the herdsman in this short story, who is unable to articulate human speech but grunts like an animal, is *Agrimis*, a word which means both wild beast and, metaphorically, an unsociable or rude person.

This chapter has sought to show how the ostensibly uncomplicated settings of Greek rural fiction were fraught with contradictions. The geography which ethographic writing envisioned was ambivalent. It mapped out a distinct, clearly bounded national space, yet projected that space simultaneously as a wilderness that needed taming, thereby remapping it as an exotic and potentially recalcitrant terrain. A reading of rural fictions reveals the extent to which boundaries between the centre and periphery are blurred. It has been argued that late nineteenth-century Greek prose fiction manifests a resistance to the state's modernizing and centralizing drive. As Artemis Leontis has argued, for example:

> It is against this current of centralization, an economic as much as a cultural one, that artists and intellectuals fought when they asserted the centrality of the local village in their literary utopias. Their narratives place at the heart of the national terrain a fiction of peasant simplicity rather than the urban capital that stood at the focal point of state geographies. The literary village serves as a topos of a shared past, a rhetorical and geographic site of return.[120]

And yet, as Dimitris Tziovas has observed, "the opposition is not so clear-cut, since one might argue that nationalist ideology propelled the narrative (re)turn to the region".[121] Rural incorporations in the fiction of the period are countered by the violent reassertion of differences; the village community is both the ideal of a "knowable community" and, at the same time, a form of imprisonment which Arjun Appadurai has called "metonymic freezing"; that process in which one aspect of a people's lives comes to epitomize them as a whole.[122] The community becomes containable and, indeed, the struggle for containment is enacted in every one of the narratives described in this chapter: the violent incorporation of the locality within the larger bounds of the nation-state, which Anthony Giddens has aptly characterized as "the pre-eminent power-container of the modern era".[123]

To summarize, I have argued that an ambivalence informs the nation-building project itself. Regionalism, which found its expression in folklore, regional geographies and histories, as well as in rural fictions, can be construed as a process whereby different groups within a nation are rendered visible or invisible. For, as Katherine Verdery has remarked, in "the project of nation-building, nonconforming elements must be first rendered visible, then assimilated or eliminated".

Regionalism, from this perspective, can be construed as a "symbolic violence[s] through which difference is highlighted and then obliterated".[124] Yet this is only half of the story, for rural fictions, no less than folkloric studies, were bent on preserving the communities they were incorporating. This ambivalence underlines the two aspects of nationalism; two tendencies contained, as Verdery further points out, within the very word "identity" itself with its contradictory root meanings of "identical" and "unique", "root meanings that, like national ideologies, simultaneously homogenize and differentiate".[125] Ethographic literature, like folklore, nurtured the diversity it sought to dispel. The local traditions it inscribed were "born disappearing".[126] As Michel de Certeau has shown in his reflection on popular French culture in the nineteenth century, the "disappearance of the object – whether newly imagined as the folk, the community, authentic voice, or tradition itself – is necessary for its ghostly reappearance in an authoritatively rendered text".[127]

Chapter Seven

Life underground: archaeology and the recovery of the present

In the late eighteenth and early nineteenth centuries, as we saw in Chapter One, an interest began to focus on archaeological remains and, more generally, on the reciprocal relations between culture and the physical environment. This marked a decisive shift away from anti-quarianism as an exclusively philological concern to archaeology's redefinition as a practice predicated upon both literary *and* material excavations. The impetus for such a reorientation in Greece came chiefly from Germany, and that it did so is hardly surprising. King Otto was a Bavarian and from the state's foundation the majority of the Greek elite was educated in Germany.[1]

August Boeckh (1785–1867), for example, at the University of Berlin, had argued that the scope of archaeological research should be broadened from its narrow base to encompass any aspect of the ancient world that might furnish useful information and bring the past back to life.[2] Boeckh's teaching was developed by his outstanding pupil, Karl Otfried Müller (1797–1840), and later by Ernst Curtius (1814–1896), who directed the excavations at Olympia (1875–1881). Müller, in particular, was influenced by Ritter's human geography which strove to:

> present a living picture of the whole land, its natural and cultivated products, its natural and human features, and to present these in a coherent whole in such a way that the most significant inferences about man and nature will be self evident, especially when they are compared side by side.[3]

In a similar way, the archaeologist sought to elucidate Ancient Greek culture through a detailed evocation of the physical environment in which it was rooted. Müller's avowed aim was to search out "in contemporary places, former human life and the ancient traces on the ground".[4] Such an approach was continued and developed by Curtius, the author of an influential study on the Peloponnese (1851–1852) who became Professor of Classical Archaeology at the University of Berlin (1868), and who consistently stressed, like Ritter, "what he took to be the essential intercourse of culture and nature, history and geography".[5] As Curtius, who was to travel around Greece in the company of Ritter, declared:

> We cannot continually limit ourselves to a comparative study of manuscripts, correct a sea of texts and quarrel over old problems! For us, the sources repose deep in the ground. That is the only way we will make a contribution to the discipline which is in danger, more than anything else, of being lost in the labyrinth of subjective tastes and predilections. In short, the archaeology of art lies in topography, in history and in linguistic investigation, a natural connection which, if we should break it, threatens genuine research.[6]

German interest in Greek archaeology, however, was not impartial. While Germans laid claims to the inheritance of Ancient Hellas, the late eighteenth and nineteenth centuries witnessed what Eliza Butler once described as "the tyranny of Greece over Germany".[7] The importance of archaeology in the rise of nationalism and its susceptibility to political exploitation have become the subjects of increasing research among archaeologists and historians of nationalism.[8] Archaeology developed out of antiquarianism as a systematic field of enquiry during the early nineteenth century, at a time when nation-states were coming into being in Europe and it functioned as a powerful institution for legitimating nationalist claims.[9] Archaeology as a discipline was, and to a certain extent remains, inextricably bound up with the quest for origins.[10] Towards the final decades of the last century it became closely connected with the prevailing debate on cultural and ethnic identities. Archaeological activities were predicated upon the demonstration of "geographically circumscribed cultural manifestations".[11] In Germany, Gustav Kossinna (1858–1931), who was originally trained as a philologist, interpreted settlement patterns within the framework of ethnic dispersion; a connection which served as a powerful nationalist tool.[12] In particular, Kossinna equated cultural continuity with ethnic continuity, construing culture as an index of ethnicity. Similarly, in Central and Eastern Europe, archaeology played an important part in undermining Russian, Prussian and Austrian hegemony and in reshaping the political configurations of the area.[13] The excavation of the land became a conclusive way of establishing a national identity by displaying the historicity of the territory claimed by the nation; as such it constituted an integral part of a larger process which Michael Herzfeld has called "the monumentalization of history".[14]

The ideological role of archaeology is particularly conspicuous in the formation of the Greek nation-state since the legitimacy of the nascent Kingdom was founded upon largely unchallenged assumptions of continuity between the modern Greeks and the Ancients. As Bruce Trigger has noted: "In countries such as Greece and Poland, and to a lesser degree Italy, where various grievances still nurture nationalism, archaeology continues to be valued as a chronicle of past glories and a source of hope for the future."[15] The first systematic excavations in Greece, as we saw in Chapter Two, date from the War of Independence, when a French scholarly expedition, which included the Orientalist Edgar Quinet, accompanied the expeditionary force sent to expel the Turks (1828). The subsequent choice of Athens as the capital of the Kingdom in 1834 (the Acropolis was formally opened to the public in 1835), together with the rebuilding of Sparta along Neoclassical lines in the 1830s and the inauguration of the Greek Archaeological Society in 1837, were reflections of the importance attached to archaeology. This tendency was strongly underlined by the emphasis on ancient geography in the school curriculum, which was first constituted in 1834, and by the early foundation of museums. As one commentator has remarked, the founding members of the Archaeological Society had "only one thing in mind":

> how, in the place which they had only a few years previously freed, they would discover and save the remains of their great and noble ancestors, remains which would enable the inhabitants of the country with its great and glorious history to join the ranks of the civilized nations.[16]

Or, as the archaeologist Kyriakos Pittakis uncompromisingly announced in the blunt title of an article that appeared in 1852 – one of a series that argued for the ideological content of archaeology: "Material to be used to demonstrate that the inhabitants of Greece are descendants of the Ancient Greeks".[17] In 1832 proposals were made, as we saw in Chapter Two, for landscaping the top of the Acropolis by Kleanthes and Schaubert, with an archaeological park to the north side of the Acropolis. Different plans were proposed by Schinkel and von Klenze for building a royal palace on the top of the Acropolis and in the Ancient Agora.[18] The first national archaeological museum was established under Capodistrias's presidency on the island of Aegina in 1829.[19]

To speak in this context of Greece's "foundations" is to speak at once figuratively and literally. As archaeologists were to demonstrate so spectacularly in the course of the nineteenth century, beneath the chaos of post-independent Greece lay a buried world which was held as tangible proof of the state's heroic foundations. In Greece, as in other emergent nation-states, archaeology constituted part of a specific project which endeavoured to affirm a distinctive, in this case Hellenic, cultural community and to celebrate the nation's glorious achievements which were indelibly inscribed in the soil. At the same time, however, the aggressive rivalries of the foreign Archaeological Schools, which established themselves in Athens from 1846 onwards, reflected deep-seated international antagonisms, especially between the French and the Germans in the aftermath of the 1870 Franco–Prussian War.[20] Archaeological activity was bound up, particularly on the part of the French and the British, with increasing political and economic interference.[21] Diffusionist views which located the origins of European culture in the Near East and saw the Northern Europeans as the legitimate heirs of earlier Eastern prehistoric cultures, overlapped, here, with nationalist ideologies that construed archaeology as a manifestation of imperial prestige.[22] As one of the protagonists in Kondylakis's novel *Les Misérables of Athens* (1893), Menelaos Vounekas, Professor of Archaeology at the University of Athens, is made to remark ironically, "the theft of archaeological artefacts [is] almost a patriotic task":

> What would civilization gain if the Ancient remains stayed in Greece? Wasn't it preferable both for Greece and for art for these Ancient monuments to be collected together in European museums, where many enlightened archaeologists and admirers of antiquity would study them and elucidate them from every angle.[23]

Archaeology needs to be seen in terms of a wider politics of place and, more specifically, in the context of nationalism as a territorial ideology that promoted the congruence of ethnic, cultural and geographic borders. In Greece archaeology became a way of laying claim to "unredeemed" territories, as much as consolidating "redeemed" ones. Thus, the archaeological remains on the island of Samos were championed as a Greek national legacy in the nineteenth century, even though the island remained formally part of the Ottoman Empire.[24] Archaeology was also a way of demonstrating the solidity of the nation's foundations, which the writer Drosinis referred to as "the granite-like foundations of Greek moral and spiritual superiority".[25] The protagonist of Drosinis's novel *Ersi*, published in 1922, the year of Greece's decisive defeat in Asia Minor, is an archaeologist who takes up arms at the end of the book to fight for his country in the Balkan Wars. The book concludes with a rousing call to arms.[26] Archaeology strove to uncover the ancient, prehistoric roots of the nation which underpinned the present, in much the same way as geography and geology (two disciplines with which archaeology were closely allied) were also used to argue for the natural unity of the nation by affirming an organic coherence that underscored, and justified, the political community. The term "prehistory" had been popularized by Sir John Lubbock (1834–1913) in his best-selling book *Pre-Historic Times, as Illustrated by Ancient Remains, and the Manners and Customs of Modern Savages* (1865), in which he proclaimed: "Archaeology forms the link between geology and history".[27] Just as geology was concerned with the decipherment of natural history, so was archaeology concerned with reading the buried traces of former times. Writing in his *History of Geology* in 1901, Konstantinos Mitsopoulos (1844–1911), Professor of Mineralogy and Geology at the University of Athens, remarked that:

> Just as the historian illuminates and interprets customs and traditions, the degree of culture, the type of culture and religion and in general the history of ancient peoples, from the ruins of temples and palaces, of inscriptions and coins, weapons and pots, so too the geologist interprets the history of the planet and of the organic life it sustains by researching the earth's fossils and the activity of past geological centuries.[28]

Similarly, the celebration of regional differences in geography, as in literature, masked a homogenizing impulse that sought to establish "the link", as Vlasios Skordelis remarked in 1890, "between nature and history".[29] In the same way, geological surveys of the regions stressed the natural unity that underscored their seeming diversity. There was a close connection, too, in this sense between geology and archaeology since they both posited an explicit correspondence between "looking back" and "looking down". These connections were implicit in the bibliography published in the newsletter of the Greek Historical and Ethnological Society (1884), which was categorized under geography, archaeology and folklore. These diverse practices served clear ideological ends. In 1896, for example, when the Macedonian struggle was intensifying, the geographer and philologist Margaritis Dimitsas (1829–1903) published his exhaustive study of Macedonia, entitled *Macedonia in Speaking Stones and Surviving Monuments*:

> The product of years of laborious library field work from one end of Macedonia to the other, this book stimulated among Greeks interest and pride in their national roots, as well as a sense of legal ownership of the land with the hidden testimonies of its Greekness.[30]

From the Kingdom's inception, therefore, nation-building involved the recovery of the landscape in two directions: vertically, through history and its material remains, and horizontally, as an irredentist ideology aimed to incorporate "unredeemed" lands into the new state. In this sense the excavation of a Classical, ideal past fused with messianic visions of a resurrected Byzantine Empire. As Steven Runciman has remarked in his elegiac account of the siege of Constantinople:

> With the Emperor fallen with his fallen city the reign of anti-Christ began and Greece was driven underground, to survive as best she could.[31]

During the last decades of the century there was growing interest in Byzantine archaeology. The Christian Archaeological Society was founded in 1888, although the Byzantine Museum in Athens was not established until 1914, and officially opened in 1930.[32] In the nineteenth century, as a Greek nation-state struggled into being, the retrieval of the nation's buried life, both Ancient and Medieval, took on an unprecedented urgency.[33] The task of archaeologists, no less than geographers, folklorists and writers, was to reactivate the landscape by bringing to light evidence of a continuous and indigenous Hellenic culture. In fact, one dominant idea of the nation is as a "deposit of the ages, a stratified or layered structure of social, political and cultural experiences and traditions laid down by successive generations of an identifiable community". According to such a view, communities are built up like ancient earthworks:

> We should regard the nationalist as a kind of archaeologist. This is not because archaeology has been central to the formation of modern nations, though it often has been, but because nationalism is a form of archaeology and the nationalist is a kind of social and political archaeologist.[34]

7.2 THE ARCHAEOLOGICAL MODEL OF GREEK CULTURE

In 1815 Grigorios Paliouritis's *Greek Archaeology* appeared, which drew parallels between Ancient and modern Greek culture, while in the first decade of the nineteenth century the pages of the newspaper *Wise Hermes*, as we saw in Chapter One, began to draw attention to the connections between geography and archaeological remains. Writing in 1829, the politician and historian Andreas Moustoxidis (1785–1860) declared that "the preservation and excavation of whatever survived the years under barbarian rule" was essential to the nation's self-respect.[35] In the decades after Independence, archaeology as a model was not restricted to the excavation of the physical environment, but was applied to folklore which paid particular attention to what Claude Fauriel (1772–1844) called, in the first volume of his *Chants Populaires de la Grèce Moderne* (1824), the "monument of the word";[36] a description which echoed Leibnitz's statement that "words are the oldest monuments of nations".[37] A complex relationship was sustained between archaeology, geology and mining as an evolving institution which came to serve as a "dominant metaphor for truth-seeking" beneath the surface.[38]

Folklore provides a striking point of connection between literature and archaeology since the orientation of Greek folklore was both "literary" and "patriotic or archaeological",[39] while both grew out of antiquarianism in much the same way as ethnology and anthropology did. If the affirmation of an archaic language reflected a desire to trace verbal roots and represented the internalization of a physical archaeology, folklore, in its search for an indigenous culture, was intent upon uncovering buried links with the Ancients as evinced in the customs and manners of the "folk". The title of Politis's chair at the University of Athens was the Professorship of Mythology and Greek Archaeology, while the very name in Greek for folklore, *laografia*, was itself an archaeological retrieval, deriving from an Ancient Alexandrian word signifying a poll tax.[40] Significantly, the Museum of Greek Folk Art was founded in 1918 on the initiative of Drosinis and the archaeologist Konstantinos Kourouniotis.[41] Beneath the accretions of four centuries of Ottoman rule, pure, ghostly vestiges of Hellenism, it was argued, had been preserved intact. As the first newsletter of the Greek Historical and Ethnographic Society affirmed in 1883, justifying its interest in the years of Greece's subjugation by the Ottomans and employing both an organic and an archaeological metaphor: "The daisy grows in the mire, in the depths of the earth [are found] precious metals".[42] The project of collecting Greek folklore, in which numerous writers participated, represented the preservation of national treasures, or heirlooms. It was an undertaking analogous to the retrieval of precious artefacts, which, from the 1840s onwards, were being yielded up to archaeologists with increasing frequency, culminating in Heinrich Schliemann's excavations in Mycenae and Troy in the 1870s and 1880s and Sir Arthur Evans's (1851–1941) work in Crete at the turn of the century (1900–1905).

An intimate relationship was perceived between the retrieval of buried artefacts and the uncovering of buried linguistic vestiges and customs. Not surprisingly, perhaps, terms such as *thisavros* (treasure) and *kimilio* (heirloom) pervaded the literature of the period. As Karkavitsas remarked in 1892: "The contemporary Greek artist, in whatever field he tries his hand, always finds himself surrounded by an inexhaustible mound of treasure and all he needs to do is to bend down and fill his arms."[43] Or, as the poet C.P. Cavafy remarked at the turn of the century: "We must study our language since we don't know it. What hidden treasures it contains, what treasures! Our thought ought to be how we can enrich it, how to bring out what it has hidden in it."[44]

7.3   SUBREADINGS: THE METAPHYSICS OF DEPTH

Strangely, although the relationship between literature and folklore is often stressed in literary histories of Greece, mention is seldom made of the links between archaeology and literature, even though a close connection was sustained between them.[45] As we saw in Chapter Two, Panayiotis Soutsos's novel *Leandros*, the first work of prose-fiction to be published in post-independent Greece in 1834, demonstrates manifest archaeological preoccupations and the landscape is evoked as a rich repository of the nation's past. Soutsos refers throughout to the historical Greek treasure interred in the national territory and the allusion to Lord Elgin's desecration of the Parthenon undermines the view that Greeks of the period were not particularly concerned about the fate of the marbles.[46] Soutsos's kinsmen, Iakovos Rizos Neroulos and Rangavis, the latter of whom was appointed to the Chair of Archaeology at the University of Athens, are other examples of writers who took an active role in Greek archaeological matters as the leading founders of the Archaeological Society. Rangavis's *Précis d'une Histoire de la Littérature Néo-Hellénique* (1877) attaches great importance to archaeology; more so than the six pages devoted to a discussion of prose-fiction.[47] Numerous other intellectuals, such as the philologist and etymologist Stephanos Koumanoudis (1818–1899) were similarly prominent in promoting archaeological interests and Koumanoudis served as the Secretary of the Greek Archaeological Society for many years.

By the 1860s important archaeological discoveries had been made, and in the following decades archaeology expanded rapidly. In 1866 construction began on the National Archaeological Museum in Athens. Literature and archaeology were further connected since the choice of sites for excavating was determined largely through reference to the Classical authors and, in particular, to Homer whose texts were "mined" for their social and historical documentation. This was certainly the case with Schliemann whose excavations were devoted to uncovering Homer's buried world, even though the tale of his own enraptured response to Homer as a child, described in the autobiographical sections of his book *Ilios: the City and the Country of the Trojans* (1880), has been proven fictitious.[48]

Excavating at Hissarlik in the early 1870s, Schliemann uncovered what he pronounced to be "Priam's Treasure" and later in the decade he turned his attention to Mycenae where he unearthed five of the six shaft graves which he identified – again mistakenly – with those of Homeric Mycenae.[49] The texts were thus used to authenticate the material remains, just as the discoveries, it was claimed, substantiated the historicity of the texts.

Close ties thus existed between archaeology, geography, folklore and literature which sustained mutually reinforcing ideological roles in promoting Greek nationalism. Distinctions between literal or physical interments, on the one hand, and figurative unearthings that extended to language and culture more broadly, on the other, were broken down. At the same time, archaeological preoccupations cannot be entirely sepa-rated from the proliferation of late nineteenth-century narratives that imagine life as a subterranean space: the city as a manufactured, inor-ganic environment, the repressive underworld of Émile Zola's *Germinal* (1885), or the imaginary descents below the surface to Stygian realms in the fiction of Jules Verne and H.G. Wells.[50] As Victor Hugo asserted in *Les Misérables* (a book which enjoyed enormous success in Greece, prompting Kondylakis to write his own Greek, version entitled *Les Misérables of Athens*), the squalid underside of society is as important for the novelist to describe as the grand narrative of historical facts: "Is the underworld of civilization, because it is deeper and gloomier, less important than the upper? Do we really know the mountain when we do not know the cavern?"[51]

Archaeological motifs and, on one occasion at least, archaeologists, make an appearance in Papadiamantis's fiction. The historical novel *The Gypsy Girl* (1884) begins with a shepherd's discovery of statues in a buried cave. There follows a brusque and ironic aside by the narrator that the antiquities will doubtless be hauled off to some museum in Europe.[52] More specifically, three archaeologists appear in the short story "At Ai-Anastasa" (1892). In this text, the etymological origin of a toponym is explicitly linked to the ambiguous historical origins of the ruins known as "Prii". The narrative accentuates a tension between the view expressed by the archaeologists, of the landscape as a static "monument" in which the ruins are perceived entirely in terms of their origins, and the narrator's own reflections on the historical evolution of the site, suggesting a dynamic syncretism.[53] Landscapes, this text hints, can never be frozen in history, just as words cannot, since both are involved in a process of continuous appropriation. It is not the site's origin that is at stake, there-fore, but its intelligibility to the present.

While archaeologists do not figure in Papadiamantis's story, "The Woman with the Black Headscarf" (1891), archaeological motifs do recur and they are central to an understanding of the narrative. Briefly,

123

the story concerns the anonymous narrator's cousin Yannios who, while fishing one day at sea, saves a young boy from drowning. The protagonist is in turn rescued from near drowning by a shepherd when he attempts to recover his boat-hook which has accidentally fallen into the water. The main action of the narrative, therefore, involves multiple resuscitations; the retrieval of two lives from the brink of death. The boy's near-fatal accident is the culmination of a web of preceding allusions to death, separation and the disruption of continuity that has pervaded the narrative up to that point. The reader is informed, for example, that Yannios himself never married and has no progeny, while his two sisters are similarly childless, and the protagonist's brother disappeared to America years previously, without sending news.

The recurrent preoccupation with the loss of children is encapsulated in the original tale of "The Woman with the Black Headscarf" (*Mavromantilou*) who gives the short story its title. According to local legend, Mavromantilou, the name given to a rock that juts out of the sea close to the shore, is the petrified figure of a grieving mother who, having lost her seven sons at sea, metamorphozed into rock. An implicit parallel is drawn between the plight of the drowning boy's anguished mother and the tale of Mavromantilou's misfortune.

In the contexts of Yannios's passionate espousal of, and later disillusionment with, the irredentist vision of the "Great Idea", as well as the prevalence of a late nineteenth-century Greek political iconography which pictured Greece as a Mother striving to save and unite her children, there are perhaps reasons for reading Mavromantilou as a symbol of Mother Greece.[54] While she has lost seven children, Yannios, we learn, named one of his former boats "Seven Hills", after the seven hills of Constantinople and the other one he called "Saint Sofia".[55] Finally, the boy who nearly drowns is, the narrator specifies, seven years old. At the same time, the passage from Book II of the *Iliad* which is quoted near the beginning of the narrative, connects Yannios's disillusion with the irredentist vision of recapturing Constantinople with Agamemnon's despair that Troy will never fall and the Greeks should sail home while they can. Home, that is, to "Agamemnon's Palace" which Schliemann had just claimed to have discovered at Mycenae.

In a narrative about loss – personal, familial and national – the resurrection of the young boy out of the watery depths has figurative resonances. Moreover, the physical resuscitation which occurs in the main action is prefaced by another, parallel, recovery. For the narrative begins with an elaborate description of Yannios's garden, where, as already mentioned, a six line passage from the *Iliad* is quoted and developed at some length, which likens the power of Agamemnon's speech to move a crowd to the wind ruffling a field or raising waves on the sea. This passage from Papadiamantis has elicited much attention. Pervaded as it is with lavish metaphors and similes, the text draws attention to its own rhetoricity, disclosing the opacity of the linguistic medium itself.[56] But the question remains unanswered: how does this passage connect to the main action of the story which is the saving of the young boy's life or, for that matter, to the tale of Mavromantilou herself?

In the first place, taking the quotation from Homer as his starting point, the narrator weaves an intricate comparison between the land and the sea. Both the garden and the sea are conceived in terms of depths and the word "depth" (*vathos*) and its cognates recur with great frequency. The wind ripples the surface of the garden and sifts through into its depth with the sun, while the Pleiads dive down to touch the bottom[57] anticipating the later description of an Austrian ship which anchors in the bay to sound the sea's depth.[58] In the passage which describes the near-drowning, great attention is paid to the relative depth and shallowness of the water; the depth being explicitly connected with antiquity through the description of the ancient marble ledge on the sea-bed which acts as a prop for Yannios's tired limbs. In short, the land and sea are associated, not only through Yannios's dual activities of gardening and fishing, but through the relative concepts of depth and surface. Finally, both passages develop an archaeological metaphor as the dextrous Yannios retrieves treasures (*thisavri*) from the garden, just as he does later from the sea.[59]

The garden is characterized by its textual properties. It has depth in the sense that the description is densely textured. As the narrator proclaims, Yannios's verdant plot resembles an "open book" – and again employing an archaeological metaphor, he adds – a book of hieroglyphs which only Yannios can decipher; a poignant reference in view of the still undeciphered Minoan Linear A script which had encouraged Evans to dig in Crete when he had come across engraved Cretan stones in Athens. Furthermore, the description of the garden as a book of hieroglyphs brings to mind W.J.T. Mitchell's thesis that landscape is "a social hieroglyph that conceals the actual basis of its value. It does so by naturalizing its conventions and conventionalizing its nature".[60] In Papadiamantis's narrative the text is naturalized at the same time that nature is textualized. Just as Yannios brings life to the earth through his meticulous cultivation, so the narrator resuscitates the life of the Homeric text. Or rather, the Homeric text is unpacked. Rather than being decoded for its historical information as archaeologists like Schliemann did, the text itself becomes a site that is metaphorically uncovered in a literary unearthing that recalls earlier literary uses of imitation.

As Thomas Greene has shown, poets in the Renaissance, like Petrarch, for example, drew heavily on notions of disinterment, producing texts which had to be "scrutinized for subterranean outlines or emergent presences or ghostly reverberations" so that "subreading the landscape came to resemble subreading a culture". As Greene concludes: "The crucial moment occurs when the poet turns from landscape to the literary remains of antiquity and struggles to pierce their verbal surfaces to reach the living particularity of the past they bear within them." The passage in Papadiamantis's short story can be read as an exploration of similar relations between the surface and the linguistic depths of an Ancient text.[61] Tradition – symbolized by the literary garden or the rock around which multiple legends have accrued and which appears both still and endlessly moving – is not a remote monument, but a living body which has to be saved from death by a continuous and hard-earned process of reinterpretation.[62] In contrast to the numerous allusions to sterility in the narrative, the garden is equated with childish friskiness and productivity.[63]

In Papadiamantis's text, then, the depth of the garden which is penetrated by the wind and light, and the depth of the sea from which the boy is saved, are implicitly connected. The short story can be read, not simply as a local drama deserving attention on the merits of its regional colour, but as a text which engages with central issues. More specifically, with the ways in which history is monumentalized and, like Mavromantilou, petrified. (Significantly, Yannios himself nearly drowns when his legs seize up like a rock.) In opposition to such an approach, Papadiamantis's text enacts what might be called a series of "critical archaeologies" to reconnect the present surface with the past depths. On another level, too, the narrative can be said to explore the organicist preoccupations of a literature which, driven by a nationalist ideology that stressed the distinctive character of an indigenous culture, aimed to "bring to the fore, hidden and internally residing qualities", as part of a project that Dimitris Tziovas has aptly called a "metaphysics of depth".[64]

7.4 MINING THE LANDSCAPE: GREECE IN THE HARZ OF GERMANY

Another example of a text which enacts a series of "critical archaeologies", albeit in a strikingly different way, is Vizyinos's short story "The Consequences of the Old Story" (1884). Appropriately for a writer whose work explores the reciprocity of place and identity, Vizyinos took his name from the village of "Vizo" or "Vizii" where he was born in Eastern Thrace, then a province of the Ottoman Empire. Of Vizyinos's six better-known short stories, only two are set in areas other than his native Thrace and Constantinople. One is set aboard a ship between Greece and Italy, while "The Consequences of the Old Story" takes place in Germany: first in Göttingen, where the author himself studied, and later in the Harz mountains. Yet, although the setting is unfamiliar, this is a text which refers frequently to Greece since it concerns two Greek students who experience homesickness abroad.

The narrative focuses on two Greeks from the Ottoman Empire who are studying in Germany after finishing school together in Athens. The narrator is studying psychology in Göttingen and his friend, Paschalis, a student of mining and mineralogy at the famous mining academy at Freiberg in Saxony – the centre of German mining since the twelfth century[65] – is gaining practical experience working in the Clausthal mines in the Harz Mountains. Invited by his German professor to visit a mental asylum, the narrator encounters a beautiful inmate called Klara who has been driven mad by unrequited love. Later on a trip to visit Paschalis in the Harz, it dawns on him that Klara may, in fact, be the girl rejected by Paschalis because of his friend's own feelings of self-disgust with which he is scarred from an earlier love affair in Athens. The narrative concludes with Paschalis's death in the mines, while coincidentally, Klara, the narrator is informed by the professor, dies on the same day.

Archaeological metaphors pervade Vizyinos's narrative and are closely connected with mining and with recurrent motifs of disinterment.[66] In the course of the narrative, national stereotypes are inverted so that the German professor recites passages from Homer, while the Greeks, who are fluent in German, allude to German poetry and recite Goethe's (1749–1832) poetry.[67] The Harz mountains are consistently associated with a cultural mythology and constitute part of a cultural landscape associated principally with German Romanticism. The professor speaks of Goethe's Classical, Homeric qualities and an implicit parallel is drawn between the Harz mountains which Goethe climbed and mined[68] and Parnassos, the mythical home of the muses which is associated with the worship of Apollo. The conflation of Homer and Goethe hints at the preoccupations of the second part of *Faust* where the hero, in his quest for Helen, journeys to Greece like a philhellene scholar elucidating mythological characters from his reading of Homer.[69] German unification in 1871 led to a spate of articles in Greek periodicals discussing German society and culture. In November 1871, for example, the journal *Pandora* ran an article in which the author suggested that many of the elements of the *Faust* legend were present in the Greek myths. Discussing Goethe's *Faust*, in particular, the writer pointed out the importance of Homer to the German poet.[70]

The description of Paschalis, the Greek miner, is also suggestive in the light of German Romanticism's preoccupation with mining. Many German writers and poets were either formally trained as mining engineers or, like Goethe – who had a lifelong interest in geology – were indirectly involved in mining. As an administrator in the Duchy of Saxe-Weimar, Goethe was responsible for the reopening of the silver mines at Ilmenau; Novalis enrolled in the mining academy at Freiberg and worked as an inspector of mines, and in 1824 Heinrich Heine visited the silver mines near Clausthal in the Harz, where Paschalis is mining. Indeed, Heine's descent is explicitly alluded to in Vizyinos's narrative and specifically the poet's playful sexual punning on the female names of the two mines he descended in the Harz called "Carolina" and "Dorothea". As Theodore Ziolkowski has observed: "it is safe to say that it would have been difficult, between 1790 and 1810, to assemble a group of intellectuals in any of the centres of German Romanticism without including at least one or two guests who were somehow involved in mining".[71] The interest in mining was stimulated by geological discoveries, but was also part of a wider phenomenon:

> The European public had only recently, in the second half of the eighteenth century, discovered the pleasures of mountain-climbing, an effort undertaken initially in pursuit of the sublime. Just as mountain elevations had become the favourite goal for hikers in English excursion poems, the mountain similarly provided the generic locus for the meditations of the classical German elegy as it was developed by Schiller, Goethe, and their contemporaries. Inevitably the initial obsession with the outsides of mountains was transferred to their inner recesses.[72]

It is ironic, given the importance of mining and specifically of the Harz mountains in German Romantic writing, that it should be Paschalis the Greek, decked out in his leather apron, who is burrowing "like a mole in the bowels of the earth" under the seams of the Romantic German landscape; "like one of those kindly creatures of Germanic folklore", the narrator remarks, "to whose hands is entrusted the production and surveillance of the treasures of the earth".[73] Significantly, the action is set during the 1870s, shortly after the unification of Germany, when archaeology functioned as a particularly important ideological tool for consolidating the new state's foundations. Ironically, at a time when Germans were endeavouring to establish the integrity of the newly incorporated lands by disclosing the national "treasures" which lay buried within them, the guardianship of that heritage is bestowed upon a Greek. The description of the Harz mountains in Vizyinos's narrative evokes the towering, misty peaks of Caspar David Friedrich's

(1774–1840) landscapes. With their dense forests and storm-torn cliffs they are also emblematic of a militant chauvinism which drew on earlier Romantic literature, and particularly on Goethe, for its inspiration; a poet who represents "not just a good and great man, but an entire culture".[74] The landscape is a place "of veneration and exaltation whose inner meanings can be fathomed only by the initiate" and it is ideologically associated with folklore and episodes from German cultural history.[75] The narrator comments on Bismarck's centralizing politics and his plans of transferring the mining academy in Clausthal to the Reich's newly established capital at Berlin. The landscape of the Harz in Vizyinos's story displays a culture and becomes the symbolic expression of German cultural values.[76] If the symbolic description of the Harz is reminiscent of Romantic literature's preoccupations with the hardy independence symbolized in mountain scenery, it also recalls the topographic myths of the fatherland which pervade the histories of nation-states. For the German Romantics, "the bonds between nature and the national character were perceived as organically melded".[77]

It is ironic that Paschalis should be digging in Germany at precisely the time when Crown Prince Friedrich of Prussia had negotiated with King George I of the Hellenes to excavate at Olympia. On his way to the opening of the Suez Canal the Crown Prince visited Athens where he noted that:

> The sea of ruins, which cover the ground, offer an unbelievable multitude of beautiful pieces of artistry, many covered with inscriptions. Every thrust of the spade will bring new remains to light, though the inhabitants show very little interest in excavations, and when foreigners wish to undertake the job, the ban on exportations, which [is] applied to newly-discovered art objects, scares them away.[78]

At around the same time Schliemann had begun "digging for the relics of the [Homeric] past" in Greece and in Turkey.[79] In 1881, three years before Vizyinos's story was published and after a protracted legal wrangle over their ownership, Schliemann formally offered his portion of the finds he had made at Troy, including "Priam's treasure", to the German state in a symbolic gesture. In return, Schliemann obtained an honorary citizenship of Bismarck's new capital at Berlin, and Kaiser Wilhelm praised the archaeologist for his "warm devotion to the fatherland".[80]

On one level, Vizyinos's text plays with, and undermines, the implications of a rigid archaeological model of culture, by showing how cultures are not exclusive, or unique, but feed into each other through underground channels, as it were. Thus, the German nationalist project in its Romantic stage was deeply influenced by and drew upon

Hellenic ideals. While the earlier, Neoclassical phase of nationalism had sought its models in Sparta, Athens and Rome, Romantic nationalism retained this admiration for the Classical past.[81] Indeed, Faust's union with Helen in Goethe's poem represents a "symbolic synthesis of [their] cultures", of the Classical and the Romantic: the assimilation of Ancient Greece into modern Western culture.[82] The repeated allusion to the Acropolis in Athens where Paschalis and the narrator studied accentuates the connection. Thus, when Ludwig I of Bavaria commissioned a memorial to German heroes, known as the Walhalla, its name was borrowed from the paradise of heroes in northern mythology, but it was designed by von Klenze along the lines of the Parthenon in Athens. The "consequences of the old story" assume a cultural resonance here: the consequences of the cultural explosion which took place in ancient Athens unfold in early nineteenth-century German Romanticism where artists and poets immersed themselves in the ancient culture of Greece as much as they did in the golden age of German Medievalism. Paschalis, dressed in his leather apron and mining away beneath the German landscape, highlights the Greek foundations of Romanticism.

While a nationalist German discourse manipulated the mythopoeic character of the territory it laid claim to, that discourse was itself shaped by a protracted engagement with a foreign, namely Greek, culture. As a contemporary American commentator observed, Greece for the Germans was used "as a stalking-horse for Teutonic psychology". [83] Similarly, Greek culture engaged profoundly with German culture: the two Greeks are, after all, studying in Germany, while Greek folklore itself originated in Germany where Nikolaos Politis studied. The connection is intimated by the German professor when he speaks in Greek of Greek demons known as *kalikantzari* and *striggles* which inhabit the Harz Mountains. The German scholar Johann Hahn "had showed convincingly" – in the words of Rennel Rodd – "how many of the popular Greek tales bear strong analogy to the German folkstory".[84] Ironically, Greek folklore was conceived as a response to the aspersions made against Greek racial continuity by Fallmerayer. These two contradictory influences are conspicuous in Politis's pioneering study *Modern Greek Mythology* – written at about the time when Vizyinos's story is set – which is manifestly indebted to German scholarship. The avowed aim, however, is to refute Fallmerayer.

Vizyinos's narrative explores and connects the retrieval of personal and collective memories, likening this experiential recovery to the literal excavation or mining of the environment. The narrator, like the author Vizyinos, is a student of psychology and the very title of the story – the consequence of the old story – accentuates the importance of past experiences and history in shaping the present. He is, in the words of Jacqueline Rose, a "reader of the psychic subtext of territoriality".[85] While Paschalis is mining for minerals "in the gloomy night of the underground", the narrator speaks of the heart's "treasures" and "foundations", as well as "the dark recesses" of his brain and the "depths" of his memory. By the same token, Klara is described as "the treasure" of Paschalis's, heart and, similarly, the "treasure" of her father's house, recalling Hölderlin's "Hyperion" (1797), where the hero announces that he cannot stay in Greece but must escape to a valley in the Alps or the Pyrenees: "in the depths of the mountain world the mystery of our heart shall rest, like the precious stone in its shaft".[86] Inside the mental hospital Klara tells the narrator that her future husband has gone out "digging to get diamonds for [their] rings".[87] Subsequently, the narrator, reading Carl Vogt's *Geology*, draws an explicit parallel between the palaeontological illustrations in the book, or the geological history of the earth, and the protagonists' own early histories. Paschalis's "Greek heart" is likened to earth which has been "plundered, stripped, [and] laid waste forever".[88]

In this way, then, Vizyinos's text lays bare the latent archaeological tropes which pervaded psychology as an emergent discipline in the late nineteenth century. Characteristically, for example, Freud likened psychoanalysis to the excavation of prehistoric sites and compared memory's stratification with the topographic layers of ancient sites. In 1896 he compared himself to an archaeologist bent upon unearthing "unconscious memories" and the excavation of "the inner subjective history of desire". In restoring or retrieving lost memories, Freud claimed, in his preface to the case history of Dora, to follow the example of "those discoverers whose good fortune it is to bring to the light of day after their long burial the priceless though mutilated relics of antiquity". Of one analytic discovery, Freud wrote that "it is as if Schliemann had dug up another Troy which had hitherto been believed to be mythical".[89] And the Wolf Man recalled Freud as claiming that "the psychoanalyst, like the archaeologist in his excavations, must uncover layer after layer of the patient's psyche, before coming to the deepest, most valuable treasure".[90] Schliemann was, in fact, the man whom Freud envied more than any other.[91] In a letter to the Austrian novelist Stefan Zweig, Freud declared that he had read more archaeology than psychology.[92] Besides being a passionate collector of antiquities, Freud's library contained numerous archaeological books by, among others, Schliemann, Evans, Wilhelm Dörpfeld and Ronald Burrows.[93]

Vizyinos's narrative further suggests the way in which landscape has been textualized. The lush, overtly poetic description of the Harz draws attention to the text's rhetoricity, to the fact that the landscape here is a literary construct and that territory has been internalized. The view of the mountains prompts Paschalis to recite Goethe's poem:

> Now we're not merely about to mimic foreign ways, to learn how the tragicomic scenes of German drunkenness are acted out, but to come to know the locations in which the most sober dramatist of this country imagined the most magical and extravagant scenes of *Faust.*[94]

Paschalis indicates the plateau of the Brocken Mountain where Goethe set the orgies and dance of the Witches' Sabbath on "Walpurgisnacht", just as he had previously pointed out the location of the inn under the peak where Goethe wrote "Über allen Gipfeln". The scenic beauty of the mountains inspires poetry and particular locations are named after fictive events.

The relationship between landscape and literature is developed through analogies of reading. Mining metaphors are employed in the text as the narrator excavates metaphorically, echoing his friend's literal mining of the earth. Not only does the narrator prompt his friend to disclose his hidden secret, but like an archaeologist, he pieces his finds together into a unified narrative. The narrator's interpretative skills are nowhere more evident than when he deciphers the ambiguous letter sent to Paschalis from Klara's aunt, in an interpretive process that suggests both the stratified nature of language and the textual characteristics of the landscape. In the account of the multiple interpretations which the letter from Klara's relative to Paschalis elicits informing of the girl's madness, notions of interment and disinterment are extended to the sub-reading of a literary text. The narrator probes below the surface of the German language, just as Paschalis digs away in the subterranean shafts below the German landscape. Vizyinos exploits here the associations between geology, religious and political freedom and literature which were developed by Romantic writers and poets such as Novalis and Goethe who "saw the Wenerian account of the history of the earth as extending backwards in time the histories written by political and cultural historians".[95] "Aesthetic theory [thus] merged with cultural geography" and it was no coincidence, as Timothy Mitchell has shown, that the golden age of German Romanticism was also the golden age of geology and geographical discovery.[96] The development of an organic concept of culture, which found expression during the last decades of the nineteenth century in folkloric studies, as we have seen in Chapter Four, was stimulated by evolutionism in the natural sciences and particularly in geology.

The narrator in Vizyinos's story unearths the meanings hidden in the very texture of the letter with such dexterity that he incites a sardonic jibe from his friend – a jibe which returns the narrative full circle to the professor's description of the Homeric Goethe. The excavation of the letter, in the context of the narrator's earlier allusion to the palaeontological illustrations in Vogt's *Geology*, recalls Johann Fichte's (1762–1814) image of the palaeontology of a living language in his *Address to the German Nation* (1808).[97] So keen are the narrator's interpretative faculties that he would make an excellent career rendering Homer and the Classics intelligible to small children.[98] The archaeological world does not appear, here, as self-evident and unmediated. Instead, it is the subject of the same hermeneutic procedures as a text which is read for its meanings, delivering what Dominic La Capra has called "a sedimented layering of readings".[99] Finally, this emphasis on interpretation challenges the authority of the Origin which dominated archaeological epistemology in the nineteenth century and indeed, into the twentieth century. Reflecting on a meeting with two women in the Harz mountains in the late 1880s, to whom he read his Greek short stories – at exactly the moment, that is, when Vizyinos's story about two Greeks in the Harz mountains was published – Drosinis employs a poignant archaeological analogy to describe the retrieval of past memories back into the present:

> Excavating below the heavy levels of forgetfulness I find beautiful fragments that fit together, in the same way that archaeologists dig and find in the deep earth of the years pieces of carved marble and colourful, shattered vases.[100]

Vizyinos explores the ways in which landscapes are constructed within specific ideological contexts. He probes the relationship between landscape and identity. The descent into the mine is a descent into subsurface histories; not only through geological time, but back into the history of Greece as a European ideal; an imaginary topos that later furnished the foundations of the Greek Kingdom when it was established in the early nineteenth century under a Bavarian monarchy and remapped by Germans. Yet Vizyinos goes further. He enquires what happens when identity is shown to be contingent, when the landscape is undermined to reveal its fictive fabric. Such a realization, he suggests, entails a descent into madness, the very madness that fuels nationalist passions. Heine visited the mines in the Harz dressed in what he called "the dark delinquent's costume"[101] and Vizyinos was to don the same clothes when he was consigned to the mental asylum at Dafni outside Athens in 1892, the same year that Maupassant was admitted to an asylum. A symptom of the author's madness was his conviction that he owned a mine in his native Thrace that would one day make him wealthy.[102]

7.5   THE ARCHAEOLOGY OF ARCHAEOLOGY

The last two sections of this chapter have sought to demonstrate the way in which the implications of an overarching archaeological model of culture in Greece gave rise to what might be called "critical archaeologies".[103] That is to say, an archaeological model is itself undermined to reveal the model's limitations. This contradiction – if it can be so called – characterized the organic conception of Greek culture. The work of the poet and literary critic Palamas is full of archaeological metaphors. Nevertheless he fervently rejected archaeology as a cultural model and would, undoubtedly, have assented to Byron's description of archaeologists as "emasculated fogies".[104] Speaking of his visions of a grand synthesis which would join the Ancient and the modern worlds in the prologue to *The Eyes of my Soul* (1892), Palamas asserted:

> If the poet turns back into the past, he seeks in it new significant images, and forms, symbols with which he expresses his thoughts and feelings; feelings and thoughts of the spirit of modern times which are influenced, although he does not suspect it, by the environment. In this union, the modern spirit becomes clearer and the old is transformed as the nature of the artistic creation requires, which is not, to be sure, like the work of the photographer or the archaeologist.[105]

Such contradictions are made explicit in Karkavitsas's last, allegorical novella *The Archaeologist* (1904), which tells the tale of two brothers, Dimitrakis and Aristodimos, the sons of Andreas Morfopoulos. While the Morfopoulos clan was once powerful and rich, lording over a vast acreage, it has since fallen into servitude, beaten by the Haganos clan which invaded from abroad. The plot is thus a polemical account of the subjugation of Greece by the Ottomans and constitutes an outspoken condemnation of excessive ancestor worship, known in Greek as *prognoplexia*. While Andreas had toiled during his own life to restore the family's fortunes, on his death his eldest son Aristodimos, intent on displaying the former glory of the Evmorfopoulos heritage, spends his time poring over and declaiming Ancient texts with foreign scholars who are symbolic of the Protecting Powers. Eventually he excavates the ground of his father's hard-earned estate, squandering his patrimony in order to uncover buried treasures and the subterranean "foundations",[106] thus demonstrating the inextricable relationship between the spectacular material "treasures" and the "treasure-trove" of the archaic language.

Karkavitsas's intent is clear in *The Archaeologist*: to parody the excesses of an archaeological approach to Greek culture which was recapitulated on the linguistic level as a blinkered preoccupation with purity and archaic forms. Aristodimos is, inevitably, crushed to death by a statue retrieved from the family plot and Dimitrakis likens his brother's library – the storehouse of Ancient literary treasures – to a tomb.[107] In opposition to the constraining archaeological interpretation of Greek history, Karkavitsas celebrates an oral folk-culture in lyrical passages associated with Dimitrakis and, particularly, with Elpida (meaning "hope" in Greek), who emerges in the narrative as the primary embodiment of an indigenous folk tradition. Elpida is herself a hybrid: the offspring of an illicit union between a Morfopoulos and a Haganos. Her house, which is appropriately situated on the borders between both estates, is reminiscent of a Byzantine church.

The view of the past expressed by Elpida is based upon a notion of genealogical continuity – as shown, for example, by the "family tree" which she depicts on an embroidery – as equally manufactured and restrictive as the reductive and preposterous archaeological conception embodied in Aristodimos.[108] As Jina Politi has shrewdly observed, the novella is marked by a pronounced contradiction. For on one hand, the narrative "conceives of history as a process admitting of radical break, change and development", on the other hand, however, "at the nationalist level…it dreams of the race as unchanging, persisting through time thanks to permanent historical factors".[109]

Karkavitsas's *The Archaeologist* is inscribed with a contradiction that lies at the very heart of the nationalist enterprise itself. Namely, that instead "of freeing the (Greek) subject from paralyzing [archaeological] representations", the subject is once again transfixed "within the a-temporal mode of filiation and repetition".[110] Like the Aryan myth which Malcolm Quinn defines as a "duo-temporal 'mythology of structure'", Greek conceptions of continuity combined ideas of synchronicity and diachronicity. Thus, Greek nationalism looked for the synchronic constants of Greek culture through the ages which it then sought to link "to a diachronic vision of the ancestors".[111] Karkavitsas dismantles the archaeological model, which banishes polysemy as dangerous and unsettling, only to fall victim to what Loukatos, in a different context, has called "archeofolklore".[112]

In their different ways, and with varying degrees of success, the writers discussed in this chapter attempted to explore what – to adapt Vizyinos's title – might be called the consequences of an old story. That is to say the consequences of the fixed, monumentalized representation of Greek culture which, from the inception of the Greek state, had been employed to legitimate and consolidate a national space. Paradoxically, I have argued, the interrogation of this representation meant, in the final analysis at least, undermining the foundations of the nation; a self-defeating task for writers like Palamas and Karkavitsas who were unashamedly endeavouring to save the nation. Karkavitsas himself was to intimate such an admission when, in 1911, he refered to *The Archae-ologist* as his "suicide".[113] But as Nietzsche observed, in an epigraph which Palamas affixed to Canto X of his epic poem *The Dodecalogue of the Gypsy* (1907), "only where there are tombs are there resurrections also".[114]

Chapter Seven has sought to explore the ideological uses to which archaeology was put in the emergent Greek state and has examined, albeit briefly, the impact of an archaeological model of culture on the rise of geography, folklore studies and literature, pointing to the underlying linkages between these practices. If archaeology and folk-lore in Greece were, from the outset, closely connected with Classical philology, lexicography and linguistic palaeontology, so, reciprocally, were literary texts shaped by an archaeological view of culture. Litera-ture, no less than archaeology and folklore, was inextricably bound up in a quest for cultural origins; origins which it sought to locate in the territory claimed by the nation.

The recent emphasis placed by post-processual archaeology on the textuality of archaeological discourse "has prompted questions concerning how the discipline writes itself"[115] and has redirected atten-tion to archaeology as "a process by means of which material evidence becomes encoded in discursive structures" to produce meaning.[116] Attention has been paid both to the rhetorical strategies employed by archaeological writing and to the manner in which material culture is written and diversely read within the constraints of specific economic, political and cultural systems. The present chapter has sought to demonstrate the manner in which archaeologies were written and read within specific social processes in Greece.[117] In so doing, it has sought to demonstrate the fictive dimension of archaeology and the archaeo-logical dimension of fiction through an excavation of nineteenth-century critical archaeologies which contemporary theorists, inadvertently perhaps, have tended to ignore.

Chapter Eight

Map mania

8.1 FRONTIER FICTIONS REVISITED: THE MACEDONIAN STRUGGLE

"Truly this period in our history has been well defined as the boundary-making era", Sir Thomas Holdich declared in 1899 at a lecture before the Royal Geographical Society, noting that "of all sources of international irritation, boundaries seem to be the most prolific".[1] A series of international conflicts from the Franco-Prussian debacle in 1870 to the costly imperial campaigns at the turn of the century in the Sudan, Afghanistan, South Africa and Burma supported Holdich's thesis.

In his Romanes Lecture delivered at Oxford in November 1907, George Curzon, Marquis of Kedleston and late Viceroy of India (1898–1905), similarly reflected on the significance of frontiers and border disputes in contemporary politics. Alluding to Frederick Jackson Turner's frontier thesis, which had been adumbrated fourteen years earlier (1893), he insisted that his audience "pause and consider what Frontiers mean, and what part they play in the life of nations".[2] Acknowledging the rejuvenative power of frontier life, he argued for the essential value of "Border literature": studies devoted to elucidating the political significance of frontier zones and to exploring the ways in which such spaces might be maintained and protected.[3] In particular, Curzon observed that frontiers were the main source of conflict in the modern age and he noted: "every Greek war is waged for the recovery of a national Frontier".[4] For Curzon, Greece was illustrative of the modern frontier problem.

In 1907 the "Eastern Question" had reached a new intensity as rival Greek, Bulgarian, Serbian and Turkish nationalist groups vied for supremacy in Macedonia. The following year the Young Turks were to lead a nationalist insurrection within the Ottoman Empire which was carried out with the avowed aim of creating a constitutional monarchy and overhauling the creaky, antiquated machinery of imperial government.[5] Central to the struggle in the Balkans were the different arguments used for laying claim to territory and the rationale behind the drawing up of national boundaries. As one geographer enquired in 1915, given the absence of any distinct national borders in the Balkans, might it not be "the destiny of the peninsula to be an annex either of a Central European state or of an Asiatic one?"[6] This was a dominant view in the second half of the nineteenth century. Writing in 1877 on the "geographical aspects of the Eastern Question", Edward Freeman observed that "the present frontier of the Austrian and Ottoman Empires, a frontier so dear in the eyes of diplomatists, is no natural or historical frontier at all, but simply comes of the wars of the last century".[7] As we saw in Chapter One, the boundaries of the Ottoman Empire were indeterminate, causing problems for cartographers who attempted to map its extent, as well as for the different national communities (particularly for the geographically dispersed Greeks) within the heterogeneous Empire who sought to map out clearly bounded homelands.

There was good reason, then, to focus on Greece in 1907 when Lord Curzon lectured on the frontier problem at Oxford. During the late 1890s, the Greek Kingdom had been much in the international news. In Britain, for example, *The Times* periodically reported trouble on Greece's northern boundaries, where brigand bands moved illegally, but freely, between the Kingdom and the Ottoman lands, making travel in the frontier regions unsafe.[8] The "Thirty Days War" against the Ottoman Empire in 1897, which ended with defeat for the Greeks, had been widely covered in the British Press and had prompted a spate of sensationalist books about the campaign. Thus, W. Kinnaird Rose, a war correspondent with Reuters, published a stirring account of the Greek conflict entitled *With the Greeks in Thessaly*, large sections of which were devoted to reflections on the Greek frontier.[9]

The Macedonian struggle, which had begun in earnest during the last decades of the nineteenth century, intensified after 1904 when protracted guerrilla warfare was waged between Greek, Bulgarian, and Serbian partisan bands. As Victor Bérard observed in his study of Macedonia (1897): "La Macédoine n'est encore à personne. Elle est a ceux qui la prendront pour la coloniser".[10] The Internal Macedonian Revolutionary Organization (IMRO), which advocated an autonomous Macedonia, had initiated a revolt against the Ottoman authorities in August 1903, known as the Ilinden uprising.[11] Although the insurrection was quickly crushed by Ottoman forces, it drew Western attention to the volatile situation in Macedonia which was characterized by a patchwork of fiercely antagonistic ethnic communities; a diversity that gave its name to the *Macédoine*, a salad of mixed fruit or vegetables.[12] Travelling through Macedonia shortly after the 1903 uprising, H.N. Brailsford observed that even "the peasant ploughs with a rifle on his back" and he concluded that "there is little to choose in bloody-mindedness between any of the Balkan races – they are all what centuries of Asiatic rule have made them." Everywhere he turned, the British journalist was confronted by the "strife between the Christian races, the rivalry of competing empires, the devastation caused in one form or another by the idea of nationality".[13]

Revolts against the Ottomans in Macedonia had occurred throughout the nineteenth century and in 1878, during the Russo-Turkish war, a revolt which aimed to join Macedonia to Greece was brutally crushed by the Ottoman Empire. In the same year, Bulgarian autonomy from the Empire was achieved (an independent Bulgarian Church, known as the Exarchate had been established earlier, in 1870) and the Bulgarians began a drive to urge the region's Slavic-speaking population to declare their allegiance to the Exarchate, as opposed to the Greek dominated Patriarchate at Constantinople. In 1897 Bulgarian bands invaded Ottoman territories and began terrorizing the population loyal to the Patriarchate. Armed Greek bands appeared soon afterwards in an effort "to conquer the territory of the souls" of the Macedonian peasants, as one contemporary commentator put it.[14] In 1904, following the ill-fated Ilinden uprising, Stefanos Dragoumis (1842–1923), Ion Dragoumis's father and one-time prime minister, had been involved in setting up the Macedonian Committee which actively supported Greek interests in the area. In the same year, moreover, Pavlos Melas, the Commander-in-Chief of all Greek bands in the areas of Kastoria and Monastir, who was, incidentally, Ion Dragoumis's brother-in-law, was killed by Turkish troops. This was an episode which Dragoumis described in a poignant chapter of his novel *The Blood of Heroes and Martyrs*.

As we have already seen in Chapter Five, the Greek defeat of 1897 exposed the inadequacies of a state ill-equipped to fulfil the grand ambitions for territorial expansion promoted by a political elite. The years that followed Greece's humiliation by the Ottomans were dominated by often heated debates about the role of the State as the custodian of Greek national interests.

8.2 MORBUS ETHNOGRAPHICUS

Brailsford prefaced his book with an ethnographic map of the region that reinforced his sympathies for the Bulgarian cause.[15] As another contemporary French observer concluded, the Balkan upheavals suggested that the region was suffering from a "morbus ethno-graphicus".[16] The use of ethnographic maps in the struggle over territory in the Balkans, however, had been established two decades earlier. A major Balkan crisis had erupted in 1876 when the Serbians, Montenegrins, and later Bulgarians had taken their lead from the Herzegovinians and Bosnians and risen against the Ottoman Empire. This was followed in April 1877 by the outbreak of a Russo-Turkish war and the diplomatic intercession of Europe.[17] Given the complex ethnic composition of the region, political significance was attached to ethnographic maps that purported to demonstrate the distribution of distinct populations and aimed at the ethnographic appropriation of the region. It was the Russians, pressing for Slav hegemony, who adhered to the principle of the ethno-political boundary when arguing for an enlarged Bulgarian state at the Conference of Constantinople (1876):

> The ambassadorial meeting at Constantinople brought home the principle of the ethnographic frontier for the peoples of Europe with all the force of a thunderbolt. It dramatized its significance and invested it with a propagandist value which the Balkan peoples were not slow to grasp.[18]

In Greece the Conference prompted a spate of studies devoted to the so-called "unredeemed" Greek lands in the Balkans and in Asia Minor.[19] Not surprisingly, perhaps, the 1870s witnessed a veritable "map mania" (*hartomania*) over possession of what one commentator called "those frontier lands of Eastern Europe where diverse races, professing conflicting faiths, meet and mingle".[20] As Evangelos Kofos has also noted, "the extensive use of Greek geographical names coincides with the peak of the Greek-Bulgarian national conflict in Macedonia during the last decade of the nineteenth and the first decade of the twentieth century".[21]

Bulgarian territorial aspirations were legitimated through an appeal to ethnographic surveys that demonstrated the preponderance of a Slavic, and in particular, of a Bulgarian population in the Balkans. In 1895 the Supreme Macedonian Committee was established in Bulgaria.[22] Bulgarian scholars insisted that Slavic speakers in Macedonia were "Bulgarian".[23] The notion that the Balkans was a predominantly Greek peninsula had "been steadily losing ground between 1821 and 1861".[24] Influential ethnographic maps by, amongst others, the Czech P.G. Safařík (1842), Ami Boué (1847) and G. Lejean (1861) significantly reduced the distribution of the Greeks in the area to the advantage of the Turks and Bulgarians, to such an extent that "Bulgarian and Balkan had become practically synonymous".[25]

Maps, then, and statistical surveys increasingly furnished important weapons "in the drawing up of political, intellectual and legal boundaries".[26] In Greece, the Association for the Propagation of Greek Letters, under the leadership of Paparrigopoulos, took an active role in accumulating statistical data and spearheaded the campaign to promote ethnographic maps of the Balkans which were propitious to the Greeks. Paparrigopoulos twice visited Germany in the 1870s on a mission to urge the cartographer Hienrich Kiepert (1818–1899), Karl Ritter's pupil and successor to the Chair of Geography at the University of Berlin in 1854, to modify his ethnographic map of 1876, which was finally used at the Congress of Berlin in the summer of 1878;[27] a mediation which was partly sought because the Germans were construed as impartial peace-brokers in the conflict.[28] In the event, Kiepert did not amend his conclusions materially and the Association was compelled to champion Edward Stanford's ethnological map (1877) which relied on data furnished by the Association[29] and which claimed most of the territory between the Adriatic coast and the Aegean, including central and southern Albania, for the Greeks. Maps by the Frenchman F. Bianconi (1877), the chief architect and engineer of the Ottoman railways, A. Synvet (1877) and Karl Sax (1878), one-time Austrian consul in Adrianople, were similarly favourable to the Greek cause. Ingeniously, Stanford had argued that the so-called "Slavs" should be considered as Greek "Bulgarophones"[30] and in 1899 Constantinos Nikolaïdis, in his book on Macedonia, was to argue that Greek ethnic territory could not, in fact, be divorced from Hellenism as a dominant cultural and commercial force in the Balkans.[31]

In the early twentieth century the Serb cause was advanced by the renowned geographer Jovan Cvijić (1865–1927), Head of the Department of Geography at the University of Belgrade, who produced a series of maps from 1906 to 1918 that later did much to legitimate Yugoslavia's incorporation of Macedonia.[32] Cvijić, who began his career as a physical geographer with an interest in the geomorphology of limestone landscapes,[33] became increasingly concerned with human geography and maintained that "the various Balkan peoples [were] practically limited to distinct natural regions",[34] even while "the different zones of civilization [had] developed in close connection with the principal geographical characteristics".[35] He asserted that the inhabitants of the area were latent Serbs[36] and his "revolutionary" 1909 map depicted the "Macedo-Slavs" as a distinct ethnic group.[37] Cvijić's findings were vigorously countered by Greek and Bulgarian scholars.[38]

The widely divergent demographic distributions represented on ethnographic maps of the Balkans point to the fluid definitions of national categories and the inconsistent criteria by which identity was determined. Proponents of the Greek cause, for example, based their assessments of the local "Greek" population upon the influence of Greek culture and religious affiliation, while Bulgarian claims were founded on language.[39] Greek identity was defined in ethno-religious terms, but increasingly in the nineteenth century "a national ethnic identity worked its way into the consciousness of increasing numbers of Greeks" scattered through the Ottoman Empire. At the same time, the "Greeks themselves by the mid-nineteenth century had several modes of association through which to express their identity". These included:

> faith, whether espoused or merely accepted as given; territory, be it a place of residence (Smyrna, Sinasos), a region (Cappadocia, Pontos), or a land (Asia Minor); culture and language, retaining a folk culture and a dialect or associating with the literary culture now being standardized by the educational institutions of the Greek nation-state; and political loyalty, be it to a single community, the governing authorities, fellow (ethnic) countrymen, or the nation.[40]

If the terms of ethnic identity were unstable, cartographic techniques and, in particular, the tendency to depict ethnic groups in colour codes as homogeneous blocs, obscured ethnic diversity.[41] Sub-groups were merged into dominant ethnographic categories and a map's scale adjusted to include or exclude specific minorities according to the map's purpose. Often substantial minority populations – in some cases populations of up to 49 percent – and dispersed communities were omitted so as to give an impression of stability and uniformity. Colour-coded maps ignored, for the most part, population density and a given group's proportion of the total population was thus concealed behind visual generalizations. Graphic images revealed numerical strengths but left out detailed distributions.[42] As H.R. Wilkinson noted: "some maps indicated comparative strengths of ethnic groups but neither their numerical strength nor their distribution".[43]

8.3   IMPERIAL GEOGRAPHIES: THE GREAT IDEA

The so-called "map mania" in Greece reflected a wider recognition of the political role of geography in laying claim to territory and consolidating the "New Lands" (*Nees Hores*), as Greek Macedonia and Western Thrace became known after their annexation by Greece following the Balkan Wars of 1912 and 1913.[44] Thus, the geographer Dimitsas, who was an outspoken critic of the cartographer Kiepert and had worked as a teacher in Macedonia before opening his own establishment in Athens, declared in 1875, on the occasion of the Second International Congress of Geography in Paris, that the Greek government demonstrated an alarming indifference to a discipline that rendered practical services and was instrumental in warfare. His school geographies of 1878 and 1885 reiterated the political importance of geography as a discipline.[45] Dimitsas, whose *Political Geography* had appeared in 1882, and his monumental study of Macedonia in 1896, argued that it was imperative to inaugurate a Greek Geographical Society and to establish a Chair of Geography at the University of Athens.[46] In the event, the Greek Society was founded in 1901 and from 1904 published a *Geographical Bulletin.*[47] In his history of the Society's foundation, Konstantinos N. Rados (1862–1931), Professor of Nautical History at the University of Athens, pointedly emphasized the role of geography in Macedonia.

Imperial campaigns at the turn of the century in Afghanistan, Burma and Sudan, and the Boer War in Southern Africa had underlined the practical uses of geography in war and prompted calls for the establishment of university chairs of geography in Britain.[48] Similarly, Charles Daly, President of the American Geographical Society (1864–1899), remarked that the Franco-Prussian conflict in 1870 had been "a war fought as much by maps as by weapons".[49] The increasing international importance of geography for the military influenced debates in Greece about the practical applications of the discipline.[50] Ifkratis Kokidis, a military geographer, cartographer and geodesist, produced a military geography of Greece in 1891 which outlined broader developments in Europe.[51] Moreover, the political importance attached to geography was manifest in the production of school textbooks that stressed the Greekness of what were represented as "unredeemed" territories.

Curzon's 1907 lecture on frontiers accentuated the close interrelationship between geography and empire; the frontier signified, in this context, not an inward-oriented territorial limit, but an outward civilizing push.[52] In turn, this interrelationship fed into the geopolitical model articulated by such geographers as Sir Halford Mackinder (1861–1947) and Ratzel, a geographer who enjoyed influence in Greece[53] and whose advocacy of *lebensraum* provided arguments that legitimized imperial expansion.[54] "Territorial growth", Ratzel asserted, "is effected on the periphery of the state by the displacement of the frontier". In Greece, territorial expansion was perceived as a Christian civilizing mission eastwards and was explicitly linked to an imperialist project: the reconstitution of the Byzantine Empire.[55] This messianic vision of expansion, of territorial growth conceived of in Ratzelian terms as an organic process, existed in tension – as we saw in Chapter Two – with notions of a fixed, clearly demarcated national space.[56]

Greece's independence had been sanctioned largely through a conscious appeal to the ancient Greek inheritance. Yet from the middle of the century this emphasis on Greece's classical legacy, centred geographi-cally on the Peloponnese and Attica, began to give way as the medieval, Byzantine past was rediscovered and increasingly celebrated. Significantly, the man at the centre of the "map mania" in the 1870s, Paparrigopoulos, a professor of history at the University of Athens, was the person largely responsible for the reassessment of Byzantium and for articulating a tripartite vision of Greek history that stretched, uninterrupted, from ancient Greece, through Byzantium, to the modern period. The shift in attitude to Macedonia, for example, owes much to Paparrigopoulos's *History of the Greek Nation*,[57] in which, as we have seen, "Byzantium and Kolettis's conception of the Great Idea [come] together as components of the political culture of 'Romantic Hellenism'".[58] Geography, at least from the 1880s, worked in the service of this imperialist vision of a Romantic Hellenism.

The enthusiasm for the "Great Idea" is poignantly evoked, as we have already seen, by the writer Voutiras in his novella *Langas* (1903), where he describes the jubilant crowds in Athens, whipped up into a patriotic fever by the militant newspapers and the nationalists of the National Society, poring over maps of Greece and the surrounding region: "The maps were spread out on the tables and everyone was bent over them trying to define the boundaries of the new Greek Empire".[59]

The idea of an expansive Greek Empire was thus articulated in a cartographic struggle in which representations functioned as impor-tant tools to lay claim to territory. Moreover, this struggle was both fuelled by, and in turn fuelled, the increasingly racist debates about national difference. The naturalization of boundaries promoted in late nineteenth- and early twentieth-century Greek geographies was, in part at least, a response to the increasing linkages being made between biology and territorial identity. National differences were explained in racial terms and Greek school geographies sought, for example, to represent the Bulgarians, no less than the Turks, as barbarous nations:

> ...as uncultured people, crude and hard. They hate the Greeks. At several periods in history they have attempted to invade Greece, but they have always been courageously repulsed.[60]

As one Greek commented in 1888, the Greeks are "superior when it comes to intellectual development and that is why nearly all of the scientists, artists, industrialists etc. in Turkey are Greek".[61]

Such views of Greek superiority were promoted, too, in the determin-istic geographical and geological studies of Mitsopoulos, who was made Professor of Natural Sciences at Athens on his return from Germany in 1875. For Mitsopoulos – who had produced amongst other works a physical geography of Thrace (1897), a region claimed by Greece but still under Ottoman rule – geology was a patriotic discipline. Mitsopoulos, like Dimitsas, and many other Greek geogrphers, had studied geology and mineralogy in Germany (1869–1875) and the influence of German ethnogeography and environmental determinism are conspicuous in his work.[62] In his *Elements of Geography for Usage in Hellenic Schools* (1892) Mitsopoulos claimed that the whole of Macedonia, as the homeland of Alexander the Great, was irrefutably and uniquely Greek, with few Turks and Bulgarians. A concept of national history was reinforced by imported racial ideas that, Mitsopoulos maintained, were linked to a nation's spatial identity. Following Ratzel, he conceived of cultures as organisms bound up in a struggle for survival and sought to identify, as he put it in 1895, "natural forces [that] have worked to shape the Greek land and to prepare the habitat of the most ingenious people on the planet".[63] The influence of Darwinian biology is manifest in Mitsopoulos's work and he was the editor of the journal *Prometheus* (1890–1892), a publication that did much to promote Darwinian thinking in Greece.[64] Such chauvinistic views, however, were not unchallenged. A report on Mitsopoulos's geography cautioned in 1885:

> Love for one's homeland should be cultivated in the soul of the pupil by the simple exposition of facts. Exaggerated, patriotic writing cools this sentiment instead of heating it. We consider the base slandering of rival nations particularly contemptible. The words of the author on the Bulgarians will inspire no sentiment other than hatred.[65]

8.4   DREAMS OF EMPIRE, MEMORIES OF PLACE

The collapse of Yugoslavia in 1991, and the continuing Balkan conflict that centres on Serbian claims to Kosovo, provide poignant contexts for a discussion of late nineteenth and early twentieth-century debates about the place of geography in the nation-building process. The contemporary Balkan map mania, reflected in the publication of rival maps and historical geographies that narrate the nation's history and emphasize its distinct identity – such as the new *Concise Atlas of Croatia*, or the maps of "United Macedonia" that circulate in Australia and Canada[66] – furnishes "a store-house of valuable information for geographers wishing to understand the construction of national identities".[67] In particular, the map mania has drawn attention to the ideological dimension of maps and to the socio-political forces that structure cartography as a discourse.[68]

Chapter Eight has sought to explore the preoccupation with mapping Greece in and around the beginning of the twentieth century. The focus has been on the manner in which Greek imperial geographies coincided with an efflorescence of regional geographies. On the one hand, the cohesion and distinctiveness of the local community was projected onto the larger national space; on the other, the particularities of place sat uncomfortably with the unifying drive of a state-sponsored nationalism.

Looking back at his schooldays on the island of Mytilini, then still part of the Ottoman Empire, the writer Myrivilis recalled with fondness his geography lessons and the teacher who instructed them:

> He gave us lessons in the geography of our island, and his hand slowly passed over the Aegean, where our islands were yellow like the whole of Turkey and neighbouring Asia Minor, and he reached Greece, free Greece. That was rose coloured. A small dot of rose on an enormous map of Europe. Mr Anagnostakis's finger, yellow from chain smoking, paused there. He stopped, hesitating, and his finger slowly wandered around the boundary of the free state. The boundaries were short, the wandering brief.
>
> Then Mr Anagnostakis went and locked the door of the class from within and we sighed with delight, for two reasons. Firstly, because we would get off the boring geography lesson, which was only about names and numbers; and secondly, because we knew how he would tell us about Greece and the Great Idea. He would pronounce those two words more slowly, which made us feel the sanctity of the idea like a religious revelation...Then the school-master's yellow finger began those long wanderings across the Balkans, Asia Minor and over the Greek seas. It was the Greek Empire which was destined to rise again on both continents....[69]

The schoolmaster's nicotine-stained finger, as yellow as the colour of the Ottoman Empire on the map, move, in Myrivilis's recollection, from the narrow boundaries of the state to the expansive frontiers of an imagined community. The map does not reflect the reality of a recon-stituted Greek Empire – Kolettis's "great fatherland" – but anticipates that reality and becomes "a model for, rather than a model of, what it [purports] to represent".[70] Significantly, for Myrivilis, this mapping of the nation is inseparable from the particularities of the place in which that mapping itself takes place: the writer's native island of Mytilini in the north Aegean. Mr Anagnostakis's wandering finger reminds us how, long after the Greek defeat in Asia Minor and the ensuing exchange of populations agreed upon in January 1923, the dreams of empire continued to be evoked within the particular memories of a place.

Conclusion

Nationalism and the location of culture

This book has explored the ways in which a Greek national space was conceptualized, represented and recorded during the nineteenth and early twentieth centuries across multiple interrelated practices. Pre-independence Greek geographical writing and the accumulation of ethnographic data, the book has argued, later fed into an irredentist ideology that sought to consolidate claims to the so-called "unre-deemed" territories beyond the frontiers of the Greek Kingdom. On the one hand, practices such as geography, cartography, folklore and archaeology became central to the nation-building project; on the other, the boundaries that separated these diverse practices gave way: literary and material archaeologies mutually reinforced each other, as did physical and fictive mappings.

A major focus of *National Histories, Natural States* has been on exploring the contingencies which shaped nineteenth and early twen-tieth-century representations of Greece.[1] As one commentator has recently observed, "the world figured through" such mappings may be "material or immaterial, actual or desired, whole or part, in various ways experienced, remembered or projected".[2] Writing at the end of the nineteenth century, Victor Bérard noted the germaneness of the term "Great Idea" since it underscored Greek nationalism as an act of conceptualization by which material obstacles were overcome.[3] The "Great Idea" stood for that process of interpolation in which individ-uals imagined themselves as members of a collective community, even when that community had not been materially realized. To this extent, at least, acts of mapping preceded the reality that was being mapped.[4]

Pervading the different mappings of Greece, however, was a funda-mental anxiety about the location of Greek culture and about where the boundaries were to be drawn to demarcate it. During the hundred years from the foundation of the state to the Greek routing in Asia Minor in 1922, different conceptualizations of Greece's identity gave rise to contending geographical visions and to conflicting interpretations of the state's relationship to the nation. One of the central concerns of *National Histories, Natural States* has been to investigate the dynamics of incorporation and exclusion, of centre and periphery, which were inscribed within these interpretations. Where did Greece belong? Where were the country's boundaries to be drawn? What defined the national space? How could differences be accommodated without the elimination of distinct regional "personalities"?

At the end of the nineteenth century, in Psycharis's *My Journey*, a book which describes the author's voyage from Paris to Constantinople, Chios and Athens in 1886, and which contributed undoubtedly more than any other to the intensification of the language debate in Greece, the narrator relates a dream he had while visiting Constantinople. He is confronted by an expansive map of Europe spread out before him with all the competing states marked out in different colours:

> In front of me I saw the map of Europe stretched out. It wasn't any old, small map, like the geographical charts that hang on the walls in schools. It seemed to me to be as large as Europe itself. It was coloured like the usual maps. Every place had a different shade and you could distinguish one from the other. Each one was painted green, red, yellow, mauve, dark or light. Europeans were standing on the map, in a row. The Frenchman on France, the German on Germany, the Italian on Italy; everyone separately on his place, and every nation wore either green, red, or yellow clothes in accordance with the colours of every country on the map.[5]

Psycharis was a philologist and linguistic reformer who was born in Odessa but lived most of his life in Paris, where he married the daughter of Ernest Renan. In Psycharis's dream, the European nations laughed at the Greeks who, possessing no unequivocal national language, had no place on the coloured board.

Some thirty years after Psycharis's mapping, the writer Theotokas imagined himself looking down at Greece from an aeroplane. The country below, he observed, blended harmoniously into the multi-coloured pattern of a European "garden" and presented an ordered "cluster of countless contrasts". It was possible from this height, Theotokas reflected, to take in the continent as a whole with one encompassing glance. The immediate context for this bird's eye visualizing of the relationship between Greece and Europe was the devastating Greek defeat in Asia Minor six years previously, known simply as the "Catastrophe" to the Greeks. The enforced exchange of Turkish and Greek populations, and the concomitant social, cultural and political transformation of Greece with the influx of well over a million refugees, gave an urgency to such mappings of the newly constituted national space. If the territorial acquisitions that followed the Balkan Wars of 1912 and 1913 had made Greece a Balkan country as much as a Mediterranean one, tensions began to emerge after 1922 between the "New Lands" which supported the policies of the Liberal politician Venizelos, and the Royalist old Kingdom.[6]

Theotokas himself was born and brought up in Constantinople and his father, a prominent lawyer, was a legal advisor to the Greek government at Lausanne in 1923 who helped draft the treaty on the exchange of populations.[7] In his novel *Leonis* (1940), set in Constantinople during the First World War, the members of the protagonist's Greek family scrutinize a map of Europe, spread out on the dining room table, as they anticipate the likely course of the military campaigns. The map contrasts to the panoramic aerial view afforded by the aeroplane. Rather than override differences, the map reinforces them. National borders mark the possibility of conflict, while ostensibly discrete spaces threaten to collapse into an endless, receding horizon of internal distinctions. As Theotokas himself observed:

> When after a journey we unfold a map of Europe, we relive easily the feeling of deep change that we experienced crossing the borders: Italy is blue, France red, Britain yellow, Germany green. Each country is separated from its neighbours, its particular shape distinguished by its artless outline. However, when we look at this map through a microscope we see that the differentiation is endless. Within each country of Europe there are many small countries each with its distinct personality which differs clearly from that of its neighbour.[8]

For Theotokas in the 1920s, the aeroplane (this seems to be the first appearance of an aeroplane in Greek literature) and the map represent two scales of mapping; two incompatible vantage points.[9] The prospect of national and supranational unity is undermined by a cartographic anxiety about the possibility of its obverse: disintegration and conflict.

In summary, then, this book has been concerned both with charting the pre-history of Theotokas's bird's-eye view of Greece back through the nineteenth century and with exploring what such grand visions overlook: "overlook" both in the sense of what they survey from above and what they disavow or "forget" in that process of surveillance.[10] For in championing the nation's unity the aerial view of high art disregards all subsidiary differences. As Renan remarked in a celebrated passage of his essay "What is a nation?" (1882): "Yet the essence of a nation is that all individuals have many things in common, and also that they have forgotten many things".[11]

A number of the issues dealt with in this study are explored by Michel Fais in his novel *Autobiography of a Book* (1989). On a basic level, the novel constitutes a local history of Komotini, a provincial town in Thrace, whence Fais himself originates. This is a region characterized historically by its heterogeneity; a territory fought over in the twentieth century by the Ottoman Empire, Greece and Bulgaria. Today its diverse populations include a Jewish community, a sizeable Turkish population, migrants from elsewhere in Greece, as well as the refugees who arrived from Asia Minor after the Catastrophe. The novel disconcertingly juxtaposes purported "testimonies" with newspaper articles and includes alternative, often contradictory, descriptions of the same place and of events that have occurred there. In this way, the reader is asked to self-consciously select from the contradictory "facts" which the narrative presents in a process that disaffirms the absolute divisions of testimony and fiction and gives rise to perspectival shifts. The manner in which place is framed, Fais suggests, determines our reading of it.

The implications of such a kaleidoscopic and discontinuous view of history are clear, especially in Thrace, a historically contested province which contains a relatively large non-Greek population and whose history has tended to be written from narrow, exclusively nationalist perspectives.[12] In the late twentieth century when the novel is set, Theotokas's all-encompassing vision is no longer possible and the novel suggests that "meanings engendered by hegemonic codes and narratives do not exist in hermetic domains but are placed at risk, revalued and distorted, through being enacted and experienced".[13] The emphasis here is on "the emergence of the interstices" where "intersubjective and collective experiences of *nationness*, community interest, or cultural value are negotiated".[14] This challenging of the narratorial authority is figured as a split between the "historicist, teleological time" of a Greek national history and the continually shifting perspectives of the individual characters recorded in the book.[15]

Fais's text probes the ideological assumptions that underpin spatial perceptions, as well as the intimate relationship between territory and community, to suggest how a literary work's engagement with place cannot be severed from society's other textualizing practices. The issue of territorial incorporation is addressed directly in the book when Fais "records" an imaginary interview:

> I would like to begin our conversation with a brief account of the diplomatic manoeuvrings that were a prelude to the liberation of Thrace, and particularly, of Komotini.
>
> Agreed. Before we begin, however, I feel it important to define the terms: liberation is one thing, incorporation another...Why do I draw this distinction between liberation and incorporation? At the

end of the war, in 1919, the entire region was occupied by the Bulgarians. They had been ceded it at the Treaty of Bucharest. When the allied troops arrived, however, they took control of the region in the name of the Allies. And we were automatically freed from the yoke of the Bulgarians. We were only incorporated, however, following the formal cessation of the area to Greece... Today we have three anniversary dates of our liberation: one at Xanthi in October 1919, with the entry of a British battalion, one at Komotini in May 1920, with the arrival of French troops, and one at Didymotichos in August, with the arrival of the Italians.[16]

This passage draws attention to the piecemeal expansion of the Greek state in the first decades of the twentieth century. The imagined interlocutors expose the assumptions that underlie concepts such as "liberation" that are deeply rooted in nationalist ideologies. The form of the imagined interview draws attention to the ways in which issues of political incorporation are inseparable from the integrative process of narration itself; a process that brings heterogeneous elements together within the cohesive structure of a story. The assimilation of diverse territories into the state finds its analogy in the absorption of different voices into the narrative. On the eve of the dissolution of Yugoslavia, Fais invites the reader to question what the consequences may be of undoing the seams of a unifying narration. Is it possible to "liberate" place from an overarching narrative when the concept of liberation itself remains "placed" at the centre of militant nationalist ideologies?

Notes

INTRODUCTION

1. See Peter Marden, "Geographies of dissent: globalization, identity and the nation", *Political Geography* 16/1 (1997): 37–64.
2. See Arjun Appadurai, "Disjuncture and difference in the global cultural economy", *Public Culture 2* (Spring 1990), pp.1–24.
3. Richard Handler, "Is 'Identity' a useful cross-cultural concept?", in *Commemorations: the politics of national identity*, ed. J.R. Gillis (Princeton: Princeton University Press, 1994), pp.27–40 (p.30). Handler rightly argues that we should be as suspicious of notions of "identity" as we are of "culture" or "nation".
4. Liah Greenfeld, *Nationalism: five roads to modernity* (Cambridge, MA: Harvard University Press, 1992), p.3.
5. Gerald M. Macdonald, "Indonesia's *Medan Merdeka*: national identity and the built environment", *Antipode* 27/3 (1995): 270–93 (p.272). The focus of this article is on the symbolic reconstruction of central Jakarta – with emphasis on the city's "Independence Square" ("Medan Merdeka") – as a way of symbolically unifying the fragmented (ethnically, religiously and geographically) independent Indonesian state and of incorporating various contradictory ideologies.
6. Benedict Anderson, *Imagined communities: reflections on the origin and spread of nationalism*, rev. edn. (London and New York: Verso, 1991 [1983]).
7. Colin Williams and Anthony D. Smith, "The National construction of social space", *Progress in Human Geography* 7 (1983): 502–518 (pp.502–503).
8. Sarah M. Gorse, *Nationalism and literature: the politics of culture in Canada and the United States* (Cambridge: Cambridge University Press, 1997), p.24 (see, particularly, note 6).
9. See Nicholas Thomas's discussion of the divisions and contradictions within colonialism as "a cultural process", *Colonialism's culture: anthropology, travel and government* (Cambridge: Polity, 1994), pp.2–3.
10. See Craig Calhoun, "Nationalism and civil society: democracy, diversity and self-determination", in *Social theory and the politics of identity*, ed. C. Calhoun (Oxford: Blackwell, 1994), pp.304–335.
11. Homi K. Bhabha, "Introduction: narrating the nation", in *Nation and narration* (London and New York: Routledge, 1990), pp.1–7 (p.2).
12. Homi K. Bhabha, *The Location of culture* (London and New York: Routledge, 1994), p.5.

13. Thomas, *Colonialism's culture*, p.4.
14. Mark Wheeler, "Not so Black as it's painted: the Balkan political heritage", in *The Changing shape of the Balkans*, eds. F.W. Carter and H.T. Norris (London: University College London, 1996), pp.1–8 (pp.4–7).
15. The expression "cartographic anxiety" is used by Sankaran Krishna in the context of India's preoccupations with borders and definitions of national space, see "Cartographic anxiety: mapping the body politic in India", in *Political geography; a reader*, ed. J. Agnew, rev. edn. (London: Arnold, 1997 [1994]), pp.81–92.
16. Calhoun, "Nationalism and civil society", p.318.
17. See Michael Holquist, "A New tour of Babel: recent trends linking comparative departments, foreign language departments and area studies programs", *Profession* (1996): 103–114.
18. Kathleen M. Kirby, "Thinking through the boundary: the politics of location, subjects, and space", *Boundary 2* 20/2 (1993): 173–189 (p.173).

CHAPTER ONE

1. Konstantinos Oikonomos, *Peri agapis patridos* (Athens: Estia, 1876 [1837]), p.7. *Patrida* has been translated throughout this book as "fatherland". For a discussion of the multiple resonances of *patrida*, however, in late eighteenth and nineteenth-century Greece, see David Holton, "Ethnic identity and patriotic idealism in the writings of General Makriyannis", *Byzantine and Modern Greek Studies* 9 (1984/5): 133–160. For the idea that forms of nineteenth-century nationalism were preceded by other pre-modern collective identities, see Anthony D. Smith, *The Ethnic origins of nations* (Oxford: Blackwell, 1986) and John A. Armstrong, *Nations before nationalism* (Chapel Hill: University of North Carolina Press, 1982).
2. Quoted in Richard Clogg, "Sense of the past in pre-Independence Greece", in *Culture and nationalism in nineteenth-century Eastern Europe*, eds. R. Sussex and J.C. Eade (Columbus, Ohio: Slavica Publishers, 1985), pp.7–30 (p.14). "Motherland" has been changed from the original translation to "Fatherland" for the sake of consistency, see note 1.
3. Walter Bagehot, *Physics and politics or thoughts on the application of the principles of 'natural selection' and 'inheritance' to political society* (London: Henry S. King, 1872), pp.20–21.
4. The first chapter is, in fact, entitled "The Dusk of nations"; Max Nordau, *Degeneration* (New York: D. Appleton, 1895), pp.1–7; Eric J. Hobsbawm, *Nations and nationalism since 1780: programme, myth, reality*, rev. edn. (Cambridge: Cambridge University Press, 1992 [1990]), p.183.
5. Ernest Gellner, *Nations and nationalism* (Oxford: Blackwell, 1983), p.56. On the relationship between geographical awareness and national identity, see generally David Hooson, ed. *Geography and national identity* (Oxford: Blackwell, 1994). For an interesting discussion of the relations between forces of globalization and the "place-bound politics of contemporary nationalisms" see Marden's article in which he argues that these are not opposing tendencies as is frequently argued, "Geographies of dissent".
6. Anderson, *Imagined communities*, p.3.
7. A. Linde-Laursen quoted in Geoffrey Cubitt, "Introduction", in *Imagining nations*, ed. G. Cubitt (Manchester: Manchester University Press, 1998), pp.1–20 (p.1).

8. On the complex history of the term "Balkans", however, see Maria Todorova, *Imagining the Balkans* (New York and Oxford: Oxford University Press, 1997), pp.21–37.
9. See *Istoria tou ellinikou ethnous* (Athens: Ekdotiki Athinon, Etairia Istorikon Ekdoseon, 1970), vol.13, pp.448–54.
10. See Richard Clogg, ed. and trans., *The Movement for Greek Independence, 1770–1821. A Collection of documents* (London: Macmillan, 1976), p.174.
11. E.M. Edmonds, ed. and trans., *Kolokotrones, the klepht and the warrior: sixty years of peril and daring: an autobiography* (London: T. Fisher Unwin, 1892), p.128.
12. Dimitri Obolensky, *The Byzantine commonwealth: Eastern Europe, 500–1453* (Crestwood, NY: St Vladimir's Seminary Press, 1982).
13. Quoted in Anastasia N. Karakasidou, *Fields of wheat, hills of blood: passages to nationhood in Greek Macedonia, 1870–1990* (Chicago: University of Chicago Press, 1997), p.54.
14. Richard Clogg, "The Greek *millet* in the Ottoman Empire", in *Christians and Jews in the Ottoman Empire: the functioning of a plural society*, eds. B. Braude and B. Lewis, 2 vols. (New York and London: Holmes and Meier, 1982), vol.1, pp.185–207 (p.185).
15. Cited in Konstantinos Th. Dimaras, *Neoellinikos diafotismos*, (Athens: Ermis, 1993 [1977]), p.62.
16. For a Balkan perspective on the Greek cultural revival, see Peter Mackridge, "The Greek intelligentsia, 1780–1830: a Balkan perspective", in *Balkan society in the age of Greek Independence*, ed. R. Clogg (London: Macmillan, 1981), pp.63–84. On centres of Greek learning before Greek Independence, see George P. Henderson, *The Revival of Greek thought, 1620–1830* (Albany: State University of New York Press, 1970).
17. Charles Eliot, *Turkey in Europe* (London: Frank Cass, 1965 [1900]), p.273.
18. Elie Kedourie, "Introduction", in *Nationalism in Asia and Africa*, ed. E. Kedourie (London: Weidenfeld and Nicolson, 1971), pp.1–152 (p.42).
19. Gregory Jusdanis, "Beyond national culture", *Boundary 2* 22/1 (1995): 23–60 (pp.33–35).
20. The relationship between cultural representations and territory has been explored in general terms by Simon Schama in *Landscape and memory* (HarperCollins: London, 1995).
21. On this, see Karakasidou, *Fields of wheat*; Loring M. Danforth, *The Macedonian conflict: ethnic nationalism in a transnational world* (Princeton: Princeton University Press, 1995); and Peter Mackridge and Eleni Yannakakis, eds. *Ourselves and others: the development of a Greek Macedonian cultural identity since 1912* (Oxford: Berg, 1997).
22. On the debates on culture and environment in the eighteenth century, see, classically, Clarence J. Glacken, *Traces on the Rhodian shore: nature and culture in Western thought from ancient times to the end of the eighteenth century* (Berkeley: University of California Press, 1967), pp.501–713. Michel Foucault analyzes what he perceives as a crucial shift from the representative function of language to its historicity whereby language becomes rooted "not in the things perceived, but in the active subject"; a process which he sees paralleled in the natural sciences. See, *The Order of things: an archaeology of the human sciences* (London: Routledge, 1974 [1966]), p.290.
23. See Dimaras, *Neoellinikos diafotismos*, p.308, *passim*. See also the review of Korais's translation of Strabo in *The Edinburgh Review* LXI (XXXL) (April 1810): 55–62, which mentions a modern Greek translation of a work by Montesquieu (p.57).

24. Edward A. Freeman, *The Historical geography of Europe*, 2 vols. (London: Longman, 1882), vol.1, p.17.
25. Henry R. Wilkinson, *Maps and politics: a review of the ethnographic cartography of Macedonia* (Liverpool: Liverpool University Press, 1951), pp.28–29.
26. See, in this context, Joseph P. Stern, *The Heart of Europe: essays on literature and ideology* (Oxford: Blackwell, 1992), pp.29–43, 63–77.
27. See Hugh Seton-Watson, *Nations and states: an enquiry into the origins of nations and the politics of nationalism* (Boulder, Colorado: Westview Press, 1977), pp.158–161.
28. See Rogers Brubaker, *Citizenship and nationhood in France and Germany* (Cambridge, MA: Harvard University Press, 1992), p.4.
29. See Rogers Brubaker, *Nationalism reframed: nationhood and the national question in the new Europe* (Cambridge: Cambridge University Press, 1996), p.114.
30. Quoted in Clogg, *The Movement for Greek Independence*, pp.81–82.
31. For an account of Balkan Orthodox merchants, see Traian Stoianovic, "The Conquering Balkan Orthodox merchant", *Journal of Economic History* 20/1 (1960): 234–313.
32. Adamantios Korais, *Apanta ta prototipa erga*, ed. Y. Valetas, 4 vols. (Athens: Dorikos, 1964), vol.2, p.xxi.
33. Adamantios Korais, *Ta Aithiopika. Vivlia deka*, 2 vols. (Paris, 1803), p.67.
34. Quoted in Foucault, *The Order of things*, p.291.
35. Quoted in Richard J. Crampton, *A Concise history of Bulgaria* (Cambridge: Cambridge University Press, 1997), p.47.
36. Quoted in Paschalis M. Kitromilides, *The Enlightenment as social criticism: Iosipos Moisiodax and Greek culture in the eighteenth century* (Princeton: Princeton University Press, 1992), p.26.
37. Seton-Watson, *Nations and states*, p.177. These events are also discussed by Anderson, *Imagined communities*, pp.67–82.
38. The grammar remained unpublished until 1970. See Dimitrios Katartzis, *Ta Evriskomena*, ed. K. Th. Dimaras (Athens: Ermis, 1970) and *Dokimia*, ed. K. Th. Dimaras (Athens: Ermis, 1974).
39. Paschalis Kitromilides, "'Imagined communities' and the origins of the national question in the Balkans", in *Modern Greece: nationalism and nationality*, eds. M. Blinkhorn and Th. Veremis (London and Athens: Sage and ELIAMEP, 1990), pp.23–66 (p.27). For arguments that maintain the historical roots of Greek nationalism, see Stephen X. Xydis, "Mediaeval origins of modern Greek nationalism", *Balkan Studies*, 9 (1968): 1–2; Apostolos E. Vacalopoulos, "Byzantanism and Hellenism. Remarks on the racial origin and the intellectual continuity of the Greek nation", *Balkan Studies*, 5/9 (1968): 101–126; Speros Vryonis, "Recent scholarship on continuity and discontinuity of culture: classical Greeks, Byzantines, Modern Greeks", in *The 'Past' in medieval and modern Greek culture*, ed. S. Vryonis (Malibu: Undena Publications, 1978), pp.237–256. For an argument against continuity, see Cyril Mango, "Byzantinism and Romantic Hellenism", *Journal of the Warburg and Courtauld Institutes*, 5/28 (1965): 29–43.
40. Anon, *Elliniki nomarhia iti logos peri eleftherias. Filoloyiki apomnimiosi*, eds. N.A. Veis and M. Sigouros, intr. G. Valetas, 3rd ed. (Athens: Aposperitis, 1982), p.216.
41. Quoted in Kitromilides, "'Imagined communities'", p.30. In places, the original translation has been changed.
42. Geoffrey Horrocks, *Greek: a history of the language and its speakers* (London: Longman, 1997), p.294. On the role of the Church during the Ottoman

period to Independence, see Steven Runciman, *The Great Church in captivity: a study of the Patriarchate of Constantinople from the eve of the Turkish conquest to the Greek War of Independence* (Cambridge: Cambridge University Press, 1968).

43. On the Church's reactions to French revolutionary ideas, see Richard Clogg, "The *Dhidhaskalia Patriki* (1798): an Orthodox reaction to the French revolutionary propaganda", *Middle Eastern Studies* 5 (1969): 87–115; and for a discussion of anti-clericism in pre-independence Greece, see Richard Clogg "Anti-clericism in pre-independence Greece, c.1750–1821", in *The Orthodox Churches and the West*, ed. D. Baker (Oxford: Blackwell, 1976), pp.257–276.

44. Quoted in Kitromilides, *The Enlightenment as social criticism*, p.74.

45. Williams and Smith, "The National construction of social space", p.507.

46. Jeremy Black, *Maps and politics* (London: Reaktion Books, 1997), pp.128–129. See, however, Colin Heywood's article "The Frontier in Ottoman history: old ideas and new myths", in *Frontiers in question: Eurasian borderlands, 700–1700*, eds. D. Power and N. Standen (Basingstoke: Macmillan, 1999), pp.228–250.

47. John Stoye, *Marsigli's Europe, 1680–1730: the life and times of Luigi Ferdinando Marsigli, soldier and virtuoso* (New Haven: Yale University Press, 1994), pp.164–215.

48. Black, *Maps and politics*, p.128. On the Ottoman Empire's uncertain boundaries in the Middle East, see Norman N. Lewis, *Nomads and settlers in Syria and Jordan, 1800–1980* (Cambridge: Cambridge University Press, 1987); see also, however, André Raymond, "The Ottoman legacy in Arab political boundaries", in *Imperial legacy*, ed. L.C. Brown (New York: Columbia University Press, 1996), pp.115–128.

49. J.R. Neroulos, *Histoire moderne de la Grèce: depuis la chute de l'Empire D'Orient* (Geneva, 1828), p.1.

50. See Dimaras, *Neoellinikos diafotismos*, pp.282–300. See also Michael Herzfeld, *Ours once more: folklore, ideology, and the making of modern Greece* (New York: Pella, 1986 [1982]), p.53.

51. On the relation between Katartzis and the *Modern Geography*, see K.Th. Dimaras, "O Protos mathitis mou: i glossiki theoria tis yeografias", in *Istorika frondismata: o diafotismos kai to korifoma tou*, ed. P. Polemi (Athens: Poria, 1992), pp.178–86.

52. On the importance of the "compendious" Georgian geographers such as Gordon, see Alan Downes, "The Bibliography of dinosaurs of Georgian geography", *Geographical Journal* 137 (1971): 379–383.

53. Other important geographies include Anthimos Gazis and Nikiforos Theotokis's *Elements of geography* (1804) which was designed for use in schools and Dionysios Pyrros's *Methodical geography of the entire inhabited world* (1818).

54. See, in this context, Aikaterina Koumarianou's introduction in Daniil Philippidis and Grigorios Konstantas, *Yeografia neoteriki* (Athens: Ermis, 1988), pp.9–79. On Barbié's mappings of Greece, see George Tolias, "The Cartographer Barbié du Bocage and the approach to the Greek World in the late 18th and early 19th centuries", *Journal of the International Map Collectors' Society* 40 (Spring 1990): 5–9.

55. On this, see Raoul Baladié, "Strabon dans la vie et l'œuvre de Coray", *O Eranistis* 11 (1974): 412–442. Korais's chief works were the seventeen volume *Greek Library* and the nine volume *Parerga*, collected between 1809 and 1827.

56. *The Edinburgh Review* XVI (XXXL) (April 1810): 55–62 (p.60).
57. George W. Stocking, "French anthropology in 1800", *Isis* 55/2 (1964):134–150.
58. Adamantios Korais, *Mémoire sur l'État Actuel de la Civilisation en Grèce* (Paris, 1833), pp.55–56.
59. Adamantios Korais, *Allilografia*, ed. K.Th. Dimaras, 6 vols. (Athens, 1964–1984), vol.1, p.279.
60. Adamantios Korais, *Prolegomena stous archaious ellines singrafis*, 4 vols. (Athens: Morfotiko Idrima Ethnikis Trapezis, 1984), vol.4, pp.554–555.
61. Korais, *Prolegomena*, vol.4, pp.692–693.
62. Timothy Webb, *English Romantic Hellenism, 1700–1824* (Manchester: Manchester University Press, 1982), p.211.
63. Webb, *English Romantic Hellenism*, p.116.
64. On this, see generally, Fani-Maria Tsigakou, *The Rediscovery of Greece: travellers and painters of the Romantic era* (London: Thames and Hudson, 1981).
65. Hans-Joachim Gehrke, "Anazitonas ti hora ton ellinon: epistimonika taxidia kai i simasia tous yia tin erevna kai tin antimetopisi tis arhaioellinikis istorias ston 19° aiona", in *Enas neos kosmos yennietai: i ikona tou ellinikou politismou sti yermaniki epistimi kata ton 19° ai.*, ed. E. Chrysos (Athens: Akritas, 1996), pp.59–82 (p.74).
66. Webb, *English Romantic Hellenism*, pp.8,166.
67. Koumarianou, "Introduction", p.13.
68. Antonios Miliarakis, "Daniil Filippidis kai i yeografia aftou (1791)", *Estia* 474/19 (1885): 115–119 (p.115).
69. Montesquieu's *Lettres Persanes* (1721) is a good example of the new comparative ethnology. More generally, see Anthony Pagden, *The Fall of natural man: the American Indian and the origins of comparative ethnology* (Cambridge: Cambridge University Press, 1982).
70. Grigorios Paliouritis, *Arhaiologia elliniki iti filoloyiki istoria*, 2 vols. (Venice, 1815), p.326.
71. Anderson emphasizes the importance of the sacral communities out of which – as well as against which – the nation came into being. See *Imagined communities*, pp.9–19. More specifically, see the articles collected in Paschalis M. Kitromilides, *Enlightenment, nationalism, Orthodoxy: studies in the culture and political thought of south-eastern Europe* (Aldershot and London: Variorum, 1994). I am much indebted to Kitromilides's argument. See also Kemal H. Karpat, "*Millets* and nationality: the roots of the incongruity of nation and state in the post-Ottoman era", in *Christians and Jews in the Ottoman Empire: the functioning of a plural society*, eds. B. Braude and B. Lewis, 2 vols. (New York and London: Holmes and Meier, 1982), vol.1, pp.141–169.
72. Karpat, "*Millets* and nationality", pp.141–145.
73. See Karakasidou, *Fields of wheat*, p.21. For a brief summary of the arguments surrounding the break-up of Ottoman society, see Traian Stoianovich, "Factors in the decline of Ottoman society in the Balkans", *Slavic Review* XXI (1962): 623–632.
74. Dimaras, *Neoellinikos diafotismos*, p.30.
75. Nikolai Iorga, *Byzance après Byzance: continuation de l'histoire de la vie Byzantine* (Bucharest: Association Internationale d'Études du Sud-Est Européen Comité National Roumain, 1971).

76. For an excellent overview, see Paschalis M. Kitromilides, "'Balkan mentality': history, legend, imagination", *Nations and nationalism* 2/2 (1996): 163–191 (pp.172–179).
77. See, generally, Kitromilides, "'Balkan mentality': history, legend, imagination".
78. See Karpat, "*Millets* and nationality", p.52. See also Karpat's *An Inquiry into the social foundation of nationalism in the Ottoman state: from social estates to classes, from millets to nations* (Princeton: Princeton University Press, 1973).
79. The Greek translation of Barthélemy's *Voyage du Jeune Anacharsis en Grèce* was begun by Yeoryios Sakellarios and taken up by Rigas (1797). It was not until some twenty years later that a seven-volume translation was published in Vienna. See Clogg, "Sense of the past", p.14.
80. Christopher M. Woodhouse, *Rhigas Velestinlis: the proto-martyr of the Greek revolution* (Athens: Denise Harvey, 1995), p.58. On the circulation of the map, see pp.55–56. Rigas also produced maps of Wallachia and Moldavia.
81. See, in this context, however, the essay by Richard Clogg which underlines the reactionary nature of the Greek merchant class, "The Greek mercantile bourgeoisie: 'progressive' or 'reactionary'?", in *Balkan society in the age of Greek independence*, pp.85–110.
82. Quoted in Kedourie, ed. *Nationalism in Asia and Africa*, p.170.
83. Quoted in Christina Koulouri, *Istoria kai yeografia sta ellinika scholia (1834–1914): gnostiko antikimeno kai ideoloyikes proektasis* (Athens: Yeniki Grammatia Neas Yeneas, 1988), p.14.
84. Philippidis and Konstantas, *Yeografia neoteriki*, pp.172–173.
85. Dimaras, *Istorika frondismata*, p.97.
86. On "textual communities" formed around "shared readings", see Brian Stock, "Reading, community and a sense of place", in *Place/culture/represen-tation*, eds. J.S. Duncan and D. Ley (London and New York: Routledge1993), pp.314–328.
87. Clogg, "Sense of the past", pp.13–14.
88. Christina Koulouri, *Dimensions idéologiques de l'historicité en Grèce (1834–1914)* (Frankfurt: Peter Lang, 1991), p.397.
89. *Ermis o Loyios* (1812), facsimile edition, vol.2 (Athens: Etairia Ellinikou Logotehnikou kai Istorikou Arhiou 1989), p.2.
90. *Ermis o Loyios*, p.340.
91. See Koumarianou, "Introduction", pp.12–18.
92. Koulouri, *Dimensions idéologiques*, p.46.
93. Paschalis M. Kitromilides, "Europe and the dilemmas of Greek conscience", in *Greece and Europe in the modern period: aspects of a troubled relationship*, ed. P. Carabott (London: Centre for Hellenic Studies, King's College London, 1995), pp.1–15 (p.4).
94. Kitromilides, "Europe and the dilemmas of Greek conscience", p.5.
95. Alki Kyriakidou-Nestoros, *I Theoria tis ellinikis laografias. Kritiki analisi* (Athens: Etairia Spoudon Neoellinikou Politismou kai Yenikis Paidias, 1986 [1978]), pp.52–57.
96. Stephanos Krinos, *Sinopsis ethniki periehousa epitomi hronoloyiki kai istorikin ton metavolon tis Ellados kai yeografian aftis para Daniil Ieromonahou kai Grigo-riou Ierodiakonou ton Dimitrieon* (Athens, 1879); Antonios Miliarakis, "Daniil Filippidis kai i yeografia aftou (1791)", pp.115–119, 131–136, 147–151, 163–167.
97. Kyriakidou-Nestoros, *I Theoria tis ellinikis laografias*, pp.31–33.
98. Brubaker, *Citizenship and nationhood*, p.8.

99. See the distinction drawn by Homi K. Bhabha between the "performative" and "pedagogic" roles of literature, "DissemiNation", in *Nation and narration*, pp.291–322.

100.Korais, *Ta Aithiopika*, p.71.

101.Stern, *The Heart of Europe*, p.30

102.See Seton-Watson, *Nations and states*, p.11.

103.Quoted in Horrocks, *Greek*, p.302.

104.Anna Avramea, "Maps of the Aegean", in *Maps and map-makers of the Aegean*, eds. V. Sphyroeras, A. Avramea, S. Asdrahas, trans. G. Cox and J. Solman (Athens: Olklos, 1985), pp.22–32 (p.29).

105.Stathis Gourgouris, *Dream nation: enlightenment, colonization and the institution of modern Greece* (Princeton: Princeton University Press, 1996), p.90.

106.D. K. Vyzandios, *I Vavilonia*, ed. S. Evangelatos, 2nd ed. (Athens: Ermis, 1996 [1972]), p.2.

107.Korais, *Aithiopika*, p.vii. The term in use today, *mythistorema*, was employed by Panayiotis Soutsos in 1865 and gained currency in the second half of the century. See Tziovas, "Apo ti mythistoria sto mythistorema", in *Apo ton Leandro ston Louki Lara: meletes yia tin pezografia tis periodou 1830–1880*, ed. N. Vayenas (Heraklion: Panepistimiakes Ekdosis Kritis, 1997), pp.9–30.

108.Cited in the introduction to Grigorios Palaiologos, *O Polypathis*, ed. A. Angelou (Athens: Ermis, 1989), p.25.

109.See Dimaras, *Istorika frondismata*, p.125.

CHAPTER TWO

1. Stephen Daniels and Denis Cosgrove, "Introduction: iconography and landscape", in *The Iconography of landscape: essays on the symbolic representation, design and use of past environments*, eds. D. Cosgrove and S. Daniels (Cambridge: Cambridge University Press, 1988), pp.1–10 (p.1).

2. For a comparative case, see Ann Jensen Adams, "Competing communities in the 'great bog of Europe': identity and seventeenth-century Dutch landscape painting", in *Landscape and power*, ed. W.J.T. Mitchell (Chicago: University of Chicago Press, 1994), pp.35–76 (p.39).

3. James S. Duncan, *The City as text: the politics of landscape interpretation in the Kandyan Kingdom* (Cambridge: Cambridge University Press, 1990), p.19.

4. Stephen Daniels, *Fields of vision: landscape imagery and national identity in England and the United States* (Cambridge: Polity, 1993), p.5.

5. Roland Barthes, *Mythologies*, trans. A. Lavers (London: Vintage, 1993 [1972]).

6. Daniels, *Fields of vision*, p.5.

7. Fred Inglis, "Nation and community: a landscape and its morality", *The Sociological Review* 25 (1977): 489–513.

8. Daniels, *Fields of vision*, p.5.

9. Doris Sommer, *Foundational fictions: the national romances of Latin America* (Berkeley: University of California Press, 1991).

10. Roderick Beaton, *An Introduction to modern Greek literature*, rev. edn. (Oxford: Clarendon Press, 1999 [1994]), p.56.

11. George Finlay, *The Hellenic Kingdom and the Greek nation* (London: John Murray, 1836), pp.17–18.

12. Quoted in William M. McGrew, *Land and revolution in modern Greece, 1800–1880: the transition in the tenure and exploitation of land from Ottoman rule to Independence* (Ohio: Kent State University Press, 1985), p.2.

13. Alexandros Soutsos, *O Exoristos tou 31: komikotrayikon istorema*, ed. L. Droulia (Athens: Idrima Kosta kai Elenis Ourani, 1994), p.131.
14. See, generally, Vasilios Ch. Petrakos, *I en Athinais Arhaioloyiki Etairia. I istoria ton 150 hronon tis, 1837–1987* (Athens: En Athinais Arhaioloyiki Etairia, 1987).
15. Panayiotis Soutsos, *O Leandros* (Athens, 1834), p.41.
16. Michael Rowlands, "Memory, sacrifice and the nation", *New Formations* 30 (1996): 8–17 (p.10).
17. Ilias G. Mikoniakis, "The Greek War of Independence on the London stage, 1821–1833", *Epistimoniki Epetirida Filosofikis Scholis Thessalonikis* 18 (1979): 331–343.
18. See in this context, Denis E. Cosgrove, *Social formation and symbolic landscape* (Madison, Wis.: University of Wisconsin Press, 1998 [1984]) and Cosgrove and Daniels, *The Iconography of landscape*.
19. Adams, "Competing communities", p.57, pp.65–66.
20. Donald W. Meinig, "Symbolic landscapes: some idealizations of American communities", in *The Interpretation of ordinary landscapes: geographical essays*, eds. D.W. Meinig *et al.* (New York and Oxford: Oxford University Press, 1979), pp.164–192 (p.164).
21. Korais, *Apanta ta prototipa erga*, A2, p.792.
22. Artemis Leontis, *Topographies of Hellenism: mapping the homeland* (Ithaca: Cornell University Press, 1995).
23. Anthony D. Smith, *National identity* (Harmondsworth: Penguin, 1991), p.65.
24. Williams and Smith, "The National construction of social space", p.511 and p.514.
25. Nasos Vayenas, "O Outopikos sosialismos ton adelfon Soutson", in *Apo ton Leandro ston Louki Lara*, pp.43–58 (p.48). See Dimitris Tziovas's chapter in the same volume in which he argues that travel is an important motif in these early Greek novels, "Apo ti mythistoria sto mythistorema", pp.9–30 (pp.18–19).
26. Edward Said, *Orientalism* (Harmondsworth: Penguin, 1985 [1978]), p.177.
27. Gehrke, "Anazitonas ti hora ton ellinon", p.63.
28. Soutsos, *O Leandros*, p.iii.
29. Thongchai Winichakul quoted in Anderson, *Imagined communities*, p.173.
30. Stephen Daniels and S. Rycroft, "Mapping the modern city: Alan Sillitoe's Nottingham novels", *Transactions of the Institute of British Geographers* 18/4 (1993): 460–480.
31. Yi-Fu Tuan, "Literature and geography: implications for geographical research", in *Humanistic geography: prospects and problems*, eds. D. Ley and M.S. Samuels (London: Croom Helm, 1978), pp.194–206 (p.205).
32. On this, see Daniels, *Fields of vision*.
33. On the connection between aestheticization and the nation, see Geoff Quilley, "'All ocean is her own': the image of the sea and the identity of the maritime nation in eighteenth-century British art", in *Imagining nations*, pp.132–152 (p.134).
34. See Ioannos A. Meletopoulos, *Ikones tou agonos. I. Makriyanni – Panayioti Zografou* (Athens: Ekdosis Istorikis kai Ethnoloyikis Etairias tis Ellados, 1972).
35. Andreas S. Ioannou, *Greek painting: the 19th century*, trans. D. Dellagrammatika (Athens: Melissa, 1974), p.42. See Chrysanthos Chrystou, *I Elliniki*

zografiki, 1832–1922 (Athens: Ethniki Trapeza tis Ellados, 1981), pp.23–24.

36. On the artistic and cultural ties between Greece and Bavaria, see the catalogue of the recent exhibition at the National Gallery in Athens; Marilena Z. Kazimati, ed. *Athina–Monaho: tehni kai politismos sti nea Ellada* (Athens: Ethniki Pinakothiki, 2000).

37. See, generally, Tsigakou, *The Rediscovery of Greece*, and more particularly: Christoph Heilmann, "Ludwig I's Munich as a centre of artistic renewal", in *The Romantic spirit in German art, 1790–1990*, eds. K. Hartley *et al.* (London: Thames and Hudson, 1994), pp.46–51; Fani Maria Tsigakou, "Yermanikes ikones i ana-parastasis tis Elladas", in *Enas neos kosmos yennietai*, pp.315–319.

38. See in this context, Fani-Maria Tsigakou, *Through Romantic eyes: European images of nineteenth-century Greece from the Benaki Museum* (Alexandria, VA: Art Services International, 1991). For a discussion of the emergence of modern Greece in European consciousness, with a chapter on painting, see Tsigakou's *The Rediscovery of Greece*. Gyzis spent most of his later life in Munich where he was a professor at the Academy of Fine Arts, as did later artists such as Yeoryios Iakovidis (1853–1932) and Symeon Savvidis (1859–1927).

39. See Francis Haskell, "Chios, the massacres, and Delacroix", in *Chios: a conference at the Homereion in Chios*, eds. J. Boardman and C.E. Vaphopoulou-Richardson (Oxford: Clarendon Press, 1986), pp.335–358. See also Nina Athanassoglou-Kallmyer, *French images from the Greek War of Independence, 1821–1830: art and politics under the Restoration* (New Haven and London: Yale University Press, 1989), pp.9–10. See also the articles collected in Claire Constans *et al.*, eds., *La Grèce en révolte: Delacroix et les peintres français, 1815–1848* (Paris: Éditions de la Réunion des Musées Nationaux, 1996).

40. Chrystou, *Elliniki zografiki*, pp.19–20.

41. On Vryzakis, see Chrystou, *Elliniki zografiki*, pp.28–30.

42. Anderson, *Imagined communities*, p.7.

43. Athanassoglou-Kallmyer, *French images*, p.84 (plate 43).

44. Barthes, *Mythologies*, p.151. See in this context, Trevor R. Pringle, "The Privation of history: Landseer, Victoria and the Highland myth", in Cosgrove and Daniels, *The Iconography of landscape*, pp.142–161 (p.146).

45. Bhabha, "DissemiNation", p.300.

46. Daniels, *Fields of vision*, p.5.

47. Roderick Beaton, "Romanticism in Greece", in *Romanticism in national context*, eds. R. Porter and M. Teich (Cambridge: Cambridge University Press, 1988), pp.92–108 (p.96).

48. Quilley, "'All ocean is her own'", p.132.

49. McGrew, *Land and revolution*, p.19.

50. Thiersch was writing in 1833. Quoted in Christina Agriandoni, *I Aparhes tis ekviomihanisis stin Ellada ton 19ᵒᵘ aiona* (Athens: Istoriko Arhio Emboriki Trapeza tis Ellados, 1986), p.25.

51. Finlay, *The Hellenic Kingdom*, p.49 and p.83.

52. McGrew, *Land and revolution*, pp.21–40.

53. As Kemal H. Karpat argues, however, from at least the eighteenth century a new social order had emerged out of the *timar* system. The *ayan* or local lord "represented the beginning of a new process of social mobility and economic relations". See "The Land regime, social structure, and modern-

izationin the Ottoman Empire", in *Beginnings of modernization in the Middle East*, eds. R.L. Chambers and W.R. Polk (Chicago: Chicago University Press, 1968), pp.69–90 (p.77).
54. George Finlay, "Turkey and its population", *Blackwood's Edinburgh Magazine* 76 (November 1854): 493–509 (p.495).
55. McGrew, *Land and revolution*, pp.53–79.
56. Alexandros Soutsos was to become an outspoken opponent of Capodistrias, however. His novel *The Exile of 1831* contains trenchant criticism of the President's authoritarian regime. Alexandros was also to protest at the illegal distribution of land during Otto's reign. See Yannis L. Lefas, *O Alexandros Soutsos kai i epidrasis tou ergou tou stous synhronous tou. Didaktoriki diatrivi* (Athens, 1979), pp.39, 44.
57. John Petropulos, *Politics and statecraft in the Kingdom of Greece, 1833–1843* (Princeton: Princeton University Press, 1968), p.20.
58. George Finlay estimated in 1854 that approximately a quarter of the population was Albanian, "King Otho and his classic kingdom", *Blackwood's Edinburgh Magazine* 76 (October 1854): 403–421 (p.416).
59. McGrew, *Land and revolution*, p.258. "National differences", observed Finlay as late as 1854, "municipal distinctions, local interests, class prejudices, and individual pretensions, divide the people", in "King Otho", p.416.
60. Finlay, *The Hellenic Kingdom*, pp.33–34, p.36.
61. On the divisions with which Capodistrias was confronted in Greece, see Christopher M. Woodhouse, *Capodistria: the founder of Greek independence* (London: Oxford University Press, 1973), p.391, *passim*.
62. See, generally, George Finlay, *History of the Greek Revolution and the reign of King Otho* (Edinburgh and London: W. Blackwood & Sons, 1861) and on the tensions between Roumeli, the Peloponnese and the islands, see Frédéric Thiersch, *De l'État actuel de la Grèce et des moyens d'arriver à sa restauration*, 2 vols. (Leipzig: F.A. Brockhaus, 1833), vol.1, pp.218–220.
63. Thiersch, *De l'État actuel de la Grèce*, p.220.
64. Thiersch, *De l'État actuel de la Grèce*, p.217.
65. Petropulos, *Politics and statecraft*, p.135.
66. Georg Ludwig von Maurer, *O Ellinikos laos: dimosio, idiotiko kai ekklisiastiko dikaio apo tin enarxi tou agona yia tin anexartisia os tin 31 Iouniou 1834*, trans., O. Robaki, ed., T. Vourna (Athens: Tolidis, 1976 [1835]). See Thiersch's comments on the "traditional" organization of Greek social and political space which centred on the family, *De l'État actuel de la Grèce*, vol.2, pp.213–267. See also Apostolos E. Vacalopoulos's comments on the pre-revolutionary Greek communities (*kinotites*) in *Istoria tou neou ellinismou*, 2nd ed., 6 vols. (Thessaloniki, 1961–1982), 2(1) pp.279–314. For a critique of Maurer's administrative reorganization, see Nikolaos Pantazopoulos, *O Ellinikos kinotismos kai i neoelliniki kinotiki paradosi* (Athens: Parousia, 1993). On the problems faced by the Bavarians who were ignorant of the language and local customs, see von Maurer's frank admissions in *O Ellinikos laos*.
67. Nikolaos Pantazopoulos, quoted in Kiriakidou-Nestoros, *Theoria tis ellinikis laografias*, p.43, *passim*.
68. See Gustave d'Eichthal, *La Langue grecque: mémoires et notices, 1864–84. Précédé d'une notice sur les services rendus par M. G. d'Eichthal à la Grèce et aux études grecques par le Marquis de Queux de Sainte-Hilaire* (Paris: Hachette, 1887) – for a description of d'Eichthal's involvement in Greece, see

pp.1–103. As d'Eichthal himself asserted: "Depuis mon arrivée en Grèce, mon désir est de la coloniser" (p.24).

69. McGrew, *Land and revolution*, p.103. See also generally, "The Land issue in the Greek War of Independence", in *Hellenism and the first Greek War of Independence*, eds. N.P. Diamandouros *et al.* (Thessaloniki: Institute for Balkan Studies, 1976), pp.111–129.

70. This is a paraphrase of N. Poulantzas's assertion that a nation's unity is achieved through the "historicity of a territory and a territorialization of a history", in *State, power and socialism* (London: New Left Books, 1978), p.114.

71. Abel Blouet, ed. *Expédition scientifique de Morée, ordonée par le gouvernement français* (sic). *Architecture, sculpture, inscriptions et vues du Péloponnèse, des Cyclades et de l'Attique*, 3 vols. (Paris, 1831–1838).

72. Quoted in Gehrke, "Anazitontas ti hora ton ellinon", p.63.

73. J.J.G. Pelet, *Carte de la Morée rédigée et gravée au dépôt général de la guerre* (Paris, 1832). On the French mission, see generally, Gehrke, "Anazitontas ti hora ton ellinon", pp.63–64.

74. See Y. Tolias, "1830–1930: o horos kai i anthropi", in *Ekato hronia hartografias tou ellinismou* (Athens, 1992), pp.25–26.

75. Koulouri, *Istoria kai yeografia*, p.27.

76. McGrew, *Land and revolution*, p.94.

77. Richard Clogg, *A Short history of modern Greece* (Cambridge: Cambridge University Press, 1986 [1979]), p.61.

78. Vilma Hastaoglou-Martinidis, "City, form and national identity: urban designs in nineteenth-century Greece", *Journal of Modern Greek Studies* 13/1 (1995): 99–123.

79. For a survey of Greek society after 1821, see *Istoria tou ellinikou ethnous*, vol.13, pp.448–454.

80. Parisatis Papadopoulou-Simeonidou, *I Epiloyi tis Athinas os protevousas tis Ellados, 1833–1834* (Thessaloniki: Adelfon Kyriakidi, 1996), pp.13–14. On the importance of the Acropolis in interpretations of Greek national identity, see Argyro Loukaki, "Whose genius loci?: contrasting interpretations of the 'sacred rock of the Athenian Acropolis'", *Annals of the Association of American Geographers* 87/2 (1997): 306–329 (pp.306–307).

81. See Eleni Bastéa, *The Creation of modern Athens: planning the myth* (Cambridge: Cambridge University Press, 2000) who explores the role of civic architecture and planning in forging a modern Greek identity.

82. Quoted in Hastaoglou-Martinidis, "City, form and national identity", p.103.

83. See Hastaoglou-Martinidis, "City, form and national identity", p.120.

84. Quoted in Hastaoglou-Martinidis, "City, form and national identity", p.107. On the relationship between city and patriotic identity, see Armstrong, *Nations before nationalism*, pp.93–128. And on Kleanthis and Schaubert's plan, see Bastéa, *The Creation of modern Athens*, pp. 85–92.

85. See Jörge Traeger, "Walhalla: the temple of fame on the Danube", in *The Romantic spirit in German art*, pp.303–306.

86. Alexandros Papayeoryiou-Venetas, "Architektoniki dimiouryia stin Athina: nei dromi tou klasikismou", in *Enas neos kosmos yennietai*, pp.277–314. See R. Carter, "K.F. Schinkel's project for a royal palace on the Acropolis", *Journal of the Society of Architectural Historians* 38/1 (March 1979): 34–46.

87. Vilma Hastaoglou-Martinidis, K. Kafkoula, N. Papamihos, "The Making of modern urban identity: the transformation of Greek towns in the nineteenth century", *Journal of Modern Hellenism* 8 (1991): 46–62 (p.50).

88. Wilkinson, *Maps and politics*, pp.20–23.
89. N.Y. Politis, "Ta Onomata ton dimon", *Epiteris Parnassou* 3 (1899): 54–80.
90. M. Chouliarakis, *Yeografiki, diikitiki kai plithismiaki exelixis tis Ellados, 1821–1971* (Athens, 1973), p.207.
91. Smith, *National identity*, pp.14–15.
92. On the process of aestheticizing territory, see the argument presented by Peter Mackridge in "Cultivating new lands: the consolidation of territorial gains in Greek Macedonia through literature, 1912–1940", in *Ourselves and others*, pp.175–186.

CHAPTER THREE

1. See, however, the comments by Paschalis Kitromilides, "On the intellectual content of Greek nationalism: Paparrigopoulos, Byzantium and the Great Idea", in *Byzantium and the modern Greek identity*, eds. D. Ricks and P. Magdalino (London and Aldershot: Ashgate, 1998), pp.25–33 (p. 26).
2. Quoted in Richard Clogg, *A Concise history of Greece* (Cambridge: Cambridge University Press, 1992), p.48.
3. Michael Llewellyn Smith, *Ionian vision: Greece in Asia Minor, 1919–1922* (London: Hurst, 1998 [1973]).
4. Gerasimos Augustinos, *The Greeks of Asia Minor: confession, community, and ethnicity in the nineteenth century* (Kent, OH: Kent State University Press, 1992), pp.19–32.
5. Charles K. Tuckerman, *The Greeks of to-day* (New York: Putnam, 1878), p.120.
6. William Miller, *Greek life in town and country* (London: William Clowes, 1905), p.44.
7. Barbara Jelavich, *History of the Balkans, Vol.1: eighteenth and nineteenth centuries* (Cambridge: Cambridge University Press, 1983), pp.244–245.
8. David Mackenzie, *The Serbs and Russian Pan-Slavism, 1875–1878* (Ithaca: Cornell University Press, 1967), p.6. See Misha Glenny, *The Balkans, 1804–1999: nationalism, war and the Great Powers* (London: Granta Books, 1999), pp.43–44.
9. Dimitrije Djordjevic and Stephen Fischer-Galati, *The Balkan revolutionary tradition* (New York: Columbia University Press, 1981), p.101.
10. Alexandros Rizos Rangavis, *Apomnimonevmata* 4 vols (Athens: Estia, 1894), vol.2, p.89, *passim*.
11. Victor Bérard, *La Turquie et l'Hellénisme contemporain* (Paris: Félix Alcan, 1893), p.1.
12. Ion Dragoumis, *O Ellinismos mou kai i ellines, 1903–1909* (Athens: Estia, 1927), p.108.
13. See Elli Skopetea, *To 'Protipo vasilio' kai i Megali Idea. Opsis tou ethnikou provlimatos stin Ellada (1830–1880)* (Athens: Politipo, 1988), p.35, *passim*.
14. See, in this context, Mark Bassin, "Imperialism and the nation state in Friedrich Ratzel's political geography", *Progress in Human Geography* 11 (1987): 473–495.
15. John Koliopoulos, *Brigands with a cause: brigandage and irredentism in modern Greece, 1821–1912* (Oxford: Clarendon Press, 1987), p.308. On the early debate surrounding Greece's boundaries, see Ioannis Poulos, "Ta Prota sinora tis neoteras Ellados", *Deltion tis Istorikis kai Ethnoloyikis Etairias tis Ellados* 18 (1966): 3–83.
16. Skopetea, *To 'Protipo vasilio'*, p.23.
17. Quoted in Skopetea, *To 'Protipo vasilio'*, p.26.

18. The Imperial Palace in Istanbul, which came to stand for the Ottoman government.
19. See Malcolm Wagstaff, "Independent Greece: the search for a frontier, 1822–35", *Kambos: Cambridge Papers in Modern Greek* 7 (1999): 59–70 (pp.63–64).
20. Quoted in Skopetea, *To 'Protipo vasilio'*, p.22. On Capodistrias and Greece's frontiers, see Woodhouse, *Capodistria*, pp.380–381, 439–440.
21. Woodhouse, *Capodistria*, p.336.
22. Korais, *Apanta*, A2, p.791.
23. Quoted in Richard Clogg, "*I Kath'imas Anatoli*: the Greek East in the eighteenth and nineteenth centuries", in *Anatolica: studies in the Greek East in the 18th and 19th centuries* (London and Aldershot: Variorum, 1996), pp.1–7 (p.1).
24. Wagstaff, "Independent Greece", p.66.
25. Quoted in Skopetea, *To 'Protipo vasilio'*, p.22.
26. Alexis Politis, *Romantika hronia: ideoloyies kai nootropies stin Ellada tou 1830–1880* (Athens: Eatairia Meletis Neou Ellinismou, 1993), p.63. On the debate about where Greece's boundaries should be drawn, see especially pp.61–65.
27. Miliarakis, "Daniil Filippidis", p.115. Miliarakis discusses the boundary issue in the article's final instalment, *Estia* 478/19 (1885): 147–151 (pp.147–148).
28. Philippidis and Konstantas, *Yeografia neoteriki*, pp.107–110.
29. Cited in Politis, *Romantika hronia*, p.45.
30. Dimitrios Vikelas, *Le Rôle et les aspirations de la Grèce dans la question d'Orient* (Paris: Au Cercle Saint Simon,1885), p.88.
31. Peter Sahlins, *Boundaries: the making of France and Spain in the Pyrenees* (Berkeley: University of California Press, 1989), p.271. See in this context, Fredrik Barth, ed. *Ethnic groups and boundaries: the social organization of cultural difference* (Oslo: Universitetsforlaget, 1994 [1969]).
32. William Miller, *Greece* (London: Ernest Benn Limited, 1928), p.28.
33. Kyriakidou-Nestoros, *Theoria tis ellinikis laografias*, p.45.
34. Ion Dragoumis, *Ellinikos politismos* (Athens: Nea Thesis, 1991a [1913] p.39.
35. Stratis Myrivilis, *I Daskala me ta Chrisa matia* (Athens: Pirsos, 1934), pp.28–29.
36. Édouard Driault, *La Grande Idée: la renaissance de l'Hellénisme*, pref. N. Politis (Paris: Félix Alcan, 1920), p.119.
37. Kostis Palamas, *Thanatos pallikariou* (Athens: Kollaros, 1927 [1891]), p.17.
38. Douglas Dakin, *The Greek struggle in Macedonia 1897–1913* (Thessaloniki: Society for Macedonian Studies and the Institute for Balkan Studies, 1993 [1966]), p.2.
39. Stratis Myrivilis, *O Palamas sti zoi mou* (Athens: Fexis, 1963), pp.26–29.
40. Stratis Myrivilis, *O Vasilis o Arvanitis* (Athens: Estia, 1987 [1943]), p.100.
41. Quoted in Sophie Basch, *Le Mirage grec: la Grèce moderne devant l'opinion française (1846–1946)* (Athens and Paris: Hatier and Kauffman, 1995), p.173.
42. Charles Stewart, *Demons and the devil: moral imagination in modern Greek culture* (Princeton: Princeton University Press, 1991), p.182.
43. Stewart, *Demons and the devil*, p.181.
44. Mary Douglas, *Purity and danger: an analysis of concepts of pollution and taboo* (London: Routledge and Kegan Paul, 1978 [1966]), p.3. For an analysis of the social and political meanings invested in the body in Greece, see Jane

K. Cowan, *Dance and the body politic in Northern Greece* (Princeton: Princeton University Press, 1990).

45. For a fuller account of "body politics" in Greece, see Robert Shannan Peckham, "Diseased bodies of the nation: suicide in *fin de siècle* Greece", in *Journal of Mediterranean Studies* 9/2 (1999) pp. 155–174.

46. A. Kokkou, *I Merimna yia tis arhaiotites stin Ellada kai to prota mousia* (Athens: Ermis, 1977), pp.283–288.

47. The second, definitive edition of Paparrigopoulos's work appeared between 1885–87.

48. Kitromilides, "On the intellectual context of Greek nationalism", p.28.

49. The fact that the richest Greek communities remained outside Greece, together with a resentment felt against the educated Greeks who moved into the Kingdom after independence, led to a controversy in the National Assembly over who should be considered "native" Greeks, or *autochthons*, as opposed to *heterochthons*, or Greeks from outside the confines of the Kingdom.

50. Koulouri, *Dimensions idéologiques*, p.407.

51. Koulouri, *Dimensions idéologiques*, p.419.

52. Quoted in Koulouri, *Istoria kai yeografia*, p.255.

53. See, for example, N. Metaxas's *Political and physical geography* (1899), cited in Koulouri, *Istoria kai yeografia*, pp. 456–457.

54. Koulouri, *Dimensions idéologiques*, p.422.

55. Nikolaos Politis, *Les Aspirations nationales de la Grèce* (Paris: Édition Spéciale de la Paix des Peuples, 1920), p.11.

56. Henri Belle, *Trois années en Grèce* (Paris: Hachette, 1881), p.105. On Greece as a border region generally during the late nineteenth century, see Robert Shannan Peckham, "The Exoticism of the familiar and the familiarity of the exotic: *fin-de-siècle* travellers to Greece", in *Writes of Passage: Reading Travel*, eds. J.S. Duncan and D. Gregory (London and New York: Routledge, 1999), pp.164–184.

57. Eleni Bastéa, "Nineteenth-century travellers in Greek lands: politics, prejudice and poetry in Arcadia", *Dialogos* 4 (1997): 47–69 (p. 61).

58. Miller, *Greece*, p.29.

59. Mihail Mitsakis, *Afiyimata*, ed. D. Lekkas (Athens: Syllogi, 1995), pp.40–42.

60. Markos Renieris, "Ti inai i Ellas; Anatoli i Disis', *Eranistis* 2/1 (1842): 187–213.

61. Georgios Varouxakis, "The Idea of 'Europe' in nineteenth-century Greek political thought", in *Greek and Europe in the modern period: aspects of a troubled relationship*, ed. P. Carabott (London: Centre for Hellenic Studies, King's College London, 1995), pp.16–37.

62. Dimitris Tziovas, *The Nationism of the demoticists and its impact on their literary theory, 1888–1939* (Amsterdam: Hakkert, 1986), pp.293–414.

63. Dimitris Tziovas, "The Politics of metaphor and the rhetoric of consensus: Europe in the *Free Spirit* of George Theotokas", in *Greece and Europe in the modern period*, pp. 70–82.

64. Varouxakis, "The Idea of 'Europe", p.20.

65. Varouxakis, "The Idea of 'Europe", p.22.

66. Varouxakis, "The Idea of 'Europe", p.24.

67. Said, *Orientalism*, pp.56–57.

68. Mark Bassin, "Russian geographers and the 'national question' in the Far East", in *Geography national identity*, ed. D. Hooson (Oxford: Blackwell, 1994), pp.112–133 (p.115). See also Mark Bassin, "Russia between Europe

and Asia: the ideological construction of geographical space", *Slavic Review* 50 (1991): 1–17.

69. Grigorios Palaiologos, *O Polypathis*, ed. A. Angelou (Athens: Ermis, 1989), p.181.

70. Franco Moretti, *Atlas of the European novel, 1800–1900* (London and New York: Verso, 1998), p.53.

71. Moretti, *Atlas of the European novel*, p.35.

72. See Denis Cosgrove, "Habitable Earth: Wilderness, Empire, and Race in America", in *Wild Ideas*, ed. D. Rothenberg (Minneapolis: University of Minnesota Press, 1995), pp.27–41 (p.32).

73. Quoted in David Trotter, *The English novel in history, 1895–1920* (London: Routledge, 1993), p.158.

74. Constantinos Sathas and Émile Legrand, eds. *Les Exploits de Degénis Akritas Epopée Byzantine du Dixième Siècle* (Paris: Maisonneuve, 1875) and K. Prousis quoted in Roderick Beaton, *Folk poetry of modern Greece* (Cambridge: Cambridge University Press, 1980), p.80. There is, however, little basis for these assumptions in the text. See Roderick Beaton and David Ricks, eds. *Digenes Akrites: new approaches to Byzantine heroic poetry* (London and Aldershot: Variorum, 1993).

75. Quoted in Michael Herzfeld, *Ours once more*, pp.120–121.

76. On the ideological significance of Diyenis Akritas for the demoticists, see Tziovas, *The Nationism of the demoticists*, pp.225–228.

77. See Andreas Karkavitsas, *Diyenis Akritas kai all adiiyimata* (Athens: Papadopoulos, n.d.), pp.9–116.

78. Herzfeld notes that "a small minority of Politis's contemporaries were uncomfortable with his conception of the Akritic hero. Karolidis (1906) was the first to point out that one might just as easily take the name as symbolizing the "twy-born culture (*politismos*)", *Ours once more*, p.120.

79. Psycharis, *To Taxidi mou*, ed. A. Angelou (Athens: Ermis, 1983) p.37.

80. Koliopoulos, *Brigands with a cause*, p.226.

81. Koliopoulos, *Brigands with a cause*, p.299. For an excellent study of the *kleftika*, see Alexis Politis's introduction to *To Dimotiko tragoudi: kleftika* (Athens: Ermis, 1973).

82. Herzfeld, *Ours once more*, p.60. For a discussion of the kleft as a figure in nationalist writing, see pp.60–70.

83. Lambros Enialis, *O Parafron erimitis, mythistorema*, 3rd edn. (Athens, 1868).

84. Gaston Deschamps, *La Grèce d'aujourd'hui* (Paris: Armand Colin, 1892), pp.125–127

85. Anastasios N. Goudas, *Vii paralthe ton epi tis Anayenniseos tis Ellados diaprepsandon andron* (Athens:1872).

86. On the nationalist interpretation of the kleft and brigand, see Koliopoulos, *Brigands with a cause*, pp.31–33, p.210 and p.322. For a brief account of the glorification of the klefts, see John C. Alexander, "The Klefts of the Morea: An Historical Essay", in *New trends in modern Greek historiography*, eds. L. Makrakis and P. N. Diamandouros (MGSA Occasional Papers, 1982), pp. 32–33.

87. H.F. Tozer, *Researches in the Highlands of Turkey*, 2 vols. (London: John Murray, 1869), vol.2, pp.46, 224.

88. George Finlay, "Brigandage in Greece", *Saturday Review*, 810/31 (1871): 561–563.

89. Herzfeld, *Ours once more*, pp.67–68. See also Koliopoulos, *Brigands with a cause*, pp.187–189

90. Moretti, *Atlas of the European novel*, p.38.
91. Skopetea, *To 'Protipo vasilio'*, p.310.
92. Andreas Karkavitsas, *Palies agapes* (Athens: Ermis, 1995), pp.93–94.
93. Andreas Karkavitsas, *Diiyimata* (Athens: Ermis, 1982), p.148.
94. Mitsakis, *Afiyimata*, p.186.
95. Mitsakis, *Afiyimata*, p.199.
96. Bhabha, "DissemiNation", p.300.
97. Reed-pipes, as symbols of continuity and pastoral celebration, pervade the rural fiction and poetry of the 1880s and 1890s in Greece. Drosinis's tale "Mitros's Reed-Pipe" appeared in 1882 and Karkavitsas's "His Reed-Pipe" was published in 1893, while a reed-pipe is central to Christovasilis's tale "Lame Yannis in Iannina" (1898). Anton Chekhov's "The Reed-Pipe" appeared in Russian in 1887. See Emmanouil Roidis's introduction to Konstantinos Metaxas-Vosporitis's *Skinai tis erimou* (Athens: Nefeli, 1988 [1899]), p.11, where he criticizes the idealization of the country in fiction pervaded with reed-pipes.
98. On the representation of the city and relations between the "real" and "idealized" country, see Pantelis Voutouris, *Os is Kathreptin...protasis kai ipothesis yia tin elliniki pezografia tou 19ου aina* (Athens: Nefeli, 1995), pp. 221–246
99. Moretti, *Atlas of the European novel*, p.40.
100. Elizabeth Mayhew Edmonds, trans. *Kolokotrones, the klepht and the warrior: sixty years of peril and daring: an autobiography* (London: T.Fisher Unwin, 1892).
101. Dimitrios Vikelas, *Loukis Laras: reminiscences of a Chiote merchant during the War of Independence*, trans. J. Gennadius (London: Macmillan and Co, 1881); Rennell Rodd, "The Poet of the klephts: Aristoteles Valaoritis", *The Nineteenth Century* 173 (1891):130–144; W. Alison Phillips, *The War of Greek Independence, 1821–1833* (London: Smith, Elder and Co, 1897); Stefanos Theodoros Xenos, *Andronike: The heroine of the Greek Revolution*, trans. E.A. Grosvenor (Boston: Roberts Brothers, 1897).
102. Significantly, in this context, the word *istoria* in Greek signifies both "history" and "story".
103. Mario Vitti, *Ideoloyiki litouryia tis ellinikis ithografias* (Athens: Kedros, 1991 [1974]), p.75.
104. See David Holton, "Ethnic identity and patriotic idealism" and Gourgouris, *Dream nation*, pp.175–200.
105. Papakostas, *To Periodiko Estia*, p.82.
106. See Papakostas, *To Periodiko Estia*, p.46. The novel had been translated into ten languages by 1884.
107. See, for example, Kondylakis's novel *In 62. Down with tyranny*, which was published in the magazine *Skrip* between 1895 and 1896; V. Nikolaïdis, *Ali Pasha Bey* (1882) which is set in Constantinople in 1821.
108. Kostis Palamas, "Istories tou Yiannou Epahtitis", in *Apanta*, 10 vols (Athens: Biris and Idrima Kosti Palama, n.d.), vol.2, pp. 179–186 (p.179)
109. On this text, see Dimitris Kokoris, "Ena pezografima tou Kosta Krystalli: 'To Simomatari tou Yerokalameniou' piran tis idilliakis ithografias", *Diavazo* 326 (January 1994): 75–79.
110. Christos Christovasilis, *Diiyimata tis stanis* (Athens: Nefeli, 1988), p.7 and p. 15, *passim*.
111. See, for example, Y. Psillas cited in Skopetea, *To 'Protipo vasilio'*, pp.48–49.

112.Politis, *Romantika hronia*, p.65.
113.Maria Korasidou, *I Athlii ton Athinon kai i therapeftes tous: ftohia kai filanthropia stin elliniki protevousa ton 19o aiona* (Athens: Kentro Neoelliniko Erevnon, 1995), p.74. [see bibliography]
114.See, in this context, Haris Exertzoglou, *Ethniki tavtotita stin Konstantinoupoli ton 19o ai: O Ellinikos Filoloyikos sillogos Konstantinoupoleos, 1861–1912* (Athens: Nefeli, 1996).
115.Eric J. Hobsbawm, *The Age of revolution, 1789–1848* (New York: Mentor, 1964), p.166.
116.Quoted in Agriandoni, *I Aparhes tis ekviomichanisis*, p.265.
117.Edmonds, *Kolokotrones*, p.vii.
118.Koliopoulos, *Brigands with a cause*, p.296.
119.*Ilios* 33 (22 October 1833), p.133. Cited in Vayenas, "O Outopikos sosialismos ton adelfon Soutson", pp.45–46.
120.Gellner, *Nations and nationalism*, p.1.
121.See W.D. Smith "Friedrich Ratzel and the origins of *Lebensraum*", *German Studies Review* 3 (1980): 51–68 and Bassin, "Imperialism and the nation ".
122.George Curzon, *Frontiers* (Oxford: Clarendon Press, 1907), p.7.
123.Trotter, *The English novel*, p.146.

CHAPTER FOUR

1. Eugen Weber, *Peasants into Frenchmen: the modernization of rural France, 1870–1914* (London: Chatto and Windus, 1976); for a qualifying critique of Weber's thesis, see Ted W. Margadant, "French rural society in nineteenth-century France: a review essay", *Agricultural History* 53/3 (July 1979): 644–651.
2. See, for example, Maurice Agulhon's study of the Var, *The Republic in the village: the people of the Var from the French Revolution to the Second Republic*, trans. J. Lloyd (Paris and Cambridge: Éditions de la Maison des Sciences de l'Homme and Cambridge University Press, 1982 [1970]).
3. Gellner, *Nations and nationalism*, p.21.
4. John Cuthbert Lawson, *Modern Greek folklore and ancient Greek religion: a study in survivals* (Cambridge: Cambridge University Press, 1910), p.28.
5. See, on this, Katerina Gardikas Alexander, "Centre and periphery in the 1874 Greek elections: competition for political control in Gortynia", *Balkan Studies* 36/1 (1995): 11–30; and the articles collected in Ernestine Friedl and Muriel Dimen-Schein, eds. *Regional variations in modern Greece and Cyprus: toward a perspective on the ethnography of Greece* (New York: New York Academy of Sciences, 1976).
6. Miller, *Greek life*, p.27.
7. Gellner, *Nations and nationalism*, pp.55–56.
8. Yorgos Skliros, *To Kinoniko mas zitima* (Athens: Anestis Konstantinidis, 1907).
9. See Stephen Kern, *The Culture of time and space, 1880–1918* (Cambridge, MA: Harvard University Press, 1983).
10. Magdalena Dabrowski, *French landscape: the modern vision, 1880–1920* (New York: Museum of Modern Art, 2000), p.12.
11. On this, see McGrew, *Land and revolution*.
12. See Koliopoulos, *Brigands with a cause*.
13. Skopetea, *To 'Protipo vasilio'*, p.72.
14. R.A.H. Bickford-Smith,*Greece under King George*, (London: Richard Bentley & Son, 1893). See also, Thomas Gallant "Murder in a Mediterranean city:

homicide trends in Athens, 1850–1936", *Journal of the Hellenic Diaspora* 25/2 (1997): 8–14.

15. See Peckham "The exoticism of the familiar", pp.164–184.
16. On this, see Romilly Jenkins, *The Dilessi murders* (London: Longman, 1961).
17. Maria Sinarelli, *Dromi kai limania stin Ellada, 1830–1880* (Athens: ETVA, 1989). On the great modernizing projects in late nineteenth-century Greece, see Vasias Tsokopoulos, *Megala tehnika erga stin Ellada: teli 19ou-arhes 20ou aiona* (Athens: Kastaniotis, 1999).
18. Kostis Moskof, *I Ethniki kai kinoniki sinidisi stin Ellada, 1830–1902: ideoloyia tou metapraktikou chorou* (Thessaloniki: 1972), pp.48–49.
19. Lefteris Papayannakis, *I Elliniki siderodromi (1882–1910)* (Athens: Morfotiko Idrima Ethnikis Trapezis, 1982).
20. Bickford-Smith, *Greece under King George*, pp.83–84.
21. See John Pemble, *The Mediterranean passion: Victorians and Edwardians in the South* (Oxford: Clarendon Press, 1992), p.29.
22. Mark Mazower, *Greece and the inter-war economic crisis* (Oxford: Clarendon Press, 1991), p.41.
23. Bickford-Smith, *Greece under King George*, pp.99–100.
24. Nikos P. Mouzelis, *Modern Greece: facets of underdevelopment* (London and Basingstoke: Macmillan, 1978), p.21.
25. On the increasing distribution of local banks in Greece from the 1870s, see S. Thomadakis, *Yeografiki katanomi ton ergasion tis Ethnikis Trapezis tis Ellados (1861–1900)* (Athens, 1984) and Robert Shannan Peckham, "O Papadiamantis kai i oikonomia tis fantasias", *Revue des Études Néo-Helleniques* IV, 1/2 (1995a): 35–69 (pp.38–40).
26. Bickford-Smith, *Greece under King George*, p.202.
27. Politis, *Romantika hronia*, p.145.
28. Dimitrios Vikelas, "I Elliniki dimosiografia kata to 1883", *Estia* 423/17 (1884): 87–91 (p.88).
29. Albeit only 51 percent, see Eric Hobsbawm, *The Age of Capital, 1848–1875* (London: Abacus, 1997 [1975]), p.205.
30. Konstantinos Tsoukalas, *Exartisi kai anaparagogi. O Kinonikos rolas ton ekpaidevtikon mihanisman Stin Ellada (1830–1922)* (Athens: Themelio, 1970), p.198.
31. Bickford-Smith, *Greece under King George*, p.6.
32. Mazower, *Greece and the inter-war economic crisis*, p.47.
33. Robert Eisner, *Travellers to an antique land: the history and literature of travel to Greece* (Ann Arbor: The University of Michigan Press, 1991), p.175. See also Lila Leontidou, *Polis tis siopis* (Athens: ETVA, 1989), P. 48.
34. Tsoukalas, *Exartisi kai anaparagogi*. See, also, Yeoryios Drosinis and Yeoryios Kasdonis, eds. *Nea Ellas: ethnikou imeroloyiou ikonografimenou* (Athens: Estia, 1894), p.59.
35. Dimitrios Chatzopoulos, "Emis kai meriki xeni", *Dionysos* 1 (1901): 82–89 (p.83).
36. Michael Herzfeld, *Anthropology through the looking-glass: critical ethnography in the margins of Europe* (Cambridge: Cambridge University Press, 1987), pp.49–76.
37. Miller, *Greek life*, p.207, p.195.
38. J. Theodore Bent, "On insular Greek customs" (1886). Quoted in Herzfeld, *Anthropology through the looking-glass*, p.74.
39. Rennell Rodd, *The Customs and lore of modern Greece*, 2nd edn. (London: David Stott, 1892), p.xi.

40. H.N. Brailsford, *Macedonia: its race and their future* (London: Methuen & Co, 1906), pp.218–219.
41. On France, see Weber, *Peasants into Frenchmen*, pp.470–471.
42. J.P. Mahaffy, *Rambles and studies in Greece*, rev. 4th edn. (London: Macmillan, 1892), p.viii.
43. Politis, *Laografia*, p.3.
44. Herzfeld, *Ours once more*, p.127.
45. Richard C. Jebb, *Modern Greece. Two lectures delivered before the Philosophical Institution of Edinburgh, with pages on 'The Progress of Greece' and 'Byron and Greece'* (London: Macmillan, 1901 [1880]), p.53.
46. See Eric J. Hobsbawn and Terence Ranger, eds. *The Invention of tradition* (Cambridge: Cambridge University Press, 1983).
47. See Robert Colls and Philip Dodds, eds. *Englishness, 1880–1920* (London: Croom Helm, 1986).
48. Weber, *Peasants into Frenchmen*.
49. See James Vernon, "Border crossings: Cornwall and the English (imagi)nation" in *Imagining nations*, pp.153–72 (p.154).
50. Yeorgios Drosinis, *Skorpia filla tis zois mou*, (Athens: Sideris, 1940), p.156.
51. Thodoros Chatzipandazis, *I Isvoli tou karayiozi stin Athina tou 1890* (Athens: Stigmi, 1984).
52. See, on this generally, Karl Nef, *Istoria tis mousikis*, ed. and trans. F. Anoyianakis, 2nd edn. (Athens: Votsis, 1985), pp.571–572, *passim.*
53. See, on this, Charalambos-Dimitris Gounelas, *I Sosialistiki sinidisi stin elliniki logotehnia, 1897–1912* (Athens: Kedros, 1984).
54. Ilhan Basgöz, "Folklore studies and nationalism in Turkey", in *Folklore, nationalism, and politics*, ed. F.J. Oinas (Columbus, Ohio: Slavica, 1978), pp.123–137 (pp.123–124, *passim*). See, also, William A. Wilson's discussion of the central role of folklore in the articulation of a Finnish national identity, "The *Kalevala* and Finnish politics" in the same volume, pp.51–75.
55. Dimaras, *Ellinikos romantismos*, p.374.
56. See Herzfeld, *Ours once more*, p.13.
57. Drosinis, *Skorpia filla*, pp.151–173.
58. Drosinis, *Skorpia filla*, p.158.
59. Politis, *Neoelliniki mytholoyia* I, p.4.
60. Politis, *Neoelliniki mytholoyia* I, p.3.
61. Politis, *Neoelliniki mytholoyia* I, p.iii. On Fallmerayer's often misunderstood centrality to the development of Greek folklore, see Mihalis Y. Meraklis, "O Fallmerayer kai i elliniki laografia", in *Enas neos kosmos yennietai*, pp.269–276, and Elli Skopetea, *Fallmerayer: tehnasmata tou antipalou deous* (Athens: Themelio, 1997).
62. See, for example, Kostis Palamas's article "I Ethniki glossa", *Apanta* vol.6 pp. 245–261 (p.248).
63. Quoted in Trotter, *The English novel*, p.158.
64. Trotter, *The English novel*, pp.157–159.
65. See, on regionalism in the Greek theatre, Chatzipantazis, *I Isvoli tou karaghiozi stin Athina*. On regionalism in Britain, see Keith Snell, ed. *The Regional novel in Britain and Ireland* (Cambridge: Cambridge University Press, 1998).
66. Cited in Dimitris Tziovas, "Heteroglossia and the defeat of regionalism in Greece", *Kambos: Cambridge Papers in Modern Greek* 2 (1994): 95–120 (pp.105–106).
67. Lawson, *Modern Greek folklore*, p.35.

68. Loring M. Danforth, "The Ideological context of the search for continuities in Greek culture", *Journal of Modern Greek Studies* 2/1 (May 1984): 53–85 (p.53).
69. Nikolaos G. Politis, "Laografia", in *Laografia symmiktra*, vol.1 (Athens, 1920 [1909]): 3–18 (p.6).
70. Quoted in Gerasimos Augustinos, *Consciousness and history: nationalist critics of Greek society, 1897–1914* (Boulder: East European Quarterly, 1977), p.30.
71. Gillian Bennett, "Geologists and folklorists: 'cultural evolution' and the science of folklore", *Folklore* 105 (1994): 29.
72. Politis, *Laografia*, vol.1, p. 9.
73. Politis, *Neoelliniki mytholoyia* I, p.3.
74. Politis, *Laografia*, vol.1, p.7.
75. Politis, *Neoelliniki mytholoyia* I, pp.5–6.
76. Argyris Eftaliotis, *Tales from the isles of Greece, being sketches of modern Greek peasant life*, W.H.D. Rouse, trans. (London: J.M. Dent, 1897), p.iv.
77. Dimitrios S. Loukatos, *Isagogi stin elliniki laografia* (Athens: Morfotiko Idrima Ethnikis Trapezis, 1978a), pp.63–64.
78. Gustav Le Bon, *The Crowd: a study of the popular mind*, intr. R.K. Merton (Harmondsworth: Penguin, 1960), pp.82–83.
79. Bhabha, "DissemiNation", p.297.
80. Linda H. Peterson, "Sage writing", in *A Companion to Victorian literature and culture*, ed. H.F. Tucker (Oxford: Blackwell, 1999) pp.373–387 (p.385).
81. Quoted in Uli Linke, "Folklore, anthropology, and the government of social life", *Comparative Studies in Society and History* 32/1 (1990): 117–148 (p.123).
82. Linke, "Folklore, anthropology, and the government of social life", p.122.
83. Linke, "Folklore, anthropology, and the government of social life", p.120.
84. Richard M. Dorson, *The British folklorists: a history* (London: Routledge and Kegan Paul, 1968), p.332.
85. Linke, "Folklore, anthropology, and the government of social life", p.121.
86. Kyriakidou-Nestoros, *Theoria tis ellinikis laografias*, pp.32–33.
87. Kyriakidou-Nestoros, *Theoria tis ellinikis laografias*, p.159.
88. See Vernon, "Border crossings", pp.155–158.
89. This appeared in the *Journal of the Anthropological Institute of Great Britain and Ireland* XXIIII, (1894): 29–44, and was republished in Greek in *Parnassos* 12 (1894): 81–87. Politis actually sent the British anthropologists signed reprints of his published work. See Herzfeld, *Ours once more*, pp.102–103.
90. Dorson, *The British folklorists*, p.194.
91. Michael Hechter, *Internal colonialism: the Celtic fringe in British national development, 1536–1966* (London: Routledge and Kegan Paul, 1975).
92. Vernon, "Border crossings", p.156.
93. Vernon, "Border crossings", p.156.
94. Michel de Certeau, *Heterologies: discourse on the other*, trans. B. Massumi, foreword by W. Godzich (Manchester: Manchester University Press, 1986), pp.119–167.
95. Weber, *Peasants into Frenchmen*, pp.485–496.
96. Dorson, *The British folklorists*, p.195.
97. Nikolaos Politis, "Dimodis kosmoyoniki mythi", *Laografia symmiktra*, vol.2 (Athens: 1921 [1894]): 77–109 (pp.82–83).
98. Politis, "On the Breaking of vessels", p.29.
99. See Loukatos, *Isagogi stin Elliniki laografia*, pp.291–292.
100. Moretti, *Atlas of the European novel*, p.40.

CHAPTER FIVE

1. Koulouri, *Dimensions idéologiques*, p.453.
2. Howard F. Andrews, "The Early life of Paul Vidal de la Blache and the makings of modern geography", *Transactions of the Institute of British Geographers* 11 (1986): 174–182 (p.178).
3. Koulouri, *Dimensions idéologiques*, pp.434–436.
4. Ion Dragoumis, *Martiron kai iroon aima*, ed. K.A. Vakalopoulos (Thessaloniki: Kiriakidis, 1991), p.247.
5. Charles Tilly, *Coercion, capital, and European states* (Oxford: Blackwell, 1990), p.107.
6. Quoted in Sahlins, *Boundaries*, p.8.
7. Pierre Nora, ed. *Les Lieux de mémoire*, 3 vols. (Paris: Gallimard, 1997 [1984–1992]).
8. Clifford Geertz, *The Interpretation of cultures* (New York: Basic Books,1973), p.259.
9. See Alun Howkins, "The Discovery of rural England", in *Englishness: politics and culture*, pp.62–88.
10. Eugen Weber, "L'Hexagone", in Nora ed., *Les Lieux de mémoire*, vol.1, pp.1171–1190 (pp.1179–1180).
11. Drosinis, *Skorpia filla*, p.61.
12. Koulouri, *Dimensions idéologiques*, pp.435–436.
13. See John K. Campbell, "Regionalism and local community", in Friedl and Dimen-Schein, eds., *Regional variation in modern Greece*, pp.18–27.
14. Panayiotis A. Komninos, *Lakonika hronon proïstorikon te kai istorikon* (Athens, 1896).
15. E. Manolakakis, *Karpathiaka periehonta tin topografian, istorian, perigrafin, arhaioloyian, fusikin katastasi, statistiki, toponimies tis nisou, itha kai ethima, idiomata tis glossis, lexiloyion, dimotiki, asmata kai dimidis primias ton katikian aftis* (Athens, 1896).
16. Stephanos N. Thomopoulos, *Istoria tis poleos Patron apo ton arhiotaton hronon mehri tou 1821* (Athens, 1888), p.v.
17. Nikos Bakounakis, *To Fandasma tis Norma: i ipodohi tou melodramatos ston elliniko horo to 19o aiona* (Athens: Kastaniotis, 1991), p.48.
18. See Vasias Tsokopoulos, *Piraias, 1835–1870: isagogi stin istoria tou ellinikou Manchester* (Athens: Kastaniotis, 1984) and "Ta Stadia tis topikis sinidisis: o Piraias, 1835–1935" in *Ta Praktika tou Diethnnous Simposiou tis Etairias Meletis Neou Ellinismou* (Athens, 1985), pp.245–248.
19. See Kyriakidou-Nestoros, *Theoria tis ellinikis laografias*, p.193.
20. J. Shaw and E. Shaw, *History of the Ottoman Empire and modern Turkey II: reform, revolution and republic: the rise of modern Turkey, 1808–1975* (Cambridge: Cambridge University Press, 1977), pp.259–263.
21. Antonios Miliarakis, *Odigos ton aplon topografikon perigrafon* (Athens: Kollaros, 1901 [1882]), p.8.
22. See, for example, Politis's famous statement on the organization of folklore in the journal *Laografia* 1(1909): 3–18.
23. Gerasimos Augustinos, *The Greeks of Asia Minor*, p.194.
24. Koulouri, *Dimensions idéologiques*, pp.404–415.
25. Ioannis Soutsos, "Peri tis epirrois ton fisikon peristaseon epi tou politismou", *Pandora* vol.17, no.386 (15 April 1867): 33–41.
26. Tziovas, *The Nationism of the demoticists*, p.398.
27. Tziovas, *The Nationism of the demoticists*, p.393.
28. Tziovas, *The Nationism of the demoticists*, p.394.

29. Dragoumis, *Ellinikos politismos*, p.84.
30. Anastasios Hourmouziadis, *Peri ton Anastenarion kai allon tinon ethimon kai prolipseon* (Constantinople, 1873).
31. *Makedonia iti meleti ikonomiki, yeografiki, istoriki kai ethnoloyiki tis Makedonias*, 2nd edn. (Piraeus, 1896), pp.i–ii.
32. Gellner, *Nations and nationalism*, p.21. This passage is discussed by Moretti, *Atlas of the European novel*, p.45.
33. Gellner, *Nations and nationalism*, p.124.
34. Tsokopoulos, "Ta Stadia tis topikis sinidisis", pp.247–248.
35. Basil Gounaris, *Steam over Macedonia, 1870–1912: socio-economic change and the railway factor* (Boulder: East European Monographs, 1993), pp.270–272. This process was especially evident in Belgium and Italy.
36. For a brief analysis of the ways in which integration and disintegration "impress their definite mark on the present dynamics of [Greek] social space", see Bernard Kayser, "Dynamics of regional integration in modern Greece", in Friedl and Dimen-Schein, eds., *Regional variation in modern Greece*, pp. 10–15 (p.11).
37. Similar ideas were articulated later in the twentieth century by K.D. Karavidas; see, for example, his *Agrotika* (Athens: Papazisis, 1977 [1931]).
38. Nikiforos Diamandouros has argued that the tension between society and state, between a regional and urban culture, continued to characterize Greece in the late twentieth century; see, for example, "Greek political culture in transition: historical origins, evolution, current trends", in *Greece in the 1980s*, ed. R. Clogg (London: Macmillan, 1983), pp.43–69 (p.55).
39. Augustinos, *Consciousness and history*, p.5.
40. Augustinos, *Consciousness and history*, p.26.
41. Konstantinos S. Sokolis, *Aftokratoria* (Athens: Roes, 1993 [1916]), p.35.
42. Sokolis, *Aftokratoria*, p.46.
43. Sokolis, *Aftokratoria*, p.47.
44. Periklis Yannopoulos, *Apanta*, ed. D. Lazoyiorgos-Ellinikos (Athens: Nea Thesis, 1993), pp.95–144.
45. Yannopoulos, *Apanta*, pp.16–32.
46. See, for example, Maurice Barrès, *Les Déracinés: le roman de l'énergie nationale*, vol.1 (Paris and London: Nelson, 1897). Barrès had, in fact, visited and written about Greece; see his *Le Voyage à Sparte* (Paris: Plon-Nourrit et Cie, 1906).
47. Juliette Adam, *Grecque* (Paris: Calmann-Lévy, 1879).
48. See, on this, Vincent Berdoulay, *La Formation de l'École Française de Géographie (1870–1914)* (Paris: Bibliothèque Nationale, 1981) and Anne Buttimer, *Society and milieu in the French geographic tradition* (Chicago: Rand McNally, 1971).
49. Andrews, "The Early life of Paul Vidal de la Blache", p.178.
50. Pavlos Nirvanas, "Emis kai i xeni", *Panathinaia* 15 (1907): 121.
51. Dragoumis, *Ellinikos politismos*, p.3.
52. Appadurai, "Disjuncture and difference", p.14.
53. Nikos Kazantzakis, *Report to Greco* (London: Faber and Faber, 1973 [1961]), p.174.
54. Kazantzakis, *Report to Greco*, p.175.

CHAPTER SIX

1. Yeoryios Drosinis, *Diiyimata kai anamnisis* (Athens: Kollaros, 1886), p.166. Originally published in *Estia* 477/19 (1885): 136–139, 151–154.

2. Ioannis Pantazidis, "Filoloyia, grammatoloyia, logotehnia", *Estia* 557/22 (1886): 545–548. Pantazidis's article is discussed by Tziovas in *The Nationism of the demoticists*, p.19.

3. See Martha Karpozilou, *Ta Ellinika ikoyeniaka filoloyika periodika* (Ioannina: Panepistimio Ioanninon, 1991), pp.236–240.

4. *Estia* 1/1 (1876), p.1. See also Papakostas's discussion of this article, *To Periodiko Estia*, p.36.

5. Drosinis, *Skorpia filla*, p.175.

6. Drosinis, *Skorpia filla*, p.26.

7. Grigorios Xenopoulos, *Stratiotika diiyimata* (Athens: Kasdonis, 1892).

8. Yeoryios K. Aspreas, *Politiki istoria tis neoteras Ellados, 1821–1928*, 3 vols. (Athens).

9. Yeoryios K. Aspreas, *Diiyimata apo tin katastrofi*, 2 vols. (Athens: Sakellariou, 1900).

10. As Tziovas seeks to do, for example, in *The Nationism of the demoticists*.

11. For an account of the importance of soldier narratives in the constitution of the nation, see Graham Dawson, *Soldier heroes: British adventure, empire and the imagining of masculinities* (London: Routledge, 1996).

12. Drosinis, *Skorpia filla*, p.167.

13. Timothy Brennan, "The National longing for form", in H.K. Bhabhka, ed., *Nation and narration*, pp.44–70 (p.53).

14. The Greek journal took its name from the French magazine, *Le Foyer*.

15. Tziovas, *The Nationism of the demoticists*, pp.102–103.

16. P.D. Mastrodimitris, ed. *O Zitianos tou Karkavitsa*, 3rd edn. (Athens: Kardamitsa, 1985), p.270.

17. Drosinis, *Skorpia filla*, p.179.

18. Alphonse Daudet, *I Vasilis en ti exoria,* trans. E. Sekiaris (Smyrna: 1880). Like many of Papadiamantis's translations, this has recently been republished (Athens: Estia, 1989).

19. See, generally, Dabrowski, *French landscape*.

20. See James McMillan, "La France profonde, modernity and national lidentity", in *Landscapes of France: Impressionism and its rivals*, ed. J. House (London: Hayward Gallery, 1995), pp.52–9.

21. For a comparison between this German movement and Greek ethographic writing, see Yeoryios Veloudis, "Vizyinos kai Auerbach", in *Mona-Ziga, deka neoellinika meletimata* (Athens: Gnosis, 1992), pp.37–42.

22. For a comparitive study of Papadiamantis with Pereda, see Robert Shannan Peckham, "O Papadiamantis kai i ennoia tou dendrou", *Ellinika* 44 (1994): 147–157 (pp.149–150).

23. See Mackridge, "The Textualization of place", p.153.

24. Papakostas, *To Periodiko Estia*, p.82.

25. E.M. Edmonds, ed. and trans. *Stories from Fairyland by George Drosines and the cup of tears and other tales by Aristotle Kourtidos* (London: T. Fisher Unwin, 1892).

26. Quoted in Tziovas, *The Nationism of the demoticists*, p.197.

27. See Kyriakidou-Nestoros, *Theoria tis ellinikis laografias*, p.96.

28. *Deltion tis Estias*, 27 March 1883, p.2. See Yeoryios Drosinis, *Odiporikai endiposis. Tris imerai en Tino* (Athens, 1883).

29. Beaton, *An Introduction to modern Greek literature*, pp.73–74.

30. See James Clifford, *Routes: travel and translation in the late twentieth century* (Cambridge, MA: Harvard University Press, 1997), p.23.

31. Joseph S. Wood, "'Build, therefore, your own world': the New England village as settlement ideal", *Annals of the Association of American Geographers* 81/1 (1991): 32–50 (pp.32, 34).
32. Raymond Williams, *The Country and the city* (London: Chatto and Windus, 1973), pp.165–181. See also Anderson, *Imagined communities*, p.6.
33. Dorson, *The British folklorists*, pp.220–221.
34. Peckham, "Memory and homelands", p.97.
35. Dorson, *The British folklorists*, p.223.
36. Poulantzas, *State, power and socialism*, p.114.
37. On urbanization, literacy, the circulation of periodicals, and the metaphorical reflection of these things in the prose literature of the 1890s, see Michalis Chryssanthopoulos, "Anticipating Modernism: Constructing a genre, a past, and a place", in *Greek Modernism and beyond: essays in honor of Peter Bien*, ed. D. Tziovas (London: Rowman and Littlefield, 1997), pp. 61–76 (pp.61–65). For a discussion of the ways in which experience of nature in nineteenth-century France – from the consumption of prints and pictures to rural excursions and country retreats – was rooted in a particular urban (Parisian) way of seeing, see Nicholas Green, *The Spectacle of nature: landscape and bourgeois culture in nineteenth-century France* (Manchester: Manchester University Press, 1990).
38. On *politismos* in nineteenth-century Greece, see Paul Sant Cassia, *The Making of the modern Greek family: marriage and exchange in nineteenth-century Athens* (Athens: Cambridge University Press, 1992), p.48.
39. Drosinis, *Diiyimata*, p.21.
40. Drosinis, *Diiyimata*, p.22.
41. Drosinis, *Diiyimata*, p.19.
42. Drosinis, *Diiyimata*, p.14.
43. Drosinis, *Diiyimata*, p.14.
44. Drosinis, *Diiyimata*, p.26.
45. Drosinis, *Diiyimata*, p.14.
46. Drosinis, *Diiyimata*, p.9.
47. Drosinis, *Diiyimata*, p.37.
48. Drosinis, *Diiyimata*, pp.38–39.
49. See James A. Boon, *Other tribes, other scribes: symbolic anthropology in the comparative study of culture* (Cambridge: Cambridge University Press, 1982).
50. See, in this context, Jill Dubisch, *In a Different place: pilgrimage, gender, and politics at a Greek island shrine* (Princeton: Princeton University Press, 1995), p.15.
51. Simon Pugh, "Loitering with intent", in *Reading landscape*, ed. S. Pugh (Manchester: Manchester University Press, 1990), pp. 145–160.
52. Drosinis, *Diiyimata*, p.16.
53. Drosinis, *Diiyimata*, p.27.
54. Green, *The Spectacle of nature*.
55. Quoted in Tziovas, *The Nationism of the demoticists*, p.196.
56. Anderson, *Imagined communities*, pp.6–7.
57. Quoted in Chris Bongie, *Islands and exiles: the Creole identities of post/colonial literature* (Stanford: Stanford University Press, 1998), p.21.
58. Fredric Jameson, *The Political unconscious: narrative as a socially symbolic act* (London: Routledge, 1981), p.79.
59. A discourse of islands was central to process of collective imagining that brought the modern nation-state into being. See generally Robert Shannan Peckham, "The Uncertain state of islands: nationalism and the discourse of islands", *Journal of Historical Geography* (in press).

60. Gillian Beer, "Discourses of the island", in *Literature and science as modes of expression*, ed. F. Amrine (Dordrecht and Boston: Kluwer Academic Publishers, 1989), pp.1–27 (p.21).

61. Alfred Russel Wallace, *Island life: or, the phenomena and causes of insular faunas and floras, including a revision and attempted solution of the problem of geological climates* (London: Macmillan & Co, 1880), pp.233–4.

62. See in this context, Jean-Jacques Rousseau's reflections on the island in the Fifth Walk of his *Reveries of the solitary walker*, trans. P. France (Harmondsworth: Penguin, 1979 [1782]), p.84.

63. Katherine Verdery, "Wither 'nation' and 'nationalism'?" in *Mapping the nation*, ed. G. Balakrishnan (London and New York: Verso 1996), pp. 226–234 (p.227).

64. Bongie, *Islands and exiles*, p.18. On the island as a utopia and dysutopia, see Fredric Jameson, "Of Islands and trenches: naturalization and the production of utopian discourse", *Diacritics* 7 (Summer 1977): 2–21.

65. Robert Louis Stevenson, *In the South Seas*, ed. N. Rennie (Harmondsworth: Penguin, 1998 [1896]), p.6.

66. John Richetti, *The English novel in history, 1700–1780* (London: Routledge, 1999), p.67.

67. Augustinos, *The Greeks of Asia Minor*, p.190.

68. See Politis, *Les Aspirations nationals de la Grèce*.

69. Alfred L. Wegener, *The Origins of continents and oceans*, trans. J.G.A. Skerl, introduction J. Evans (London: Methuen & Co, 1924), p.11, p.31.

70. Anthony Hope, *Phroso. A Romance* (London: Methuen, 1897).

71. See M. Green, *The Robinson Crusoe story* (Pennsylvania: Pennsylvania State University Press, 1990).

72. Richard H. Grove, *Green imperialism: colonial expansion, tropical island Edens and the origins of environmentalism, 1600–1860* (Cambridge: Cambridge University Press, 1995), pp.32–33.

73. Grove, *Green imperialism*, pp.32–33.

74. See Diana Loxley, *Problematic shores: the literature of islands* (New York: St. Martin's Press, 1990), p.xi. For a summary list of Robinsonnades, see p.178.

75. Loxley, *Problematic shores*, p.3.

76. Ion Dragoumis, *Samothraki (to nisi)* (Athens, 1909 [1907]), pp.19–20.

77. See Sofia Denisi, *Metafrasis mythistorimaton kai diiyimaton, 1830–1880. Isayoyiki meleti kai katagrafi* (Athens: Periplous, 1995), pp.29–32.

78. Psycharis, *Zoi kai agapi sti monaxia* (Athens: Estia, 1904), pp.293–326.

79. Mitsakis, *Afiyimata*, p.57.

80. Drosinis, *Skorpia filla*, p.69

81. Drosinis, *Diiyimata*, p.23.

82. Alphonse Daudet, *Letters from my windmill*, trans. F. Davies (Harmondsworth: Penguin, 1978), pp.33, 37, 45.

83. Daudet, *Letters*, p.220.

84. Daudet, *Letters*, p.33.

85. Mackridge, "The Textualization of place", p.149. On the "backwardness" of the Italian islands, see Daniel Pick, *Faces of degeneration: a European disorder, c. 1848–c.1918* (Cambridge: Cambridge University Press, 1989), p.114.

86. Argyris Eftaliotis, *Modern tales of the Greek islands*, trans. W.H.D. Rouse (London: Thomas Nelson and Sons, 1942 [1897]), p.9.

87. James Theodore Bent, *The Cyclades or life among the insular Greeks* (London, Longman, Green and Co 1885), pp.v–viii.

88. James Theodore Bent, "A Christening on Karpathos", *Macmillan's Magazine* LIV (1886): 199–205 (p.199).
89. Brailsford, *Macedonia*, pp.218–9.
90. Lawson, *Modern Greek folklore*, p.27. Recent anthroplogical studies of Greece, by amongst others Michael Herzfeld, Charles Stewart and Jill Dubisch, continue to privilege the island as a site for anthropological study. Significantly, in her study of Macedonia, Anastasia Karakasidou's avowed aim is to expose "ethnographic island(s) to the crosscurrents of history", *Fields of wheat*, p.xv.
91. Argyris Eftaliotis, *Nisiotikes istories*, ed. S. Kokkinis (Athens: Estia, n.d. [1894]), p.36.
92. Drosinis, *Diiyimata*, p.7.
93. Vizyinos's short stories were almost certainly written in London during a visit there in the 1880s. A collection of Vizyinos's poetry was also published in London in 1883.
94. Discussed by Mackridge, "The Textualization of place", p.154.
95. Compare this incident to Vizyinos's short story in which two Greeks travel to the Harz mountains.
96. See Mackridge, "The Textualization of place", p.155.
97. Eftaliotis, *Nisiotikes istories*, pp.34–35.
98. Declan Kiberd, "Modern Ireland: Postcolonial or European?", in *Not on any map: essays on postcoloniality and cutural nationalism*, ed. S. Murray (Exeter: University of Exeter Press, 1997), pp.81–100 (p.83).
99. *Margarita Stefa* was not published in book form until 1906. For a discussion of this preface, see Mackridge, "The Textualization of place", p.156.
100. Drosinis, *Skorpia filla*, p.11.
101. Drosinis, *Diiyimata*, p.14.
102. *My Mother's sins and other stories by Georgios Vizyenos*, trans. W.F. Wyatt (Hanover and London: University Press of New England, 1988), p.66.
103. For a comparative study of the ways in which the Celtic Fringe was both celebrated and "colonized", see Hechter, *Internal colonialism*.
104. See, generally, Henrika Kuklick, *The Savage within: the social history of British anthropology, 1885–1945* (Cambridge: Cambridge University Press, 1991).
105. Pick, *Faces of degeneration*, p.40.
106. Pick, *Faces of degeneration*, p.126.
107. Drosinis, *Diiyimata*, p.9.
108. Yeoryios Drosinis, *Ersi* (Athens: Sideris, 1922), p.83.
109. Johannes Fabian, *Time and the other: how anthropology makes its object* (New York: Columbia University Press, 1983), p.143.
110. On this, see Peckham, "The exoticism of the familiar".
111. "Epistolai tou Stanley", *Estia Ikonografimeni* 1/4 (1890): 59–60.
112. Andreas Rigopoulos quoted in Varouxakis, "The idea of 'Europe'", p.37.
113. Although not published in novel form until 1916. See Ioannis Kondylakis, *O Patouchas* (Athens: Almopos, n.d.).
114. See, for example, Ioannis Dambergis's collection, *I Krites mou*, which was serialized in the journal *Evdomada* in 1898.
115. Jean Baudrillard, *Symbolic exchange and death*, trans. I. Hamilton Grant, intr. M. Gane (London: Sage, 1993 [1976]), p.126.
116. This story was translated into English in 1897.
117. Karkavitsas, *Diiyimata*, p.90.

118.Jina Politi, "I Mythistorimatiki katergasia tis ideoloyias: analysi tis *Lygeris tou Andrea Karkavitsa*", in *Sinomilontas me to kimena* (Athens: Agras, 1996 [1981]), pp.63–127.

119.Stewart, *Demons and devils*, p.xv.

120.Artemis Leontis, "The Diaspora of the novel", *Diaspora* 2/1 (1992): 131–146 (p.136).

121.Tziovas is here commenting on Leontis's article; "Heteroglossia and the defeat of regionalism", p.117.

122.Quoted in Clifford, *Routes*, p.24.

123.Anthony Giddens, *The Nation-state and violence* (Cambridge: Polity Press, 1985), p.120.

124.Verdery, "Wither 'nation' and 'nationalism'?", p.230.

125.Verdery, "Wither 'nation' and 'nationalism'?", p.229.

126.See the discussion of Maryon McDonald's thesis in *"We are not French!': language, culture and identity in Brittany* (1989), cited in Danforth, *The Macedonian conflict*, p.21.

127.This is Marilyn Ivy's summary, see her chapter, "Ghostlier demarcations: textual phantasm and the origins of Japanese nativist ethnology", in *Culture/contexture: explorations in anthropology and literary studies*, eds. E.V. Daniel and J.M. Peck (Berkeley: University of California Press, 1996), pp.296–322 (p.297).

CHAPTER SEVEN

1. See Fanis Kakridis, "I Yermaniki diahirisi tis ellinikis klironomias", in *Enas neos kosmos yennietai*, pp.25–39 (pp.38–39).

2. Gehrke, "Anazitontas ti hora ton ellinon", p.68.

3. Quoted from George Tatham in David N. Livingstone, *The Geographical tradition: episodes in the history of a contested enterprise* (Oxford: Blackwell, 1992), p.141.

4. Gehrke, "Anazitontas ti hora ton ellinon", p.72.

5. Livingstone, *The Geographical tradition*, p.141.

6. Gehrke, "Anazitontas ti hora ton ellinon", p.77.

7. Eliza Marian Butler, *The Tyranny of Greece over Germany: a study of the influence exercised by Greek art and poetry over the great German writers of the eighteenth, nineteenth and twentieth centuries* (Cambridge: Cambridge University Press, 1935).

8. Philip L. Khol and Clare Fawcett, eds. *Nationalism, politics and the practice of archaeology* (Cambridge: Cambridge University Press, 1996).

9. See Neil Asher Silberman, ed. *Between past and present: archaeology, ideology and nationalism in the modern Middle East* (New York: Holt, 1989), Bruce G. Trigger, "Alternative archaeologies: nationalist, colonialist, imperialist", *Man* 19/3 (1984): 355–370 (pp.358–360) and *A History of archaeological thought* (Cambridge: Cambridge University Press, 1990), pp.174–186.

10. Stephen Shennan, ed., *Archaeological approaches to cultural identity* (London and New York: Routledge 1994 [1989]), p.2.

11. Trigger, *A History of archaeological thought*, p.187.

12. Ulrich Veit, "Ethnic concepts in German prehistory: a case study on the relationship between cultural identity and archaeological objectivity", in S. Shennan, *Archaeological approaches*, pp.35–56 (pp.35–42 on Kossinna).

13. K. Sklenár, "The History of archaeology in Czechoslovakia", in *Towards a history of archaeology*, ed. G. Daniel (London and New York: Thames and Hudson, 1981), pp.150–158 and *Archaeology in Central Europe: the first 500*

years, trans. I. Lewitová, foreword S. Piggott (Leicester and New York: Leicester University Press, St Martin's Press), pp.63–69, *passim*. See also Barbara G. Scott, "Archaeology and national identity: the Norwegian example", *Scandinavian Studies* 68/3: 321–342.

14. Michael Herzfeld, *A Place in history: social and monumental time in a Cretan town* (Princeton: Princeton University Press, 1991), p.9.
15. Trigger, *A History of archaeological thought*, p.185.
16. Petrakos, quoted in Athanasios E. Kalpaxis, *Arhaioloyia kai politiki II: i anaskafi tou naou tis Artemidos (Kerkyra 1911)* (Rethymno: Panepistimiakes Ekdosis Kritis, 1993), p.19.
17. Quoted in Kalpaxis, *Arhaioloyia kai politiki II*, p.19. See also Skopetea, *To 'Protipo vassilio'*, p.196.
18. See Loukaki, "Whose genius loci?"
19. Kokkou, *Merimna yia tis arhaiotities*, pp.61–68.
20. On this, see Athanasios Kalpaxis, "Epirroes tis galloyermanikis antiparathesis tou 19ou aiona stin kataskevi tis ikonas tis arhais Elladas", in *Enas neos kosmos yennietai*, pp.41–58.
21. Neil Asher Silberman, *Digging for God and country* (New York: Knopf, 1982).
22. Trigger, *A History of archaeological thought*, p.150–155.
23. Ioannis D. Kondylakis, *I Athlii ton Athinon*, ed. Y. Gotsi, 2 vols. (Athens: Nefeli, 1999), vol.1, pp.217–8.
24. See Athanasios E. Kalpaxis, *Arhaioloyia kai politiki I: Samiaka arhaioloyika, 1850–1914* (Rethymno: Panepistimiakes Ekdosis Kritis, 1990), p.22, *passim*.
25. Quoted in Augustinos, *Consciousness and history*, p.30.
26. Drosinis, *Ersi*, p.332.
27. Rosalind Williams, *Notes on the underground: an essay on technology, society, and the imagination* (Cambridge, MA: MIT, 1990), p.38.
28. Konstantinos Mitsopoulos, *Yeoloyiki istoria tis ellinikis horas* (Athens: 1901), p.10. On the close relationship between archaeology and geology, see John A. Gifford and George Rapp, eds. *Archaeological geology* (New Haven and London: Yale University Press, 1985).
29. Koulouri, *Istoria kai yeografia*, p.364.
30. Evangelos Kofos, "National heritage and national identity in nineteenth and twentieth-century Macedonia", in Blinkhorn and Veremis, eds., *Modern Greece: nationalism and nationality*, pp.103–141 (p.107). On the relationship between archaeology and folklore generally, see Skopetea, *To 'Protipo vasilio'*, pp.190–204.
31. Steven Runciman, *The Fall of Constantinople 1453* (Cambridge: Cambridge University Press, 1965), p.xiii.
32. See Kokkou, *Merimna yia tis arhaiotites*, pp.283–286; Fotis Dimitrakopoulos, *Vyzandio kai neoelliniki dianoisi sta mesa tou dekatou enatou aionas* (Athens: Kastaniotis, 1996).
33. During the last decades of the century there was growing interest in Byzantine archaeology. The Christian Archaeological Society was founded in 1888, although the Byzantine Museum in Athens was not founded until 1914 and officially opened in 1930; see Kokkou, *Merimna yia tis arhaiotites*, pp.283–286.
34. Anthony Smith, "Gastronomy or geology? The role of nationalism in the reconstruction of nations", *Nations and Nationalism* 1/1 (1995): 3–23 (p.15).
35. Quoted in Kalpaxis, *Arhaioloyia kai politiki I*, p.21.

36. Herzfeld, *Ours once more*, pp.10–11. On archaeology and folklore, see Kyriakidou-Nestoros, *Theoria tis ellinikis laografias*, pp.91–97.
37. Juroslav Malina and Zdenek Vasicek, *Archaeology yesterday and today: the development of archaeology in the sciences and humanities* (Cambridge: Cambridge University Press, 1990), p.59.
38. Williams, *Notes on the underground*, p.50.
39. A. Orlandos quoted in Herzfeld, *Ours once more*, p.11.
40. Kyriakidou-Nestoros, *Theoria tis ellinikis laografias*, p.152.
41. Kokkou, *Merimna yia tis arhaiotities stin Ellada kai to prota mousia*, p.299.
42. Quoted in Kyriakidou-Nestoros, *Theoria tis ellinikis laografias*, p.157.
43. Quoted in Tziovas, *The Nationism of the demoticists*, p.196.
44. I.A. Sareyannis, *Scholia ston Kavafi* (Athens: Ikaros, [1964] 1973), p.42.
45. For a cursory review of archaeological themes in English literature, see Alison Girdwood, "The imaginative response to archaeology in nineteenth and early twentieth-century literature", *Archaeological Review from Cambridge* 3 (1984), pp.29–37. For a more detailed discussion, see Wendy Lesser, *The Life below the ground: a study of the subterranean in literature and history* (London: Faber and Faber, 1987).
46. Soutsos, *Leandros*, p.21.
47. Alexandros Rizos Rangavis, *Précis d'une histoire de la littérature néo-Hellénique* (Berlin: S. Calvary, 1877), pp.177–183.
48. William M. Calder and David A. Traill, eds., *Myth, scandal and history: the Heinrich Schliemann controversy* (Detroit: Wayne State University Press, 1986); David A. Traill, *Schliemann of Troy: Treasure and Deceit* (London: John Murray, 1995).
49. David Traill notes that reviewers of Schliemann's book *Ilios* in 1881 criticized the author "for drawing on quotations from the *Iliad* to illustrate the artefacts and buildings of the 'burnt city' when he acknowledged that that stratum had been buried before Homer was born"; *Schliemann of Troy*, pp.207–208.
50. Williams, *Notes on the underground*, pp.1–16.
51. As Williams remarks, crucial events in the novel take place underground in sewers, *Notes on the underground*, p.47.
52. Alexandros Papadiamantis, *Apanta*, ed. N.D. Triantafillopoulos, 5 vols. (Athens: Domos, 1981) II, p.347.
53. On the issues raised by syncretism in Greece, in particular, see Charles Stewart, "Syncretism as a dimension of nationalist discourse in modern Greece", in *Syncretism/anti-syncretism: the politics of religious synthesis*, eds. C. Stewart and R. Shaw (London: Routledge, 1994), pp.127–144.
54. Sant Cassia, *The Making of the modern Greek family*, p.244.
55. Papadiamantis, *Apanta*, II, p.161.
56. Yeoryia Farinou-Malamatari, *Afiyimatikes tehnikes ston Papadiamanti, 1887–1910* (Athens: Kedros, 1987), pp.108–110.
57. Papadiamantis, *Apanta*, II, p.155.
58. Papadiamantis, *Apanta*, II, p.160.
59. Papadiamantis, *Apanta*, II, pp.155, 161.
60. W.J.T. Mitchell, "Imperial landscape", in *Landscape and power*, pp.5–35 (p.5).
61. Thomas M. Greene, *The Light of Troy: imitation and discovery in Renaissance poetry* (New Haven and London: Yale University Press, 1982), pp.92–93.
62. The rock in Papadiamantis's story as a symbolic landmark recalls Dan Sperber's observations on the metaphorical expression "a landmark" used by the Ndembu to designate symbols; *Rethinking symbolism*, trans. A. L. Morton (Cambridge: Cambridge University Press, 1975), p.33.

63. In the reflecting surface of the garden, there are perhaps echoes, too, of another Greek poet, Dionysios Solomos, whom Kostis Palamas once described as the poet of the garden. The description of the garden and the sea recalls the passage in "The Cretan", a poem, like Papadia- mantis's "The Woman with the Black Headscarf", about near-drowning and loss, where the sea is likened to a garden; Dionysios Solomos, *Apanta*, vol.1, *piimata*, ed. L. Politis, rev. edn. (Athens: Ikaros 1986 [1960]), p.199.

64. Tziovas, *The Nationism of the demoticists*, p.407. The notion here of "depth" is taken from Foucault; see Dimitris Tziovas, "The Organic discourse of nationistic demoticism: a tropological approach", in *The Text and its margins: post-structuralist approaches to twentieth-century Greek literature*, eds. M. Alexiou and V. Lambropoulos (New York: Pella, 1985), pp.253–277 (p.258).

65. Theodore Ziolkowski, *German Romanticism and its institutions* (Princeton: Princeton University Press, 1990), p.26.

66. The theme of mining recurs in Greek fiction at the end of the last century. See, for example, Mitsakis's story that focuses on the gold mines of Lavrion, "Eis Athnaios chrisothiras"(1890), in *Afiyimata*, pp.21–64.

67. On Vizyinos and German culture see, generally, William F. Wyatt, "Viziinos in Germany", *Modern Greek Studies Yearbook* 9 (1993): 281–296.

68. On Goethe's interest in geology and his friendship with Johann Voigt, who was a student of the great geologist Werner at the Freiburg Mining Academy where Paschalis is a student, and with whom Goethe visited the Harz, see Nicholas Boyle, *Goethe; the poet and the age* (Oxford: Oxford University Press, 1991), vol.1, p.336 and p.347.

69. For an analysis of Goethe's engagement with Homer and the Greeks, see, classically, H. Trevelyan, *Goethe and the Greeks* (Cambridge: Cambridge University Press, 1941).

70. See Peckham "Memory and homelands", p.105.

71. Ziolkowski, *German Romanticism*, p.20.

72. Ziolkowski, *German Romanticism*, p.22.

73. Vizyinos, *My Mother's sin*, p.124.

74. Boyle, *Goethe*, p.6.

75. Smith, *National identity*, p.9.

76. Meinig, *The Interpretation of ordinary landscapes*, p.3.

77. Timothy F. Mitchell, *Art and science in German landscape painting, 1770–1840* (Oxford: Clarendon Press, 1993), p.149.

78. Suzanne L. Marchand, "The Excavations at Olympia, 1868–1881: an episode in Greco-German cultural relations", in *Greek society in the making, 1863–1913: realities, symbols and visions*, ed. P. Carabott (London: King's College London, Centre for Hellenic Studies), pp.73–85 (p.78). See also, Suzanne L. Marchand, *Down from Olympus: archaeology and philhellenism in Germany, 1750–1970* (Princeton: Princeton University Press, 1996).

79. Heinrich Schliemann, *Ilios: the city and the country of the Trojans: the results of researches and discoveries on the site of Troy and throughout the Troad in the years 1871–1879* (London: John Murray, 1880), p.5.

80. Traill, *Schliemann of Troy*, pp.209–214 (p.211). Schliemann's identifica- tion of the swastika symbol which he discovered on artefacts at Hissarlik as Aryan was later used by German nationalists and Nazis in their endeavours to prove the nation's Aryan descent. On this see Malcolm

Quinn, *The Swastika: constructing the symbol* (London: Routledge, 1994), pp.24–49.

81. J. Hutchinson and Anthony Smith, eds. *Nationalism* (Oxford: Oxford University Press, 1994), p.5.
82. J.R. William, *Goethe's Faust* (London: Allen and Unwin, 1988), p.171.
83. J.J. Chapman, quoted in Herzfeld, *Ours once more*, p.5.
84. Rodd, *The Customs and lore*, p.xiii. Birgit Olsen has further explored the German appropriation of the Greek tales translated by Hahn, see "I Yermanoprepia ton ellinikon paramithion sto sillogi tou J.G. Hahn", *Ellinika* 41 (1990): 79–93.
85. Jacqueline Rose, *States of fantasy* (Oxford: Clarendon Press, 1996), p.34.
86. Ziolkowski, *German Romanticism*, pp.20–21.
87. Vizyinos, *My Mother's sin*, p.106.
88. Vizyinos, *My Mother's sin*, p.136.
89. David Lowenthal, *The Past is a foreign country* (Cambridge: Cambridge University Press, 1985), pp.252–253. For an account of Freud's engagement with archaeology, see Donald Kuspit, "A Mighty metaphor: the analogy of archaeology and psychoanalysis", in *Sigmund Freud and art: his personal collection of antique*, eds. L. Gamwell and R. Wells (London: Thames and Hudson/ State University of New York/Freud Museum, 1989), pp.131–151. See also Carl E. Schorsek, "Freud: the psychoarchaeology of civilizations", in *The Cambridge companion to Freud*, ed. J. Neu (Cambridge: Cambridge University Press, 1992), pp.8–24.
90. Peter Gay, *Freud: a life for our time* (London: Dent, 1988), p.16.
91. Gay, *Freud*, p.172.
92. Gay, *Freud*, p.16.
93. Wendy Booting and J. Keith Davies, "Freud's library and an appendix of texts related to antiquities", in Gamwell and Wells, eds. *Sigmund Freud and art*, pp.184–192.
94. Vizyinos, *My Mother's sins*, p.121.
95. Rachel Laudan, *From Mineralogy to geology: the foundations of a science, 1650–1830* (Chicago: University of Chicago Press, 1987), pp.111–112.
96. Mitchell, *Art and science*, pp.2, 6.
97. Quinn, *The Swastika*, pp.29–30.
98. Vizyinos, *My Mother's sin*, p.145.
99. Dominic LaCapra, *Rethinking intellectual history: texts, contexts, language* (Ithaca: Cornell University Press, 1983), p.45.
100. Drosinis, *Skorpia filla*, p.444.
101. Ziolkowski, *German Romanticism*, p.22.
102. V. Athanasopoulos, *I Mythi tis zois kai tou ergou tou Y. Viyzinou* (Athens: Kardamitsa, 1992), pp.26–27.
103. See Mark P. Leone et al., "Toward a critical archaeology", *Current Anthropology* 28/3 (1987): 283–302.
104. Byron's remark was recorded by E.J. Trelawny. Quoted in Richard Stoneman, ed. *A Literary companion to travel in Greece* (Harmondsworth: Penguin, 1984), p.35.
105. Thanasis Maskaleris, *Kostis Palamas* (New York: Twayne Publishers, 1972), p.24.
106. Andreas Karkavitsas, *O Arheologos* (Athens: Pella, n.d.), p.16.
107. Karkavitsas, *O Arheologos*, p.18.
108. The trope of "weaving" recurs in nationalist rhetoric and in writing about nationalism, see Greenfeld, *Nationalism*, p.40.

109.Jina Politi, "The Tongue and the pen: a reading of Karkavítsas's *O Arhe-ológos*", in *The Greek novel AD 1–1985*, ed. R. Beaton (London: Croom Helm, 1988), pp.42–53 (p.42).

110.Politi, "The Tongue and the pen", p.44.

111.Quinn, *The Swastika*, p.26.

112.Demetrios Loukatos, "Archeofolklore", in *Folklore in the modern world*, ed. R. M. Dawson (The Hague: Mouton, 1978), pp.175–182.

113.Quoted in William Wyatt, "Andreas Karkavitsas's *The Beggar* and *The Archaeologist*", *Modern Greek Studies Yearbook* 1 (1985): 114–130 (p.128).

114.Kostis Palamas, *The Twelve lays of the gipsy*, trans. G. Thomson (London: Lawrence and Wishart, 1969), p.117.

115.Christopher Evans, "Digging with the pen: novel archaeolgies and literary traditions", in *Interpretative archaeology*, ed. C. Tilley (Oxford: Berg, 1993), pp. 417–447 (p.417).

116.Christopher Tilley, ed., *Material culture and text: the art of ambiguity* (London: Routledge, 1991), p.77.

117.Ian Hodder, *Reading the past: current approaches to interpretation in archaeology* (Cambridge: Cambridge University Press, 1991) and Ian Hodder *et al.*, eds., *Interpreting archaeology: finding meaning in the past* (London: Routledge, 1995).

CHAPTER EIGHT

1. Thomas Holdich, "The Use of practical geography illustrated by recent frontier operations", *Geographical Journal* 13/5 (1899): 465–480 (p.467).

2. Curzon, *Frontiers*, p.5.

3. On Curzon's arguments about the centrality of geography to Oriental Studies, see Said, *Orientalism*, pp.213–216. On Curzon's later involvement in Greece's Asia Minor catastrophe, see Llewellyn Smith, *Ionian vision*, pp.64–6, *passim*. Quotation, Curzon, *Frontiers*, p.54.

4. Curzon, *Frontiers*, p.6.

5. Alan Palmer, *The Decline and fall of the Ottoman Empire* (London: John Murray, 1992), pp.200–211.

6. Marion I. Newbigin, *Geographical aspects of Balkan problems in their relation to the Great European War* (London: Constable & Co, 1915), pp.19–20.

7. Edward A. Freeman, "Geographical aspects of the Eastern Question", *The Fortnightly Review* 122 (1877): 73–87 (p.81).

8. On the relative danger and safety of travel to Greece at the end of the nineteenth century, see Peckham, "The Exoticism of the familiar".

9. Other titles include: George W. Steevens, *With the Conquering Turk: the confessions of a Bashi-Bazouk* (Edinburgh: W. Blackwood, 1897), Henri Turot, *L'Insurrection crétoise et la guerre gréco-turque* (Paris: Hachette, 1898) and Henry W. Nevinson, *Scenes in the thirty days war between Greece and Turkey, 1897* (London: J.M. Dent and Co, 1898).

10. Victor Bérard, *La Macédoine* (Paris: Calmann Lévy, 1897), p.15.

11. The 1903 Ilinden uprising was so named after the Slavic for St Elijah's day on which the insurrection took place; see Richard J. Crampton, *A Short history of modern Bulgaria* (Cambridge: Cambridge University Press, 1987), p.48.

12. W.K. Rose, *With the Greeks in Thessaly* (London: Methuen and Co, 1897), pp.25–47. For a full account of the Macedonian struggle, see Dakin, *The Greek struggle in Macedonia*.

13. Brailsford, *Macedonia*, pp.x–xi.

14. Quoted in Dimitris Livanios, "'Conquering souls': nationalism and Greek guerrilla warfare in Ottoman Macedonia, 1904–1908", *Byzantine and Modern Greek Studies* 23 (1999): 195–221 (p.196).
15. For a discussion of Brailsford's map, see Wilkinson, *Maps and politics*, pp.139–143.
16. Konstantinos Th. Dimaras, *Konstantinos Paparrigopoulos: i epohi, i zoi, to ergo tou* (Athens: Morfotiko Idrima Ethnikis Trapezis, 1986), p.335.
17. See M.S. Anderson, *The Eastern Question 1774–1923: a study in international relations* (London: Macmillan, 1966), pp.178–219. For a detailed analysis of Greece's part in the Eastern Crisis, see Evangelos Kofos, *Greece and the Eastern Crisis* (Thessaloniki: Institute for Balkan Studies, 1975).
18. Wilkinson, *Maps and politics*, p.64.
19. Papakostas, *To Periodiko Estia*, p.70.
20. Anonymous, *Slavs and Turks: the borderlands of Islam in Europe* (London: The Leisure Hour Office, 1876), p.1.
21. Kofos, "National heritage and national identity", p.137, note 10.
22. Karakasidou, *Fields of wheat*, p.100.
23. Karakasidou, *Fields of wheat*, p.15.
24. Wilkinson, *Maps and politics*, p.45.
25. Wilkinson, *Maps and politics*, p.64.
26. Dimaras, *Konstantinos Paparrigopoulos*, p.335.
27. Dimaras, *Konstantinos Paparrigopoulos*, p.335.
28. Wilkinson, *Maps and politics*, p.68.
29. Kofos, *Greece and the Eastern Crisis*, p.194. Stanford's map, however, was dismissed by many cartographers, such as Karl Sax. On Kiepert's revised "ethnocratic" map of 1878, which was more favourable to the Greeks, see Wilkinson, *Maps and politics*, pp.74–75.
30. Wilkinson, *Maps and politics*, p.71.
31. Wilkinson, *Maps and politics*, pp.120–125.
32. Jovan Cvijić, *La Péninsule Balkanique: géographie humaine* (Paris: A. Colin, 1918).
33. T.W. Freeman, *The Geographer's craft* (Manchester and New York: Manchester University Press and Barnes and Noble, 1967), pp.72–84.
34. Jovan Cvijić, "The Geographical distribution of the Balkan peoples", *Geographical Review* V/5 (1918a): 345–361 (p.345).
35. Jovan Cvijić, "The Zones of civilization of the Balkan Peninsula", *Geographical Review* V/6 (1918b): 470–482 (p.470).
36. Wilkinson, *Maps and politics*, pp.163–165.
37. Peter J. Taylor takes Cvijić's project as exemplary: "There is probably no other example of a man influencing national definition so completely as Cvijić but this extreme case clarifies the general process", *Political geography: world-economy, nation-state and locality* (Harlow: Longman, 1993 [1985]), p.212.
38. See, for example, V. Colocotronis, *La Macédoine et l'hellénisme: étude historique et ethnologique* (Paris: Berger-Levrault, 1919) and A. Ischirkov, *Les Confins occidentaux des terres Bulgares* (Lausanne: Librairie Nouvelle, 1916).
39. Karakasidou, *Fields of wheat*, p.16.
40. Augustinos, *The Greeks of Asia Minor*, p.190.
41. See M. Monmonier, *How to lie with maps* (Chicago: University of Chicago Press, 1991) and Black, *Maps and politics*, p.48.
42. Wilkinson, *Maps and politics*, p.316.

43. Wilkinson, *Maps and politics*, p.316. For a Greek discussion of the ideological context of cartographic representations, see Vangelis Pantazis, *Hartes kai ideoloyies* (Athens: Kalvos, 1989).
44. Mackridge and Yannakakis, eds., *Ourselves and others*, p.175.
45. Koulouri, *Istoria kai yeografia*, pp.28–29.
46. Koulouri, *Dimensions idéologiques*, p.416. This was a position which he repeated, for example, in his *Political geography* of 1878.
47. The Society was actually dissolved in 1907, but re-established in 1919 by P.D. Kaloyeropoulos.
48. Holdich, "The Use of practical geography".
49. B. Hudson, "The New Geography and the New Imperialism, 1870–1918", *Antipode* 9/2 (1977): 12–19 (p.13).
50. D.R. Stoddart, "Geography and war: the 'New Geography' and the 'New Army' in England, 1899–1914", *Political Geography* 11/1 (1992): 87–99.
51. I. Kokidis, *Sratiotiki yeografia tis Ellados. Meta sindomos exetaseos tis Evropis pros ta stratiotikas epihirisis* (Athens: 1891).
52. Taylor, *Political geography*, p.163. For more detailed discussions of the differences between frontiers and boundaries, see John R.V. Prescott, *The Geography of boundaries and frontiers* (London: Hutchinson).
53. Koulouri, *Dimensions idéologiques*, pp.428–431.
54. Friedrich Ratzel, "The Territorial growth of states", *Scottish Geographical Magazine* 12 (1896): 351–361 (p.356).
55. See Skopetea, *To 'Protipo vasilio'*, pp.273–286. There are similarities here with Russia's inheritance of the Byzantine legacy and her civilizing mission eastwards, see Bassin, "Russian geographers and the 'national question', pp.112–133.
56. Bassin, "Imperialim and the nation space".
57. The second, definitive, edition of Paparrigopoulos's work appeared from 1885–1887.
58. Kitromilides, "On the Intellectual content of Greek nationalism", p.28.
59. Voutiras, *Apanta*, vol.1, p.107.
60. Koulouri, *Dimensions idéologiques*, p.445.
61. Koulouri, *Dimensions idéologiques*, p.443.
62. On the influence of translated German geographies in Greece, see Koulouri, *Dimensions idéologiques*, pp.411, 430.
63. Koulouri, *Dimensions idéologiques*, p.429.
64. Koulouri, *Dimensions idéologiques*, p.425.
65. Koulouri, *Dimensions idéologiques*, p.446.
66. Danforth, *The Macedonian conflict*, p.177.
67. Peter Vujakovic, "Drawing on a Balkan dream", *Geographical* LXV/11 (1993): 38–40 (p.40).
68. J.B. Harley, "Deconstructing the map", in *Writing worlds: discourse, text and metaphor in the representation of landscape*, eds. T.J. Barnes and J.S. Duncan (London and New York: Routledge, 1992), pp.231–247 (pp. 232–233), for a study in Greek, see Pantazis, *Hartes kai ideoloyies*.
69. Stratis Myrivilis, *Ap'tin Ellada. Taxidiotika* (Athens: Estia, 1949), p.13.
70. Thongchai Winichakul, quoted in Anderson, *Imagined communities*, p.173.

CONCLUSION

1. Denis Cosgrove, "Introduction: mapping meaning", in *Mappings*, ed. D. Cosgrove (London: Reaktion Books, 1999), pp.1–23 (p.1).
2. Cosgrove, "Introduction", p.2.

3. Bérard, *La Turquie et l'hellénisme*, p.240.
4. See, in this context, Jean Baudrillard's comment "it is the map that precedes the territory" which is discussed in James Corner, "The Agency of mapping: speculation, critique and invention", in Cosgrave, ed., *Mappings*, pp.213–252 (p.213, p.222).
5. Psycharis, *To Taxidi mou*, p.77.
6. Mazower, *Greece and the inter-war economic crisis*, p.43.
7. Thomas Doulis, *George Theotokas* (New York: Twayne, 1975), p.18.
8. Yorgos Theotokas, *Free spirit*, trans. S.G. Stavrou, *Modern Greek Studies Yearbook 2* (1986): 153–200 (p.155).
9. On the map and the aeroplane, see Dimitris Tziovas, "The Politics of metaphor and the rhetoric of consensus: Europe in the *Free spirit* of George Theotokas", in *Greece and Europe*, pp.70–82 (pp.76–77).
10. Bhabha, *The Location of culture*, p.236.
11. Ernest Renan "What is a nation?", trans. M. Thom, in *Nation and narration*, pp.8–22 (p.11).
12. Michel Fais, *Aftoviografia enos vivliou* (Athens: Kastaniotis, 1994 [1989]).
13. Thomas, *Colonialism's culture*, p.4.
14. Bhabha, *The Location of culture*, p.2.
15. Bhabha, *The Location of culture*, p.35.
16. Fais, *Aftoviografia enos vivliou*, p.79.

Bibliography

Adam, Juliette (née Lamber) 1879 *Grecque* (Paris: Calmann-Lévy)

Adams, Ann Jensen 1994 "Competing communities in the 'great bog of Europe': identity and seventeenth-century Dutch landscape painting", in *Landscape and power*, ed. W.J.T. Mitchell (Chicago: University of Chicago Press), pp.35–76.

Agnew, John, ed. 1997 [1994] *Political geography: a reader*, rev. edn (London: Arnold). 1987 *Place and politics: the geographical mediation of state and society* (Boston: Allen and Unwin).

Agnew, John A. and James S. Duncan, eds. 1989 *The Power of place: bringing together geographical and sociological imaginations* (Boston: Unwin Hyman).

Agriandoni, Christina 1986 *I Aparhes tis ekviomihanisis stin Ellada ton 19⁰ aiona* (Athens: Istoriko Arhio Emboriki Trapeza tis Ellados).

Agulhon, Maurice 1982 [1970] *The Republic in the village: the people of the Var from the French Revolution to the Second Republic*, trans. J. Lloyd (Paris and Cambridge: Éditions de la Maison des Sciences de l'Homme and Cambridge University Press).

Alexander, John C. 1982 "The Klefts of the Morea: an historical essay", in *New trends in modern Greek historiography*, eds. L. Makrakis and P.N. Diamandouros (MGSA Occasional Papers), pp.32–33.

Alexander, Katerina Gardikas 1995 "Centre and periphery in the 1874 Greek elections: competition for political control in Gortynia", *Balkan Studies* 36/1: 11–30.

Alexiou, Margaret and V. Lambropoulos, eds. 1985 *The Text and its margins: post-structuralist approaches to twentieth-century Greek literature* (New York: Pella).

Allen, G. 1880 "Geology and history", *Fraser's Magazine* XXI: 769–780.

Amrine, F., ed. 1989 *Literature and science as modes of expression* (Dordrecht and Boston: Kluwer Academic Publishers).

Anderson, Benedict 1991 [1983] *Imagined communities: reflections on the origin and spread of nationalism*, rev. edn. (London and New York: Verso).

Anderson, M.S. 1966 *The Eastern Question, 1774–1923: a study in international relations* (London: Macmillan).

Andrews, Howard F. 1986 "The Early Life of Paul Vidal de la Blanche and the makings of modern geography", *Transactions of the Institute of British Geographers* 11: 174–182.

Anonymous 1876 *Slavs and Turks: the borderlands of Islam in Europe* (London: The Leisure Hour Office).

Anonymous 1982 *Elliniki nomarhia iti logos peri eleftherias. Filoloyiki apomnimiosi*, eds. N.A. Veis and M. Sigouros, intr. G. Valetas, 3rd edn. (Athens: Aposperitis).

Appadurai, Arjun 1990 "Disjuncture and difference in the global cultural economy", *Public Culture* 2: 1–24.

Armstrong, John A. 1982 *Nations before nationalism* (Chapel Hill, NC: University of North Carolina Press).

Aspreas, Yeoryios K. 1900 *Diiyimata apo tin katastrofi*, 2 vols. (Athens: Sakellariou). 1922–30 *Politiki istoria tis neoteras Ellados, 1821–1928*, 3 vols. (Athens).

Athanasopoulos, V. 1992 *I Mythi tis zois kai tou ergou tou Y. Vizyinou* (Athens: Kardamitsa).

Athanassoglou-Kallmyer, Nina 1989 *French images from the Greek War of Independence, 1821–1830: art and politics under the Restoration* (New Haven, CT and London: Yale University Press).

Augustinos, Gerasimos 1992 *The Greeks of Asia Minor: confession, community, and ethnicity in the nineteenth century* (Kent, OH: Kent State University Press). 1977 *Consciousness and history: nationalist critics of Greek society, 1897–1914* (Boulder, CO: East European Quarterly).

Avramea, Anna 1985 "Maps of the Aegean", in *Maps and map-makers of the Aegean*, trans. G. Cox and J. Solman, eds. V. Sphyroeras, A. Avramea and S. Asdrahas (Athens: Olklos), pp.22–32.

Bagehot, Walter 1872 *Physics and politics or thoughts on the application of the principles of 'natural selection' and 'inheritance' to political society* (London: Henry S. King).

Baker, Derek, ed. 1976 *The Orthodox churches and the West* (Oxford: Blackwell).

Bakounakis, Nikos 1991 *The Fandasma tis Norma: i ipodohi tou melodramatos ston elliniko horo to 19° aiona* (Athens: Kastaniotis).

Baladié, Raoul 1974 "Strabon dans la vie et l'oeuvre de Coray", *O Eranistis* 11: 412–442.

Balakrishnan, Gopal, ed. 1996 *Mapping the nation* (London and New York: Verso).

Barnes, T.J. and James S. Duncan, eds. 1992 *Writing worlds: discourse, text and metaphor in the representation of landscape* (London and New York: Routledge).

Barrès, Maurice 1906 *Le Voyage à Sparte* (Paris: Plon-Nourrit et Cie). 1906a *Alsace-Lorraine* (Paris: E. Sansot). 1897 *Les Déracinés: le roman de l'énergie nationale* (Paris and London: Nelson).

Barth, Fredrik, ed. 1994 [1969] *Ethnic groups and boundaries: the social organization of cultural difference* (Oslo: Universitetsforlaget).

Barthes, Roland 1993 [1972] *Mythologies*, trans. A. Lavers (London: Vintage).

Basch, Sophie 1995 *Le Mirage grec: la Grèce moderne devant l'opinion française (1846–1946)* (Paris and Athens: Hatier and Kauffman).

Basgöz, Ilhan 1978 "Folklore studies and nationalism in Turkey", in *Folklore, nationalism and politics*, ed. F.J. Oinas (Columbus, OH: Slavica), pp.123–137.

Bassin, Mark 1994 "Russian geographers and the 'national question' in the Far East", in *Geography and national identity*, ed. D. Hooson (Oxford: Blackwell), pp.112–133. 1991 "Russia between Europe and Asia: the ideological construction of geographical space", *Slavic Review* 50: 1–17. 1987 "Imperialism and the nation state in Friedrich Ratzel's political geography", *Progress in Human Geography* 11: 473–495.

Bastéa, Eleni 2000 *The Creation of modern Athens: planning the myth* (Cambridge: Cambridge University Press). 1997 "Nineteenth-century travellers in Greek lands: politics, prejudice and poetry in Arcadia", *Dialogos* 4 (1997): 47–69. 1994–1995 "Forging a national image: building a modern Athens", *Modern Greek Studies Yearbook* 10/11: 297–317.

Baudrillard, Jean 1993 [1976] *Symbolic exchange and death*, trans. I. Hamilton Grant, intr. M. Gane (London: Sage).

Beaton, Roderick 1999 *An Introduction to modern Greek literature*, rev. edn. (Oxford: Oxford University Press). 1988 "Romanticism in Greece", in *Romanticism in national context*, eds. R. Porter and M. Teich (Cambridge: Cambridge University Press), pp.92–108. 1982–1983 "Realism and folklore in nineteenth-century Greek fiction", *Byzantine and Modern Greek Studies* 8: 103–122. 1980 *Folk poetry of modern Greece* (Cambridge: Cambridge University Press).

Beaton, Roderick, ed. 1988 *The Greek novel AD 1–1985* (London: Croom Helm).

Beaton, Roderick and David Ricks, eds. 1993 *Digenes Akrites: New approaches to Byzantine heroic poetry* (London and Aldershot: Variorum).

Beer, Gillian 1989 "Discourses of the island", in *Literature and science as modes of expression*, ed. F. Amrine (Dordrecht and Boston: Kluwer Academic Publishers), pp.1–27.

Belle, Henri 1881 *Trois années en Grèce* (Paris: Hachette).

Bennett, Gillian 1994 "Geologists and folklorists: 'cultural evolution' and the science of folklore", *Folklore* 105: 25–37.

Bent, James Theodore 1886 "A Christening on Karpathos", *Macmillan's Magazine* LIV: 199–205. 1885 *The Cyclades or life among the insular Greeks* (London: Longman, Green and Co).

Bérard, Victor 1897 *La Macédoine* (Paris: Calmann Lévy). 1893 *La Turquie et l'Hellénisme contemporain* (Paris: Félix Alcan)

Berdoulay, Vincent 1981 *La Formation de l'École Française de Géographie (1870–1914)* (Paris: Bibliothèque Nationale).

Bhabha, Homi K. 1994 *The Location of culture* (London and New York: Routledge). 1990 "Introduction: narrating the nation", in *Nation and narration*, ed. H.K. Bhabha (London and New York: Routledge), pp.1–7.

Bhabha, Homi K., ed. 1990 *Nation and narration* (London and New York: Routledge).

Bickford-Smith, R.A.H. 1893 *Greece under King George* (London: Richard Bentley and Son).

Black, Jeremy 1997 *Maps and politics* (London: Reaktion Books).

Blinkhorn, Martin and Thanos Veremis, eds. 1990 *Modern Greece: nationalism and nationality* (London and Athens: Sage and ELIAMEP).

Blommart, Jan and Jef Verschveren 1992 "The Role of language in European nationalist ideoloies", *Pragmatics* 2/3: 255–275.

Blouet, Abel *et al.*, eds. 1831–1838 *Expédition scientifique de Morée, ordonée par le gouvernement français. Architecture, sculpture, inscriptions et vues du Péloponèse* (sic), *des Cyclades et de l'Attique*, 3 vols. (Paris).

Boardman, John and C.E. Vaphopoulou-Richardson, eds. 1986 *Chios: a conference at the Homereion in Chios* (Oxford: Clarendon Press).

Bongie, Chris 1998 *Islands and exiles: the Creole identities of post-colonial literature* (Stanford, CA: Stanford University Press).

Boon, James A. 1982 *Other tribes, other scribes: symbolic anthropology in the comparative study of culture* (Cambridge: Cambridge University Press).

Booting, Wendy and J. Keith Davies 1989 "Freud's library and an appendix of texts related to antiquities", in *Sigmund Freud and art: his personal collection of antiques*, eds. L. Gamwell and R. Wells (London: Thames and Hudson/State University of New York/Freud Museum), pp.184–192.

Boyle, Nicholas 1991 *Goethe: the poet and the age Vol.1: the poetry of desire (1749–1790)* (Oxford: Oxford University Press).

Brailsford, H.N. 1906 *Macedonia: its races and their future* (London: Methuen and Co).

Braude, Benjamin and Bernard Lewis, eds. 1982 *Christians and Jews in the Ottoman Empire: the functioning of a plural society*, 2 vols. (New York and London: Holmes and Meier).

Brennan, Timothy 1990 "The National longing for form", in *Nation and narration*, ed. H.K. Bhabha (London and New York: Routledge), pp.44–70.

Brown, L.C., ed. 1996 *Imperial legacy* (New York: Columbia University Press).

Burbaker, Roger 1996 *Nationalism reframed: nationhood and the nation question in the new Europe* (Cambridge: Cambridge University Press). 1992 *Citizenship and nationhood in France and Germany* (Cambridge, MA: Harvard University Press).

Butler, Eliza M. 1935 *The Tyranny of Greece over Germany: a study of the influence exercised by Greek art and poetry over the great German writers of the eighteenth, nineteenth and twentieth centuries* (Cambridge: Cambridge University Press).

Buttimer, Anne 1971 *Society and milieu in the French geographic tradition* (Chicago: Rand McNally).

Calder, William and David A. Traill, eds. 1986 *Myth, scandal and history: the Heinrich Schliemann controversy* (Detroit: Wayne State University Press).

Calhoun, Craig 1994 "Nationalism and civil society: democracy, diversity and self-determination", in *Social theory and the politics of identity*, ed. C. Calhoun (Oxford: Blackwell), pp.304–335.

Calhoun, Craig, ed. 1994 *Social theory and the politics of identity* (Oxford: Blackwell).

Campbell, John K. 1976 "Regionalism and local community", in *Regional variation in modern Greece and Cyprus: toward a perspective on the ethnography of Greece*, eds. M. Dimen-Schein and E. Friedl (New York: Annals of the New York Academy of Sciences 264), pp.18–27.

Carabott, Philip, ed. 1997 *Greek society in the making, 1863–1913: realities, symbols and visions* (London and Aldershot: Ashgate). 1995 *Greece and Europe in the modern period: aspects of a troubled relationship* (London: Centre for Hellenic Studies, King's College London).

Carter, F.W. and H.T. Norris, eds. 1996 *The Changing shape of the Balkans* (London: University College London Press).

Carter, R. 1979 "K.F. Schinkel's project for a royal palace on the Acropolis", *Journal of the Society of Architectural Historians* 38/1 (March): 34–46.

Certeau, Michel de 1986 *Heterologies: discourse on the other*, trans. B. Massumi, foreword W. Godzich (Manchester: Manchester University Press).

Chatzipantazis, Theodoros 1984 *I Isvoli tou karaghiozi stin Athina tou 1890* (Athens: Stigmi).

Chatzopoulos, Dimitrios 1901 "Emis kai meriki xemi", *Dionysos* 1: 82–89.

Chouliarakis, Mihalis 1973 *Yeografiki, diikitiki kai plithismiaki exelixis tis Ellados, 1821–1971* (Athens: Ethniko Kentro Kinonikon Erevnon).

Christovasilis, Christos 1988 *Diiyimata tis stanis* (Athens: Nefeli).

Chrysos, Evangelos, ed. 1996 *Enas neos kosmos yennietai: i ikona tou ellin-ikou politismou sti yermaniki epistimi kata ton 19° ai* (Athens: Akritas).

Chrystou, Chrysanthos 1981 *I Elliniki zografiki, 1832–1922* (Athens: Ethniki Trapeza tis Ellados).

Claval, Paul 1994 "From Michelet to Braudel: personality, identity and organization of France", in *Geography and national identity*, ed. D. Hooson (Oxford: Blackwell), pp.39–57.

Clifford, James 1997 *Routes: travel and translation in the late twentieth century* (Cambridge, MA: Harvard University Press).

Clogg, Richard 1996 *Anatolica: studies in the Greek East in the 18th and 19th centuries* (London and Aldershot: Variorum). 1992 *A Concise history of Greece* (Cambridge: Cambridge University Press). 1988 "The Byzantine legacy in the modern Greek world: the *Megali Idea*", in *The Byzantine legacy in Eastern Europe*, ed. L. Clucas (Boulder, CO: East European Monographs), pp.253–281. 1986 [1979] *A Short history of modern Greece* (Cambridge: Cambridge University Press). 1985 "Sense of the past in pre-independence Greece", in *Culture and nationalism in nineteenth-century Eastern Europe*, eds. R. Sussex and J.C. Eade (Columbus, OH: Slavica), pp.7–30. 1982 "The Greek *millet* in the Ottoman Empire", in *Christians and Jews in the Ottoman Empire: the functioning of a plural society*, eds. B. Braude and B. Lewis, 2 vols. (New York and London: Holmes and Meier), pp.185–207. 1981 "The Greek mercantile bourgeoisie: 'progressive' or 'reactionary'?", in *Balkan society in the age of Greek Independence*, ed. R. Clogg (London: Macmillan), pp.85–110. 1976 "Anti-clericism in pre-independence Greece, c. 1750–1821", in *The Orthodox churches and the West*, ed. D. Baker (Oxford: Blackwell), pp.257–276. 1966 "The *Dhidhaskalia Patriki* (1798): an Orthodox reaction to the French revolutionary propaganda", *Middle Eastern Studies* 5: 87–115.

Clogg, Richard, ed. 1983 *Greece in the 1980s* (London: Macmillan). 1981 *Balkan society in the age of Greek Independence* (London: Macmillan). 1976 *The Movement for Greek Independence, 1770–1821. A collection of documents* (London: Macmillan).

Colls, Robert and Philip Dodd, eds. 1986 *Englishness: politics and culture, 1880–1920* (London: Croom Helm).

Colocotronis, V. 1919 *La Macédoine et l'Hellénisme: étude historique et ethnologique* (Paris: Berger-Levrault).

Constans, Claire *et al.*, eds. 1996 *La Grèce en révolte: Delacroix et les pein-tres français, 1815–1848* (Paris: Éditions de la Réunion de Musées Nationaux).

Corner, James 1999 "The Agency of mapping: speculation, critique and invention", in *Mappings*, ed. D.E. Cosgrove (London: Reaktion Books), pp.213–252.

Cosgrove, Denis E. 1998 [1984] *Social formation and symbolic landscape* (Madison, WI: University of Wisconsin Press). 1995 "Habitable earth: wilderness, empire, and race in America", in *Wild ideas*, ed. D. Rothenberg (Minneapolis: University of Minnesota Press), pp.27–41.

Cosgrove, Denis E., ed. 1999 *Mappings* (London: Reaktion Books).

Cosgrove, Denis E. and Stephen Daniels, eds. 1988 *The Iconography of landscape: essays on the symbolic representation, design and use of past environments* (Cambridge: Cambridge University Press).

Cowan, Jane K. 1990 *Dance and the body politic in northern Greece* (Princeton, NJ: Princeton University Press).

Crampton, Richard J. 1997 *A Concise history of Bulgaria* (Cambridge: Cambridge University Press). 1987 *A Short history of modern Bulgaria* (Cambridge: Cambridge University Press).

Cubitt, Geoffrey, ed. 1998 *Imagining nations* (Manchester: Manchester University Press).

Curzon, George 1907 *Frontiers* (Oxford: Clarendon Press).

Cvijić, Jovan 1918 *La Péninsule Balkanique: géographic humaine* (Paris: A. Colin). 1918a "The Geographic distribution of the Balkan peoples", *Geographical Review* V/5: 345–361. 1918b "The Zones of civilization of the Balkan Peninsula", *Geographical Review* V/6: 470–482.

Dabrowski, Magdalena 2000 *French landscape: the modern vision, 1880–1920* (New York: Museum of Modern Art).

Dakin, Douglas 1993 [1966] *The Greek struggle in Macedonia* (Thessaloniki: Society for Macedonian Studies and Institute for Balkan Studies).

Danforth, Loring M. 1995 *The Macedonian conflict: ethnic nationalism in a transnational world* (Princeton, NJ: Princeton University Press). 1984 "The Ideological context of the search for continuities in Greek culture", *Journal of Modern Greek Studies* 2/1: 53–85.

Daniel, E. Valentine and Jeffrey M. Peck, eds. 1996 *Culture/contexture: explorations in anthropology and literary studies* (Berkeley, CA: University of California Press).

Daniel, Glyn, ed. 1981 *Towards a history of archaeology* (London and New York: Thames and Hudson).

Daniels, Stephen 1993 *Fields of vision: landscape imagery and national identity in England and the United States* (Cambridge: Polity).

Daniels, Stephen and S. Rycroft 1993 "Mapping the modern city: Alan Sillitoe's Nottingham novels", *Transactions of the Institute of British Geographers* 18/4: 460–480.

Daudet, Alphonse 1989 [1880] *I Vasilis en ti exoria*, trans. E. Sekiaris (Athens: Estia). 1978 *Letters from my windmill*, trans. F. Davies (Harmondsworth: Penguin).

Dawson, Graham 1996 *Soldier heroes: British adventure, empire and the imagining of masculinities* (London: Routledge).

D'Eichthal, Gustave 1887 *La Langue grecque: mémoires et notices, 1864–84. Précédé d'une notice sur les services rendus, par M.G. d'Eichthal, à la Grèce et aux études grecques. Par le Marquis de Queux de Sainte-Hilaire* (Paris: Hachette).

Denisi, Sofia 1995 *Metafrasis mythistorimaton kai diiyimaton 1830–1880. Isayoyiki meleti kai katagrafi* (Athens: Periplous).

Deschamps, Gaston 1892 *La Grèce d'aujourd'hui* (Paris: Armand Colin).

Diamandouros, P. Nikiforos 1983 "Greek political culture in transition: historical origins, evolution, current trends", in *Greece in the 1980s*, ed. R. Clogg (London: Macmillan), pp.43–69.

Diamandouros, P. Nikiforos *et al.*, eds. 1976 *Hellenism and the first Greek war of liberation (1821–1830): continuity and change* (Thessaloniki: Institute for Balkan Studies).

Dimaras, Konstantinos Th. 1994 [1982] *Neoellinikos romantismos* (Athens: Ermis). 1993 [1977] *Neoellinikos diafotismos* (Athens: Ermis). 1992 *Istorika frondismata: o diafotismos kai to korifoma tou*, ed. P. Polemi (Athens: Poria). 1986 *Konstantinos Paparrigopoulos: i epohi, i zoi tou, to ergo tou* (Athens: Morfotiko Idrima Ethnikis Trapezis).

Dimen-Schein, Muriel and Ernestine Friedl, eds. 1976 *Regional variation in modern Greece and Cyprus: towards a perspective on the ethnography of Greece*, (New York: Annals of the New York Academy of Sciences 264).

Dimitrakopoulos, Fotis 1996 *Vizandio kai neoelliniki dianoisi sta mesa tou dekatou aionas* (Athens: Kastaniotis).

Djordjevic, Dimitrije and Stephen Fischer-Galati 1981 *The Balkan revolutionary tradition* (New York: Columbia University Press).

Dorson, Richard M. 1968 *The British folklorists: a history* (London: Routledge and Kegan Paul). 1978 *Folklore in the modern world* (The Hague: Mouton).

Douglas, Mary 1978 [1966] *Purity and danger: an analysis of concepts of pollution and taboo* (London: Routledge and Kegan Paul).

Doulis, Thomas 1975 *George Theotokas* (New York: Twayne).

Downes, Alan 1971 "The Bibliography of dinosaurs of Georgian geography", *Geographical Journal* 137: 379–383.

Dragoumis, Ion 1991 [1907] *Martiron kai iroon aima*, ed. A. Vakalopoulos (Thessaloniki: Kiriakidis). 1991a [1913] *Ellinikos politismos* (Athens: Nea Thesis). 1927 [1913] *Erga kinonika – politika. O Ellinismos mou kai i Ellines (1903–1909)* (Athens: Estia). 1909 [1907] *Samothraki: to nisi* (Athens).

Dragoumis, Julia 1912 *Tales of a Greek island* (Boston: Houghton, Miffin Co).

Driault, Édouard 1920 *La Grande Idée: la renaissance de l'Hellénisme*, pref. N. Politis (Paris: Felix Alcan).

Drosinis, Yeoryios 1940 *Skorpia filla tis zois mou* (Athens: Sideris). 1922 *Ersi* (Athens: Sideris). 1910 [1882] *Diiyimata ton agron kai tis poleos*

(Athens: Kollaros). 1903 "I Ethniki simasis tis dimotikis ekpaid-evseos", *Ethniki Agogi* 6: 241–242. 1886 *Diiyimata kai anamnisis* (Athens: Kollaros). 1883 *Odiporikai endiposis. Tris imerai en Tino* (Athens).

Drosinis, Yeoryios and Yeoryios Kasdonis, eds. 1894 *Nea Ellas: ethnikou imeroloyiou ikonografimenou* (Athens: Estia).

Dubisch, Jill 1995 *In a different place: pilgrimage, gender, and politics at a Greek island shrine* (Princeton, NJ: University of Princeton Press).

Duncan, James S. 1990 *The City as text: the politics of landscape interpretation in the Kandyan kingdom* (Cambridge: Cambridge University Press).

Duncan, James S. and David Ley, eds. 1993 *Place/culture/representation* (London and New York: Routledge).

Edmonds, E.M., ed. 1892 *Stories from Fairyland by George Drosines and the cup of tears and other tales by Aritotle Kourtidos* (London: T. Fisher Unwin).

Eftaliotis, Argyris 1942 [1897] *Modern tales of the Greek islands*, trans. W.H.D. Rouse (London: Thomas Nelson and Sons). 1897 *Tales from the isles of Greece, being sketches of modern Greek peasant life*, trans. W.H.D. Rouse (London: J.M. Dent). n.d. [1894] *Nisiotikes istories*, ed. S. Kokkinis (Athens: Estia).

Eisner, Robert 1991 *Travelers to an antique land: the history and literature of travel to Greece* (Ann Arbor, MI: The University of Michigan Press).

Eliot, Charles 1965 [1900] *Turkey in Europe* (London: Frank Cass).

Ellinismos 1896 *Makedonia iti meleti ikonomiki, yeografiki, istoriki kai ethnoloyiki tis Makedonias*, 2nd edn. (Piraeus).

Enialis, Lambros 1868 *O Parafron erimitis, mythistorema*, 3rd edn. (Athens).

Evans, Christopher 1993 "Digging with the pen: novel archaeologies and literary traditions", in *Interpretative archaeology*, ed. C. Tilley (Oxford: Berg), pp.417–447.

Exertzoglou, Haris 1996 *Ethniki tavtotita stin Konstantinoupoli ton 19° ai.: O Ellinikos Filoloyikos Sillogos Konstantinopoleos, 1861–1912* (Athens: Nefeli).

Fabian, Johannes 1983 *Time and the other: how anthropology makes its object* (New York: Columbia University Press).

Fais, Michel 1994 [1989] *Aftoviografia enos vivliou* (Athens: Kastaniotis).

Farinou-Malamatari, Yeoryia 1987 *Afiyimatikes tehnikes ston Papadiamanti, 1887–1910* (Athens: Kedros).

Filippidis, S.N. 1997 *Topi: meletimata yia ton afiyimatiko logo epta neoellinon pezografon* (Athens: Kastaniotis).

Finlay, George 1871 "Brigandage in Greece", *Saturday Review* 810/31: 561–563. 1861 *History of the Greek revolution and the reign of King Otho* (Edinburgh and London: W. Blackwood and Sons). 1854 "Turkey and its population", *Blackwood's Edinburgh Magazine* 76 (November): 493–509. 1854a "King Otho and his classic Kingdom", *Blackwood's Edinburgh Magazine* 76 (October): 403–421. 1836 *The Hellenic Kingdom and the Greek nation* (London: John Murray).

Foucault, Michel 1974 [1966] *The Order of things: an archaeology of the human sciences* (London: Routledge).

Frangoudakis, A. and Th. Dragona, eds. 1997 *'Ti Ein 'i patrida mas': ethnokentrismos stin ekpaidevisi* (Athens: Alexanria).

Freeman, Edward A. 1882 *The Historical geography of Europe*, 2 vols. (London: Longmans). 1877 "Geographical aspects of the Eastern Question", *The Fortnightly Review* 122: 73–87.

Freeman, T.W. 1967 *The Geographer's craft* (Manchester and New York: Manchester University Press and Barnes and Noble).

Friedl, Ernestine and Muriel Dimen-Schein, eds. 1976 *Regional variation in modern Greece and Cyprus: toward a perspective on the ethnography of Greece* (New York: New York Academy of Sciences).

Gallant, Thomas 1997 "Murder in a Mediterranean city: homicide trends in Athens, 1850–1936", *Journal of the Hellenic Diaspora* 25/2: 8–14.

Gamwell, Lynn and Richard Wells, eds. 1989 *Sigmund Freud and art: his personal collection of antiques* (London: Thames and Hudson/State University of New York/Freud Museum).

Gay, Peter 1988 *Freud: a life for our time* (London: Dent).

Geertz, Clifford 1973 *The Interpretation of cultures* (New York: Basic Books).

Gehrke, Hans-Joachim 1996 "Anazitontas ti hora ton ellinon: epistimonika taxidia kai i simasia tous yia tin erevna kai tin antimetopisi tis arhioellinikis istorias ston 19° aiona", in *Enas neos kosmos yennietai: i ikona tou ellinikou politismou sti yermaniki epistimi kata ton 19° ai.*, ed. E. Chrysos (Athens: Akritas), pp.59–82.

Gellner, Ernest 1983 *Nations and nationalism* (Oxford: Blackwell).

Giddens, Anthony 1985 *The Nation-state and violence* (Cambridge: Polity Press).

Gifford, John A. and George Rapp, eds. 1985 *Archaeological geology* (New Haven, CT and London: Yale University Press).

Gillis, J.R., ed. 1994 *Commemorations: the politics of national identity* (Princeton, NJ: Princeton University Press).

Girdwood, Alison 1984 "The imaginative response to archaeology in nineteenth and early twentieth-century literature", *Archaeological Review from Cambridge* 3: 29–37.

Glacken, Clarence J. 1967 *Traces on the Rhodian shore: nature and culture in western thought from ancient times to the end of the eighteenth century* (Berkeley, CA: University of California Press).

Glenny, Misha 1999 *The Balkans, 1804–1999: nationalism, war and the Great Powers* (London: Granta Books).

Gorse, Sarah M. 1997 *Nationalism and literature: the politics of culture in Canada and the United States* (Cambridge: Cambridge University Press).

Goudas, Anastasios N. 1872 *Vii parallili ton epi tis anayenniseos tis Ellados diaprepsandon andron* (Athens).

Gounaris, Basil 1993 *Steam over Macedonia, 1870–1912: socio-economic change and the railway factor* (Boulder, CO: East European Monographs).

Gounelas, Charalambos-Dimitris 1984 *I Sosialistiki sinidisi stin elliniki logotehnia, 1897–1912* (Athens: Kedros).

Gourgouris, Stathis 1996 *Dream nation: enlightenment, colonization and the institution of modern Greece* (Princeton, NJ: Princeton University Press).

Green, M. 1990 *The Robinson Crusoe story* (Pennsylvania: Pennsylvania State University Press).

Green, Nicholas 1990 *The Spectacle of nature: landscape and bourgeois culture in nineteenth-century France* (Manchester: Manchester University Press).

Greene, Thomas M. 1982 *The Light of Troy: imitation and discovery in Renaissance poetry* (New Haven, CT and London: Yale University Press).

Greenfield, Liah 1992 *Nationalism: five roads to modernity* (Cambridge, MA: Harvard University Press).

Gregory, Derek 1994 *Geographical imaginations* (Oxford: Blackwell).

Grove, Richard H. 1995 *Green imperialism: colonial expansion, tropical island Edens and the origins of environmentalism, 1600–1860* (Cambridge: Cambridge University Press).

Handler, Richard 1994 "Is 'Identity' a useful cross-cultural concept?", in *Commemorations: the politics of national identity*, ed. J.R. Gillis (Princeton, NJ: Princeton University Press), pp.27–40.

Harley, J.B. 1992 "Deconstructing the Map", in *Writing worlds: discourse, text and metaphor in the representation of landscape*, eds. T.J. Barnes and J.S. Duncan (London and New York: Routledge), pp.231–247.

Hartley, Keith *et al.*, eds. 1994 *The Romantic spirit in German art, 1790–1990* (London: Thames and Hudson).

Haskell, Francis 1986 "Chios, the massacres, and Delacroix", in *Chios: a conference at the Homereion in Chios*, eds. J. Boardman and C.E. Vaphopoulou-Richardson (Oxford: Clarendon Press), pp.335–358.

Hastaoglou-Martinidis, Vilma 1995 "City, form and national identity: urban designs in nineteenth-century Greece", *Journal of Modern Greek Studies* 13/1: 99–123.

Hastaoglou-Martinidis, V., K. Kafkoula and N. Papamihos 1991 "The Making of modern urban identity: the transformation of Greek towns in the nineteenth century", *Journal of Modern Hellenism* 8: 49–62.

Hechter, Michael 1975 *Internal colonialism: the Celtic fringe in British national development, 1536–1966* (London: Routledge and Kegan Paul).

Heilmann, Christoph 1994 "Ludwig I's Munich as a centre of artistic renewal", in *The Romantic spirit in German art, 1790–1990*, eds. K. Hartley *et al.* (London: Thames and Hudson), pp.46–51.

Henderson, George P. 1970 *The Revival of Greek thought, 1620–1830* (Albany, NY: State University of New York Press).

Herzfeld, Michael 1991 *A Place in history: social and monumental time in a Cretan town* (Princeton, NJ: Princeton University Press). 1987 *Anthropology through the looking-glass: critical anthropology in the margins of Europe* (Cambridge: Cambridge University Press). 1986 [1982] *Ours once more: folklore, ideology and the making of modern Greece* (New York: Pella).

Heywood, Colin 1999 "The Frontier in Ottoman history: old ideas and new myths", in *Frontiers in question: Eurasian borderlands, 700–1700*, eds. D. Power and N. Standen (Basingstoke, UK: Macmillan), pp.228–250.

Hirschfeld, G. 1890 "Wzur geschichte der geographie bei den Neugriechen", *Berlinier Philologische Wochenschrift* 9/10: 3–15.

Hobsbawm, Eric J. 1997 [1975] *The Age of capital, 1848–1975* (London: Abacus). 1992 *Nations and nationalism since 1780: programme, myth, reality* (Cambridge: Cambridge University Press). 1964 *The Age of revolution, 1789–1848* (New York: Mentor)

Hobsbawm, Eric J. and Terence Ranger, eds. 1983 *The Invention of tradition* (Cambridge: Cambridge University Press).

Hodder, Ian 1991 *Reading the past: current approaches to interpretation in archaeology* (Cambridge: Cambridge University Press).

Hodder, Ian *et al.*, eds. 1995 *Interpreting archaeology: finding meaning in the past* (London: Routledge).

Holdich, Thomas 1899 "The Uses of practical geography illustrated by recent frontier operations", *Geographical Journal* 13/5: 465–480.

Holquist, Michael 1996 "A New tour of Babel: recent trends linking comparative departments, foreign language departments and area studies programs", *Profession*: 103–114.

Holton, David 1984/5 "Ethnic identity and patriotic idealism in the writings of General Makriyannis", *Byzantine and Modern Greek Studies* 9: 133–160.

Hooson, David, ed. 1994 *Geography and national identity* (Oxford: Blackwell).

Hope, Anthony 1897 *Phroso. A Romance* (London: Methuen).

Horrocks, Geoffrey 1997 *Greek: a history of the language and its speakers* (London: Longman).

Hourmouziadis, Anastasios 1873 *Per ton Anastenarion kai allon tinon ethimon kai prolipseon* (Constantinople).

House, John, ed. 1995 *Landscapes of France: Impressionism and its rivals* (London: Hayward Gallery).

Howkins, Alun 1986 "The Discovery of rural England", in *Englishness: politics and culture, 1880–1920*, eds. R. Colls and P. Dodd (London: Croom Helm), pp.62–88.

Hudson, B. 1977 "The new geography and the new Imperialism, 1870–1918", *Antipode* 9/2: 12–19.

Hutchinson, J. and Anthony D. Smith, eds. 1994 *Nationalism* (Oxford: Oxford University Press).

Inglis, Fred 1977 "Nation and community: a landscape and its morality", *The Sociological Review* 25: 489–513.

Ioannou, Andreas S., ed. 1974 *Greek painting, 19th century*, trans. D. Dellagrammatika (Athens: Melissa).

Iorga, Nikolai 1971 *Byzance après Byzance: continuation de l'histoire de la vie Byzantine* (Bucharest: Association Internationale d'Études du Sud-Est Européen Comité National Roumain).

Ischirkov, A. 1916 *Les Confins Occidentaux des terres Bulgares* (Lausanne: Librairie Nouvelle).

Ivy, Marilyn 1996 "Ghostlier demarcations: textual phantasm and the origins of Japanese natavist ethnology", in *Culture/contexture: explorations in anthropology and literary studies*, eds. E.V. Daniel and J.M. Peck (Berkeley, CA: University of California Press), pp.296–322.

Jackson, J.B. and Donald W. Meinig, eds. 1979 *The Interpretation of ordinary landscapes: geographical essays* (New York and London: Oxford University Press).

Jameson, Fredric 1983 [1981] *The Political unconscious: narrative as a socially symbolic act* (London: Routledge). 1977 "Of Islands and trenches: naturalization and the production of utopian discourse", *Diacritics* 7 (Summer): 2–21.

Jebb, Richard C. 1901 [1880] *Modern Greece. Two lectures delivered before the Philosophical Institution of Edinburgh, with pages on 'The progress of Greece' and 'Byron and Greece'* (London: Macmillan).

Jelavich, Barbara 1983 *History of the Balkans: Vol.1: eighteenth and nineteenth centuries* (Cambridge: Cambridge University Press).

Jenkins, Romilly 1961 *The Dilessi murders* (London: Longman).

Jusdanis, Gregory 1995 "Beyond national culture?" *Boundary 2* 22/1: 23–60. 1987 "East is East – West is West: it's a matter of Greek literary history" *Journal of Modern Greek Studies* 5/1: 1–14.

Kakridis, Fanis 1996 "I Yermaniki diachirisi tis ellinikis klironomias", in *Enas neos kosmos yennietai: i ikona tou elinikou politismou sti yermaniki epistimi kata ton 19º ai*, ed. E. Chrysos (Athens: Akritas), pp.25–39.

Kalpaxis, Athanasios E. 1996 "Epirroes tis galloyermanikis antiparath-esis tou 19ou aiona stin kataskevi tis ikonas tis arhaias elladas", in *Enas neos kosmos yennietai: i ikona tou ellinikou politismou sti yermaniki epistii kata ton 19° ai.*, ed. E. Chrysos (Athens: Akritas, 1996), pp.41–58. 1993 *Arhaioloyia kai politiki: II i anaskafi tou naou tis Artemidos (Kerkira 1911)* (Rethymno: Panepistimiakes Ekdosis Kritis). 1990 *Arhaioloyia kai politiki: I Samiaka arhaioloyika, 1850–1914* (Rethymno: Panepistimiakes Ekdosis Kritis).

Karakasidou, Anastasia N. 1997 *Fields of wheat, hills of blood: passages to nationhood in Greek Macedonia, 1870–1990* (Chicago: University of Chicago Press).

Karavidas, K.D. 1977 [1931] *Agrotika* (Athens: Papazisis).

Karkavitsas, Andreas 1995 *Palies agapes* (Athens: Ermis). 1982 *Diiyimata* (Athens: Ermis). n.d. *Diyenis Akritas kai alla diiyimata* (Athens: Papa-dopoulos). n.d. *O Arheologos* (Athens: Pella).

Karpat, Kemal H. 1982 "*Millets* and nationality: the roots of the incon-gruity of nation and state in the post-Ottoman era" in *Christians and Jews in the Ottoman Empire: the functioning of a plural society*, eds. B. Braude and B. Lewis, 2 vols. (New York and London: Holmes and Meier), vol.1, pp.141–169. 1973 *An Inquiry into the social foundation of nationalism in the Ottoman state: from social estates to classes, from millets to nations* (Princeton, NJ: Princeton University Press). 1968 "The Land regime, social struc-ture, and modernization in the Ottoman Empire", in *Beginnings of modernization in the Middle East*, eds. R.L. Chambers and W.R. Polk (Chicago: University of Chicago Press, 1968), pp.69–90.

Karpozilou, Martha 1991 *Ta Ellinika ikoyeniaka filoloyika periodika* (Ioan-nina: Panepistimio Ioanninon).

Katartzis, Dimitrios 1974 *Dokimia*, ed. K.Th. Dimaras (Athens: Ermis). 1970 *Ta Evriskomena*, ed. K.Th. Dimaras (Athens: Ermis).

Kayser, Bernard 1976 "Dynamics of regional integration in modern Greece", in *Regional variation in Modern Greece and Cyprus: toward a perspective on the ethnography of Greece*, eds. M. Dimen-Schein and E. Friedl (New York: Annals of the New York Academy of Sciences 268), pp.10–15.

Kazantzakis, Nikos 1973 [1961] *Report to Greco* (London: Faber and Faber).

Kazimati, Marilena Z., ed. 2000 *Athina – Monacho: techni kai politismos stin Ellada* (Athens: Ethniki Pinakothiki).

Kedourie, Elie, ed. 1971 *Nationalism in Asia and Africa* (London: Weidenfeld and Nicolson).

Kern, Stephen 1983 *The Culture of time and space, 1880–1918* (Cambridge, MA: Harvard University Press).

Khol, Philip L. and Clare Fawcett, eds. 1996 *Nationalism, politics and the practice of archaeology* (Cambridge: Cambridge University Press).

Kiberd, Declan 1997 "Modern Ireland: postcolonial or European?", in *Not on any map: essays on postcoloniality and cultural nationalism*, ed. S. Murray (Exeter, UK: University of Exeter Press), pp.81–100.

Kirby, Kathleen M. 1993 "Thinking through the boundary: the politics of location, subjects, and space", *Boundary 2* 20/2: 173–189.

Kitromilides, Paschalis M. 1998 "On the Intellectual content of Greek nationalism: Paparrigopoulos, Byzantium and the Great Idea", in *Byzantium and the modern Greek identity*, eds. D. Ricks and P. Magdalino (London and Aldershot: Ashgate), pp.25–33. 1996 "Balkan mentality: history, legend, imagination", *Nations and nationalism* 2/2: 163–191. 1995 "Europe and the dilemmas of Greek conscience", in *Greece and Europe in the modern period: aspects of a troubled relationship*, ed. P. Carabott (London: Centre for Hellenic Studies, King's College London), pp.1–15. 1994 *Enlightenment, nationalism, orthodoxy: studies in the culture and political thought of South-eastern Europe* (London and Aldershot: Variorum). 1992 *The Enlightenment as social criticism: Iosopos Moisiodax and Greek culture in the eighteenth century* (Princeton, NJ: Princeton University Press). 1990 "'Imagined communities' and the origins of the national question in the Balkans", in *Modern Greece: nationalism and nationality*, eds. M. Blinkhorn and Th. Veremis (London and Athens: Sage and ELIAMEP), pp.23–66.

Kofos, Evangelos 1990 "National heritage and national identity in nineteenth and twentieth-century Macedonia", in *Modern Greece: nationalism and nationality*, eds. M. Blinkhorn and Th. Veremis (London and Athens: Sage and ELIAMEP), pp.103–141. 1975 *Greece and the Eastern Crisis* (Thessaloniki: Institute for Balkan Studies).

Kokidis, Ifikratis 1891 *Stratiotiki yeografia tis Ellados, Meta sindomos exetaseos tis Evropis pros ta stratiotikas epihirisis* (Athens).

Kokkou, A. 1977 *I Merimna yia tis arhaiotites stin Ellada kai ta prota mousia* (Athens: Ermis).

Kokoris, Dimitris 1994 "Ena pezografima tou Kosta Krystalli: 'To Simomatari tou Yerokalameniou' piran tis idilliakis ithografias", *Diavazo* 326: 75–79.

Koliopoulos, John 1987 *Brigands with a cause: brigandage and irredentism in modern Greece, 1821–1912* (Oxford: Clarendon Press).

Kolokotronis, Theodoros 1892 *Kolokotrones, the klepht and the warrior: sixty years of peril and daring: an autobiography*, trans. E.M. Edmonds (London: T. Fisher Unwin).

Komninos, Panayiotis A. 1896 *Lakonika hronon proïstorikon te kai istorikon* (Athens).

Kondylakis, Ioannis D. 1999 [1894] *I Athlii ton Athinon*, ed. Y. Gotsi, 2 vols. (Athens: Nefeli). n.d. *O Patouchas* (Athens: Almopos).

Korais, Adamantios 1984 *Prolegomena stous arhaious ellines syngrafis kai I aftoviografia tou*, 4 vols. (Athens: Morfotiko Idrima Ethnikis Trapezis).

1964 *Apanta ta prototipa erga*, ed. Y. Valetas, 4 vols. (Athens: Dorikos).
1964a *Allilografia*, ed. K.Th. Dimaras, 6 vols. (Athens). 1833 *Mémoire sur l'état actuel de la civilisation en Grèce* (Paris). 1803 *Ta Aithiopika Vivlia deka*, 2 vols. (Paris).

Korasidou, Maria 1995 *I Athlii ton Athinon kai i therapeftes tous: ftohia kai filanthropia stin elliniki protevousa ton 19° aiona* (Athens: Kentro Neoellinikon Erevnon E.I.E.).

Koulouri, Christina 1991 *Dimensions idéologiques de l'historicité en Grèce (1834–1914)* (Frankfurt: Peter Lang). 1988 *Istoria kai yeografia sta ellinika scholia (1834–1914): gnostiko antikimeno kai ideoloyikes proektasis* (Athens: Yeniki Grammatia Neas Yeneas).

Krinos, Stefanos 1879 *Sinopsis ethniki periehousa epitomi hronoloyiki kai istorikin ton metavolon tis Ellados kai yeografian aftis para Daniil Ieromonahou kai Grigoriou Ierodiakonou ton Dimitrieon* (Athens).

Krishna, Sankaran 1997 [1994] "Cartographic anxiety: mapping the body politic in India", in *Political geography: a reader*, ed. J. Agnew (London: Arnold), pp.81–92.

Kuklick, Henrika 1991 *The Savage within: the social history of British anthropology, 1885–1945* (Cambridge: Cambridge University Press).

Kuspit, Donald 1989 "A Mighty metaphor: the analogy of archaeology and psychoanalysis", in *Sigmund Freud and art: his personal collection of antiques*, eds. L. Gamwell and R. Wells (London: Thames and Hudson/State University of New York/Freud Museum), pp.131–151.

Kyriakidou-Nestoros, Alki 1986 [1978] *I Theoria tis ellinikis laografias. Kritiki analisi* (Athens: Etairia Spoudon Neoellinkou Politismou kai Yenikis Paidias).

LaCapra, Dominick 1983 *Rethinking intellectual history: texts, contexts, language* (Ithaca, NY: Cornell University Press).

Laudan, Rachel 1987 *From Mineralogy to geology: the foundations of a science, 1650–1830* (Chicago: University of Chicago Press).

Lawson, John C. 1910 *Modern Greek folklore and ancient Greek religion: a study in survivals* (Cambridge: Cambridge University Press).

Le Bon, Gustave 1960 *The Crowd: a study of the popular mind*, intr. R.K. Merton (Harmondsworth: Penguin).

Lefas, Yannis L. 1979 *O Alexandros Soutsos kai i epidrasis tou ergou tou stous synhronous tou. Didaktoriki diatrivi* (Athens).

Leone, Mark *et al.* 1987 "Toward a critical archaeology", *Current Anthropology* 28/3: 283–302.

Leontidou, Lila 1989 *The Mediterranean city in transition: social change and urban development* (Cambridge: Cambridge University Press).

Leontis, Artemis 1995 *Topographies of Hellenism: mapping the homeland* (Ithaca, NY: Cornell University Press). 1992 "The Diaspora of the novel", *Diaspora* 2/1: 131–146.

Lesser, Wendy 1987 *The Life below the ground: a study of the subterranean in literature and history* (London: Faber and Faber).

Lewis, Norman N. 1987 *Nomads and settlers in Syria and Jordan, 1800–1980* (Cambridge: Cambridge University Press).

Ley, David and Marwyn S. Samuels, eds. 1978 *Humanistic geography: prospects and problems* (London: Croom Helm).

Linke, Uli 1990 "Folklore, anthropology, and the government of social life", *Comparative Studies in Society and History* 32/1: 117–148.

Livanios, Dimitris 1999 "'Conquering souls': nationalism and Greek guerrilla warfare in Ottoman Macedonia, 1904–1908", *Byzantine and Modern Greek Studies* 23: 195–221.

Livingstone, David N. 1992 *The Geographical tradition: episodes in the history of a contested enterprise* (Oxford: Blackwell).

Llewellyn Smith, Michael 1998 [1973] *Ionian vision: Greece in Asia Minor, 1919–1922* (London: Hurst).

Loukaki, Argyro, 1997 "Whose Genius loci?: Contrasting interpretations of the 'sacred rock of the Athenian Acropolis'", *Annals of the Association of American Geographers* 87/2: 306–329.

Loukatos, Dimitrios 1978 "Archeofolklore", in *Folklore in the modern world*, ed. R.M. Dorson (The Hague: Mouton), pp.175–182. 1978a *Isagogi stin ellinki laografia*, 2nd edn. (Athens: Morfotiko Idrima Ethnikis Trapezis).

Lowenthal, David 1985 *The Past is a foreign country* (Cambridge: Cambridge University Press).

Loxley, Diana 1990 *Problematic shores: the literature of islands* (New York: St. Martin's Press).

Macdonald, Gerald M. 1995 "Indonesia's *Medan Merdeka*: national identity and the built environment", *Antipode* 27/3: 270–93.

Mackenzie, David 1967 *The Serbs and Russian Pan-Slavism, 1875–1878* (Ithaca, NY: Cornell University Press).

Mackridge, Peter 1997 "Cultivating new lands: the consolidation of territorial gains in Greek Macedonia through literature, 1912–1940", in *Ourselves and others: the development of a Greek Macedonian cultural identity since 1912*, ed. P. Mackridge and E. Yannakakis (Oxford: Berg), pp.175–186. 1992 "The Textuality of place in Greek fiction, 1883–1903", *Journal of Mediterranean Studies* 2/2: 148–168. 1981 "The Greek intelligentsia, 1780–1830: a Balkan perspective", in *Balkan society in the age of Greek Independence*, ed. R. Clogg (London: Macmillan), pp.63–84.

Mackridge, Peter and Eleni Yannakakis, eds. 1997 *Ourselves and others: the development of a Greek Macedonian cultural identity since 1912* (Oxford: Berg).

Mahaffy, John P. 1892 *Rambles and studies in Greece*, rev. 4th edn. (London: Macmillan).

Makrakis, Lily and P. Nikiforos Diamandouros, eds. 1982 *New trends in modern Greek historiography* (MGSA Occasional Papers).

Malina, Juroslav and Zdenek Vasicek 1990 *Archaeology yesterday and today: the development of archaeology in the sciences and humanities* (Cambridge: Cambridge University Press).

Mango, Cyril 1965 "Byzantinism and Romantic Hellenism", *Journal of the Warburg and Courtauld Institutes* 5/28: 29–43.

Manolakakis, E. 1896 *Karpathiaka periehonta tin topografian, istorian, perigrafin, arhaioloyian, fusikin katastasi, statistiki, toponymies tis nisou, itha kai ethima, idiomata tis glossis, lexiloyion, dimotiki, asmata kai dimidis primias ton katikian aftis* (Athens).

Marchand, Suzanne L. 1998 "The Excavations at Olympia, 1868–1881: an episode in Greco-German cultural relations", in *Greek society in the making, 1863–1913: realities, symbols and visions*, ed. P. Carabott (London and Aldershot: Variorum), pp.73–85. 1996 *Down from Olympus: archaeology and philhellenism in Germany, 1750–1970* (Princeton, NJ: Princeton University Press).

Marden, Peter 1997 "Geographies of dissent: globalization, identity and the nation", *Political Geography* 16/1: 37–64.

Margadant, Ted W. 1979 "French rural society in nineteenth-century France: a review essay", *Agricultural History* 53/3 (July): 644–651.

Maskaleris, Thanasis 1972 *Kostis Palamas* (New York: Twayne).

Mastrodimitris, P.D., ed. 1985 *O Zitianos tou Karkavitsa*, 3rd edn. (Athens: Kardamitsa).

von Maurer, Georg Ludwig 1976 [1835] *O Ellinikos laos: dimosio, idiotiko kai ekklisiastiko dikaio apo tin enarxi tou agona yia tin anexartisia os tin 31 Iouniou 1834*, trans. O. Robaki, ed. T. Vourna (Athens: Tolidis).

Mazower, Mark 1991 *Greece and the inter-war economic crisis* (Oxford: Oxford University Press).

McGrew, William W. 1985 *Land and revolution in modern Greece, 1800–1881: the transition in the tenure and exploitation of land from Ottoman rule to Independence* (Columbus, OH: Kent State University Press). 1976 "The Land issue in the Greek War of Independence", in *Hellenism and the first Greek war of liberation (1821–1830): continuity and change*, ed. N.P. Diamandouros *et al.* (Thessaloniki: Institute for Balkan Studies), pp.111–129.

McMillan, James 1995 "La France profonde: modernity and national identity", in *Landscapes of France: Impression and its rivals*, ed. J. House (London: Hayward Gallery).

Meinig, Donald W. 1979 "Symbolic landscapes: some idealizations of American communities", in *The Interpretation of ordinary landscapes: geographical essays*, eds. D.W. Meinig *et al.* (New York and London: Oxford University Press), pp.164–192.

Meletopoulos, Ioannis A. 1972 *Ikones tou agona: I. Makriyanni-Panayioti Zografou* (Athens: Ekdosis Istorikis kai Ethnoloyikes Etairias tis Ellados).

Meraklis, Mihalis Y. 1996 "O Fallmerayer kai i elliniki laografia", in *Enas neos kosmos yennietai: i ikona tou ellinikou olitismou sti yermaniki epistimi kata ton 19⁰ ai.*, ed. E. Chrysos (Athens: Akritas), pp.269–276.

Metaxas-Vosporitis, Konstantinos 1988 [1899] *Skinai tis erimou* (Athens: Nefeli).

Mikoniakis, Ilias G. 1979 "The Greek War of Independence on the London stage, 1821–1833", *Epistimoniki Epitirida Filosofikis Scholis Thessalonikis* 18: 331–343.

Miliarakis, Antonios 1901 [1882] *Odigos ton aplon topografikon perigrafon* (Athens: Kollaros). 1889 *Neoelliniki yeografiki filoloyia itoi katalogos ton apo tou 1800–1889 yeografithendon ipo ellinon* (Athens: Estia). 1885 "Daniil Filippidis kai i yeografia aftou (1791)", *Estia* 474/19: 115–119. 1877 "Peri tis ofelias ton yeografikon epistimon", *Estia* 79/4: 423–426.

Miller, William 1928 *Greece* (London: Ernst Benn Limited). 1905 *Greek life in town and country* (London: William Clowes).

Mitchell, Timothy F. 1993 *Art and science in German landscape painting, 1770–1840* (Oxford: Clarendon Press).

Mitchell, W.J. Thomas 1994 "Imperial landscape", in *Landscape and power*, ed. W.J.T. Mitchell (Chicago: Chicago University Press), pp.5–35.

Mitchell, W.J. Thomas, ed. 1994 *Landscape and power* (Chicago: University of Chicago Press).

Mitsakis, Mihail 1995 *Afiyimata*, ed. D. Lekkas (Athens: Silloyi).

Mitsopoulos, Konstantinos 1901 *Yeoloyiki istoria tis ellinikis horas* (Athens).

Monmonier, M.S. 1991 *How to lie with maps* (Chicago: University of Chicago Press).

Morreti, Franco 1998 *Atlas of the European novel, 1800–1900* (London and New York: Verso).

Moskof, Kostis 1972 *I Ethniki kai kinoniki sindisi stin Ellada, 1830–1902: ideoloyia tou metapraktikou horou* (Thessaloniki).

Mouzelis, Nikos P. 1978 *Modern Greece: facets of underdevelopment* (London and Basingstoke, UK: Macmillan).

Murray, Stuart, ed. 1997 *Not on any map: essays on postcoloniality and cultural nationalism* (Exeter, UK: University of Exeter Press).

Myrivilis, Stratis 1987 [1943] *O Vasilis o Arvanitis* (Athens: Estia). 1963 *O Palamas sti zoi mou* (Athens: Fexis). 1949 *Ap 'tin Ellada. Taxidiotika* (Athens: Estia). 1934 *I Daskala me ta hrisa matia* (Athens: Pirsos).

Nef, Karl 1985 *Istoria tis mousikis*, ed. and trans. F. Anoyianakis, 2nd edn. (Athens: Votsis).

Neroulos, J.R. 1828 *Histoire moderne de la Grèce: depuis la chute de l'Empire d'Orient* (Geneva).

Neu, Jerome, ed. 1992 *The Cambridge companion to Freud* (Cambridge: Cambridge University Press).

Nevinson, Henry W. 1898 *Scenes in the Thirty Days War between Greece and Turkey, 1897* (London: J.M. Dent and Co).

Newbigin, Marion I. 1915 *Geographical aspects of Balkan problems in their relation to the Great European War* (London: Constable and Co).

Nirvanas, Pavlos 1907 "Emis kai i xeni", *Panathinaia* 15: 121.

Nora, Pierre 1997 [1984–1992] *Les Lieux de mémoire*, 3 vols. (Paris: Gallimard).

Nordau, Max 1895 *Degeneration* (New York: D. Appleton).

Obolensky, Dimitri 1982 *The Byzantine commonwealth: Eastern Europe, 500–1453* (Crestwood, NY: St. Vladimir's Seminary Press).

Oikonomos, Konstantinos 1876 [1837] *Peri agapis patridos* (Athens: Estia).

Oinas, F.J., ed. 1978 *Folklore, nationalism, and politics* (Columbus, OH: Slavica).

Olsen, Birgit 1990 "I Yermanoprepia ton ellinikon paramithion sto silloyi tou J.G. Hahn", *Ellinika* 41: 79–93.

Pagden, Anthony 1982 *The Fall of natural man: the American Indian and the origins of comparative ethnology* (Cambridge: Cambridge University Press).

Palaiologos, Grigorios 1989 *O Polipathis*, ed. A. Angelou (Athens: Ermis).

Palamas, Kostis 1969 *The Twelve lays of the Gipsy*, trans. G. Thomson (London: Lawrence and Wishart). 1927 [1891] *Thanatos pallikariou* (Athens: Kollaros). n.d. *Apanta*, vols. 2 and 6 (Athens: Biris and Idrima Kosti Palama).

Paliouritis, Grigorios 1815 *Arhaioloyia elliniki iti filoloyiki istoria*, 2 vols. (Venice).

Palmer, Alan 1992 *The Decline and fall of the Ottoman Empire* (London: John Murray).

Panayiotopoulos, A. 1980 "The 'Great Idea' and the vision of eastern federation: a propos of the views of I. Dragoumis and A. Souliotis-Nikolaidis", *Balkan Studies* 21/2: 331–365.

Pantazidis, Ioannis 1886 "Filoloyia, grammatoloyia, logotehnia", *Estia* 557/22: 545–548.

Pantazis, Vangelis 1989 *Hartes kai ideoloyies* (Athens: Kalvos).

Pantazopoulos, Nikolaos I. 1993 *O Ellinikos kinotismos kai i elliniki kinotiki paradosi* (Athens: Parousia).

Papadiamantis, Alexandros 1981 *Apanta*, ed. N.D. Triantafillopoulos, 5 vols. (Athens: Domos).

Papadopoulou-Simeonidou, Parisatis 1996 *I Epiloyi tis Athinas os protevousas tis Ellados, 1833–1834* (Thessaloniki: Adelfon Kyriakidi).

Papakostas, Yannis 1982 *To Periodiko Estia kai to diiyima* (Athens: Ekpe-deftiria Kostea-Yitona).

Papayannakis, Lefteris 1982 *I Elliniki siderodromi (1882–1910)* (Athens: Morfotiko Idrima Ethnikis Trapezis).

Papayeoryiou-Venetas, Alexandros 1996 "Arhitectoniki dimiouryia stin Athina: nei dromi tou klasikismou", in *Enas neos kosmos yennietai: i ikona tou ellinikou politismou sti yermaniki epistimi kata ton 19⁰ ai.*, ed. E. Chrysos (Athens: Akritas), pp.277–314.

Peckham, Robert Shannan (In press) "The Uncertain state of islands: nationalism and the discourse of islands", *Journal of Historical Geography*. 1999 "Diseased bodies of the nation: suicide in *fin-de-siècle* Greece", *Journal of Mediterranean Studies* 9/2: 155–174. 1999a "'Map mania': nationalism and the politics of place in Greece, 1870–1922", *Political Geography* 19: 77–95. 1999b "The Exoticism of the familiar and the familiarity of the exotic: *fin-de-siècle* travellers to Greece", in *Writes of passage: reading travel*, eds. J.S. Duncan and D. Gregory (London and New York: Routledge), pp.164–184. 1996 "Between East and West: the border writing of Yeoryios Vizyinos", *Ecumene* 3/2: 167–180. 1995 "Memory and homelands: Vizyinos, Papadiamantis and geographical imagination", *Kambos: Cambridge Papers in Modern Greek* 3: 95–123. 1995a "O Papadiamantis kai i oikonomia tis fantasias", *Revue des Études Néo-Helleniques* IV, 1/2: 35–69. 1994 "O Papadiamantis kai i ennoia tou dendrou", *Ellinika* 44: 147–157.

Pelet, J.J.G. 1832 *Carte de la Morée rédigée et gravée au dépôt general de la guerre* (Paris).

Pemble, John 1987 *The Mediterranean passion: Victorians and Edwardians in the South* (Oxford: Clarendon Press).

Peterson, Linda H. 1999 "Sage writing", in *Victorian literature and culture*, ed. H.F. Tucker (Oxford: Blackwell), pp.373–387.

Petrakos, Vasilios Ch. 1987 *I en Athinais Arhaioloyiki Etairia. I istoria ton 150 hronon tis, 1837–1987* (Athens: En Athinais Arhaioloyiki Etairia).

Petropulos, John A. 1968 *Politics and statecraft in the Kingdom of Greece, 1833–1843* (Princeton, NJ: Princeton University Press).

Philippidies, Daniil and Gregorios Konstantas 1988 *Yeografia neoteriki*, ed. A. Koumarianou (Athens: Ermis).

Phillips, Alison W. 1897 *The War of Greek Independence, 1821–1833* (London: Smith, Elder and Co).

Pick, Daniel 1989 *Faces of degeneration: a European disorder, c.1848–c.1918* (Cambridge: Cambridge University Press).

Ploumidis, Yeoryios S. 1981 *Yeografia tis istorias tou neoellinikou horou* (Athens: Vivliothiki Istorikon Meleton).

Politi, Jina 1996 *Sinomilontas me ta kimena* (Athens: Agras). 1988 "The Tongue and the pen: a reading of Karkavítsas's *O Arheológos*", in *The*

Greek novel AD 1–1985, ed. R. Beaton (London: Croom Helm), pp.42–53.

Politis, Alexis 1993 *Romantika hronia: ideoloyies kai nootropies stin Ellada tou 1830–1880* (Athens: Etairia Meletis Neou Ellinismou). 1973 *To Dimotiko tragoudi: kleftika* (Athens: Ermis).

Politis, Nikolaos 1920 *Les Aspirations nationales de la Grèce* (Paris: Édition Spéciale de la Paix des Peuples).

Politis, Nikolaos Y. 1921 [1894], "Dimodis kosmoyoniki mythi", *Laografia Simiktra* 2: 77–109. 1920 [1909] *Laografia symmikta*, vol.1 (Athens). 1899 "Ta onomata ton dimon", *Epiteris Parnassou* 3: 54–80. 1894 "On the breaking of vessels as a funeral rite in modern Greece", trans. L. Dyer, *Journal of the Anthropological Institute of Great Britain and Ireland* XXIII: 29–41. 1871 *Meleti epi tou viou ton neoteron Ellinon, vol.1, Neoelliniki mytholoyia* (Athens: Karl Wilberg and N.A. Nakis).

Porter, Roy and M. Teich, eds. 1988 *Romanticism in national context* (Cambridge: Cambridge University Press).

Poulantzas, Nikos 1978 *State, power and socialism* (London: New Left Books).

Poulos, Ioannis 1966 "Ta Prota Sinora tis neoteras Ellados", *Deltion tis Istorikis kai Ethnoloyikis Etairias tis Ellados* 18: 3–83.

Power, Daniel and Naomi Standen, eds. 1999 *Frontiers in question: Eurasian borderlands, 700–1700* (Basingstoke, UK: Macmillan).

Prescott, John R.V. 1965 *The Geography of boundaries and frontiers* (London: Hutchinson).

Pringle, Trevor R. 1988 "The Privation of history: Landseer, Victoria and the Highland myth", in *The Iconography of landscape: essays on the symbolic representation, design and use of the past environments*, eds. D.E. Cosgrove and S. Daniels (Cambridge: Cambridge University Press), pp.142–161.

Psycharis 1983 [1888] *To Taxidi mou*, ed. A. Angelou (Athens: Ermis). 1904 *Zoi kai agapi sti monaxia* (Athens: Estia). Pugh, Simon 1990 "Loitering with intent", in *Reading landscape*, ed. S. Pugh (Manchester: Manchester University Press), pp.145–160.

Pugh, Simon, ed. 1990 *Reading landscape* (Manchester: Manchester University Press).

Quilley, Geoff 1998 "'All ocean is her own': the image of the sea and the identity of the maritime nation in eighteenth-century British art", in *Imagining nations*, ed. G. Cubitt (Manchester: Manchester University Press), pp.132–152.

Quinn, Malcolm 1994 *The Swastika: constructing the symbol* (London: Routledge).

Rados, Konstantinos 1902 *Yeografiki Etairia: istoria tis idriseos* (Athens: Nomiki).

Rangavis, Alexandros R. 1894, *Apomnimonevmata*, 4 vols. (Athens: Estia). 1877 *Précis d'une histoire de la littérature néo-Hellénique* (Berlin: S. Calvary).

Ratzel, Friedrich 1896 "The Territorial growth of states", *Scottish Geographical Magazine* 12: 351–361.

Raymond, André 1996 "The Ottoman legacy in Arab political boundaries", in *Imperial legacy*, ed. L.C. Brown (New York: Columbia University Press), pp.115–128.

Renan, Ernest 1990 "What is a nation?", trans. M. Thom, in *Nation and narration*, ed. H.K. Bhabha (London and New York: Routledge), pp.8–22.

Renieris, Markos 1842 "Ti inai I Ellas; Anatoli I Disis", *Eranistis* 2/1: 187–213.

Richetti, John 1999 *The English novel in history, 1700–1780* (London: Routledge).

Ricks, David and Paul Magdalino, eds. 1998 *Byzantium and the modern Greek identity* (London and Aldershot: Ashgate).

Rodd, Rennell 1892 *The Customs and lore of modern Greece*, 2nd edn. (London: David Stott). 1891 "The Poet of the klephts: Aristoteles Valaoritis", *The Nineteenth Century* 173: 130–144.

Rose, Jacqueline 1996 *States of fantasy* (Oxford: Clarendon Press).

Rose, W.K. 1897 *With the Greeks in Thessaly* (London: Methuen and Co).

Rothenberg, David, ed. 1995 *Wild ideas* (Minneapolis: University of Minnesota Press).

Rousseau, Jean-Jacques 1979 *Reveries of the solitary walker*, trans. P. France (Harmondsworth: Penguin).

Rowlands, Michael 1996 "Memory, sacrifice and the nation", *New Formations* 30: 8–17.

Runciman, Steven 1968 *The Great church in captivity: a study of the Patriarchate of Constantinople from the eve of the Turkish conquest to the Greek War of Independence* (Cambridge: Cambridge University Press). 1965 *The Fall of Constantinople 1453* (Cambridge: Cambridge University Press).

Sahlins, Peter 1989 *Boundaries: the making of France and Spain in the Pyrenees* (Berkeley, CA: University of California Press).

Said, Edward W. 1985 [1979] *Orientalism* (Harmondsworth: Penguin).

Sakellarakis, Yannis 1998 *Arhaioloyikes agonies stin Kriti tou 19^{ou} aiona: 51 engrafa yia tis kritikes arhaiotites (1883–1898)* (Iraklion: Panepistimiakes Ekdosis Kritis).

Sant Cassia, Paul 1992 *The Making of the modern Greek family: marriage and exchange in nineteenth-century Athens* (Cambridge: Cambridge University Press).

Sareyiannis, I.A. 1973 [1964] *Scholia ston Kavafi* (Athens: Ikaros).

Sathas, Constantinos and Émile Legrand, eds. 1875 *Les Exploits de Degénis Akritas Epopée Byzantine du dixième siècle* (Paris: Maisonneuve).

Schama, Simon 1995 *Landscape and memory* (London: HarperCollins).

Schliemann, Heinrich 1880 *Ilios: the city and the country of the Trojans: the results of researches and discoveries on the site of Troy and throughout the Troad in the years 1871–1879* (London: John Murray).

Schorsek, Carl E. 1992 "Freud: the psychoarchaeology of civilizations", in *The Cambridge Companion to Freud*, ed. J. Neu (Cambridge: Cambridge University Press), pp.8–24.

Scott, Barbara G. 1996 "Archaeology and national identity: the Norwegian example", *Scandinavian Studies* 68/3: 321–342.

Seton-Watson, Hugh 1977 *Nations and states: an enquiry into the origins of nations and the politics of nationalism* (Boulder, CO: Westview Press).

Shaw, J. and E. Shaw 1977 *History of the Ottoman Empire and modern Turkey II: reform, revolution and republic: the rise of modern Turkey, 1808–1975* (Cambridge: Cambridge University Press).

Shennan, Stephen, ed. 1994 [1989] *Archaeological approaches to cultural identity* (London and New York: Routledge).

Silberman, Neil A. 1989 *Between past and present: archaeology, ideology and nationalism in the modern Middle East* (New York: Holt). 1982 *Digging for God and country* (New York: Knopf).

Sinarelli, Maria 1989 *Drom kai limani stin Ellada, 1830–1880* (Athens: ETVA).

Sklenár, Karel 1983 *Archaeology in Central Europe: the first 500 years*, trans. I. Lewitová, foreword S. Piggott (Leicester, UK and New York: Leicester University Press and St Martin's Press). 1981 "The History of archaeology in Czechoslovakia", in *Towards a history of archaeology*, ed. G. Daniel (London: Thames and Hudson), pp.150–158.

Skliros, Yiorgos 1907 *To Kinoniko mas zitima* (Athens: Anestis Konstantinidis).

Skopetea, Elli 1997 *Fallmerayer: tehnasmata tou antipalou deous* (Athens: Themelio). 1988 *To 'Protipo vasilo' kai i Megali Idea. Opsis tou ethnikou provlimatos stin Ellada (1830–1880)* (Athens: Politipo).

Smith, Anthony D. 1995 "Gastronomy or geology? The role of nationalism in the reconstruction of nations", *Nations and Nationalism* 1/1: 3–23. 1991 *National Identity* (Harmondsworth: Penguin). 1986 *The Ethnic origins of nations* (Oxford: Blackwell).

Smith, W.D. 1980 "Friedrich Ratzel and the origins of *Lebensraum*", *German Studies Review* 3: 51–68.

Snell, Keith, ed. 1998 *The Regional novel in Britain and Ireland* (Cambridge: Cambridge University Press).

Sokolis, Konstantinos S. 1993 [1916] *Aftokratoria* (Athens: Roes).

Solomos, Dionysios 1986 [1960] *Piimata*, ed. L. Politis (Athens: Ikaros).

Sommer, Doris 1991 *Foundational fictions: the national romances of Latin America* (Berkeley, CA: University of California Press).

Soutsos, Alexandros 1994 [1835] *O Exoristos tou 31: komikotrayikon istorema*, ed. L. Droulia (Athens: Idrima Kosta kai Elenis Ourani).

Soutsos, Ioannis 1867 "Peri tis epirrois ton fisikon peristaseon epi tou politismou", *Pandora* 386/17: 33–41.

Soutsos, Panayiotis 1834 *O Leandros* (Athens).

Sperber, Dan 1975 *Rethinking symbolism*, trans. A.L. Morton (Cambridge: Cambridge University Press).

Sphyroeras, V. *et al.*, eds. 1985 *Maps and map-makers of the Aegean*, trans. G. Cox and J. Solman (Athens: Olkos).

Spiridonakis, Basile G. 1977 *Essays on the historical geography of the Greek world in the Balkans during the Turkokratia* (Thessaloniki: Institute of Balkan Studies).

Steevens, George W. 1897 *With the Conquering Turk: the confessions of a Bashi-Bazouk* (Edinburgh, UK: W. Blackwood).

Stern, Joseph P. 1992 *The Heart of Europe: essays on literature and ideology* (Oxford: Blackwell).

Stevenson, Robert Louis 1998 [1896] *In the South Seas*, ed. N. Rennie (Harmondsworth: Penguin).

Stewart, Charles 1994 "Syncretism as a dimension of nationalist discourse in modern Greece", in *Syncretism/anti-syncretism: the politics of religious synthesis*, eds. C. Stewart and R. Shaw (London: Routledge), pp.127–144. 1991 *Demons and the devil: moral imagination in modern Greek culture* (Princeton, NJ: Princeton University Press).

Stewart, Charles and Rosalind Shaw, eds. 1994 *Syncretism/anti-syncretism: the politics of religious synthesis* (London: Routledge).

Stock, Brian 1993 "Reading community and a sense of place", in *Place/culture/representation*, eds. J.S. Duncan and D. Ley (London and New York: Routledge), pp.314–328.

Stocking, George W. 1964 "French anthropology in 1800", *Isis* 55/2: 134–150.

Stoddart, D.R. 1992 "Geography and war: the 'New Geography' and the 'New Army' in England, 1899–1914", *Political Geography* 11/1: 87–99.

Stoianovic, Traian 1962 "Factors in the decline of Ottoman society in the Balkans", *Slavic Review* XXI: 623–632. 1960 "The Conquering Balkan Orthodox merchant", *Journal of Economic History* 20/1: 234–313.

Stoneman, Richard, ed. 1984 *A Literary companion to travel in Greece* (Harmondsworth: Penguin).

Stoye, John 1994, *Marsigli's Europe, 1680–1730: the life and times of Luigi Ferdinando Marsigli, soldier and virtuoso* (New Haven, CT: Yale University Press).

Taylor, Peter J. 1993 [1985] *Political geography: world-economy, nation-state and locality* (Harlow, UK: Longman).

Theotokas, Yorgos 1990 [1940] *Leonis* (Athens: Kollaros). 1986 "Free spirit", trans. S.G. Stavrou, *Modern Greek Studies Yearbook* 2: 153–200. 1973 [1929] *Elefthero pnevma* ed. K. Th. Dimaras (Athens: Ermis).

Thiersch, Frédéric 1833 *De l'État actuel de la Grèce et des moyens d'arriver à sa restauration*, 2 vols. (Leipzig, Germany: F.A. Brockhaus).

Thomadakis, S. 1984 *Yeografiki katanomi ton ergasion tis Ethnikis Trapezis tis Ellados (1861–1900)* (Athens).

Thomas, Nicholas 1994 *Colonialism's culture: anthropology, travel and government* (Cambridge: Polity).

Thomopoulos, S.N. 1888 *Istoria tis poleos Patron apo ton arhiotaton hrnonon mehri tou 1821* (Athens).

Tilley, Christopher, ed. 1993 *Interpretative archaeology* (Oxford: Berg). 1991 *Material culture and text: the art of ambiguity* (London: Routledge).

Tilly, Charles 1990 *Coercion, capital, and European states* (Oxford: Blackwell).

Todorova, Maria 1997 *Imagining the Balkans* (New York and Oxford: Oxford University Press).

Tolias, Y. 1992 "1830–1939: o horos kai i anthropi", in *Ekato hronia hartografias tou ellinismou* (Athens). 1990 "The Cartographer Barbié du Bocage and the approach to the Greek world in the late 18th and early 19th centuries", *Journal of the International Map Collectors' Society* 40: 5–9.

Tozer, H.F. 1869 *Researches in the Highlands of Turkey*, 2 vols. (London: John Murray).

Traeger, Jörg 1994 "Walhalla: the temple of fame on the Danube", in *The Romantic spirit in German art, 1790–1990*, eds. K. Hartley *et al.* (London: Thames and Hudson), pp.303–306.

Traill, David A. 1995 *Schliemann of Troy: treasure and deceit* (London: John Murray).

Trevelyan, H. 1941 *Goethe and the Greeks* (Cambridge: Cambridge University Press).

Trigger, Bruce G. 1990 *A History of archaeological thought* (Cambridge: Cambridge University Press). 1984 "Alternative archaeologies: nationalist, colonialist, imperialist", *Man* 19/3: 355–370.

Trotter, David 1993 *The English novel in history, 1895–1920* (London: Routledge).

Tsigakou, Fani-Maria 1991 *Through Romantic eyes: European images of nineteenth-century Greece from the Benaki Museum* (Alexandria, VA: Art Services International). 1981 *The Rediscovery of Greece: travellers and painters of the Romantic era* (London: Thames & Hudson).

Tsokopoulos, Vasias 1999 *Megala tehnika erga stin Ellada: teli 19^{ou} – arhes 20^{ou} aiona* (Athens: Kastaniotis). 1985 "Ta Stadia tis topikis sinidisis: o Piraias, 1835–1935", *Ta Praktika tou diethnous simposio istorias Neoelliniki Poli tis Etairias Meletis Neou Ellinismou* (Athens), pp.245–249. 1984 *Piraias, 1835–1870: isagogi stin istoria tou ellinkou Manchester* (Athens: Kastaniotis).

Tsoukalas, Konstantinos 1970 *Exartisi kai anaparagogi. O Kinonikos rolos ton ekpaidevtikon mihanismon stin Ellada (1830–1922)* (Athens: Themelio).

Tuan, Yi-Fu 1978 "Literature and geography: implications for geographical research", in *Humanistic geography: prospects and problems*, eds. D. Ley and M.S. Samuels (London: Croom Helm), pp.194–206.

Tucker, Herbert F., ed. 1999 *Victorian literature and culture* (Oxford: Blackwell).

Tuckerman, Charles K. 1878 *The Greeks of to-day* (New York: Putnam).

Turot, Henri 1898 *L'Insurrection crétoise et la guerre gréco-turque* (Paris: Hachette).

Tziovas, Dimitris 1997 "Apo ti mythostiria sto mythistorema", in *Apo ton Leandro ston Louki Lara: meletes yia tin pezografia tis periodou 1830–1880*, ed. M. Vayenos (Heraklion: Panepistimiakes Ekdosis Kritis), pp.9–30. 1995 "The Politics of metaphor and the rhetoric of consensus: Europe in the 'Free spirit' of George Theotokas", in *Greece and Europe in the modern period: aspects of a troubled relationship*, ed. P. Carabott (London: Centre for Hellenic Studies, King's College London), pp.70–82. 1994 "Heteroglossia and the defeat of regionalism in Greece", *Kambos: Cambridge Papers in Modern Greek* 2: 95–120. 1986 *The Nationalism of the demoticists and its impact on their literary theory, 1888–1939* (Amsterdam: Hakkert). 1985 "The Organic discourse of nationistic demoticism: a tropological approach", in *The Text and its margins: post-structuralist approaches to twentieth-century Greek literature*, eds. M. Alexiou and V. Lambropoulos (New York: Pella), pp.253–277.

Tziovas, Dimitris, ed. 1997 *Greek modernism and beyond* (Lanham, MD: Rowman and Littlefield).

Unwin, Tim 1992 *The Place of geography* (Harlow, UK: Longman).

Vacalopoulos, Apostolos E. 1961–1982 *Istoria tou neou ellinismou*, 2nd edn., 6 vols. (Thessaloniki). 1968 "Byzantinism and Hellenism. Remarks on the racial origin and the intellectual continuity of the Greek nation", *Balkan Studies* 9: 101–126.

Valetas, Yorgos 1981 *I Yenia tou '80: o neoellinikos natouralismos kai i arhes tis ithgrafias* (Athens).

Varouxakis, Georgios 1995 "The Idea of 'Europe' in nineteenth-century Greek political thought", in *Greece and Europe in the modern period: aspects of a troubled relationship*, ed. P. Carabott (London: Centre for Hellenic Studies, King's College London), pp.16–37.

Vayenas, Nasos 1997 "Outopikos sosialismos ton adlefon Soutson", in *Apo ton Leandro ston Louki Lara: meletes yea tin pezografia tis periodou 1830–1880*, ed. N. Vayenas (Heraklion: Panepstimiakes Ekdosis Kritis), pp.43–58.

Vayenas, Nasos, ed. 1997 *Apo ton Leandro ston Louki Lara: meletes yia tin pezografia tis periodou 1830–1880* (Heraklion: Panepistimiakes Ekdosis Kritis).

Veit, Ulrich 1994 [1989] "Ethnic concepts in German prehistory: a case study of the relationship between cultural identity and archaeological objectivity", in *Archaeological approaches to cultural identity*, ed. S. Shennan (London and New York: Routledge), pp.35–56.

Veloudis, Yeoryios 1992 *Mona-Ziga, deka neoellinika meletimata* (Athens: Gnosis).

Ventoura, L. 1997 "Ta Vivlia yeografias: andifasis sto anthropistiko kai eksinchroniko minima", in *'Ti Ein 'i patrida mas': ethnokentrismos stin ekpaidevsi*, eds. A. Frangoudakis and Th. Dragona (Athens: Alexanria), pp.401–441.

Verdery, Katherine 1996 "Wither 'nation' and 'nationalism'?", in *Mapping the nation*, ed. G. Balakrishnan (London and New York: Verso), pp.226–234.

Vernon, James 1998 "Border crossings: Cornwall and the English (imagi)nation", in *Imagining nations*, ed. G. Cubitt (Manchester: Manchester University Press), pp.153–172.

Vikelas, Dimitrios 1885 *Le Rôle et les aspirations de la Grèce dans la question d'Orient* (Paris: Au Cercle Sain Simon). 1884 "I Elliniki dimosiografia kata to 1883", *Estia* 423/17: 87–91. 1881 *Loukis Laras: reminiscences of a Chiote merchant during the War of Independence*, trans. J. Gennadius (London: Macmillan and Co).

Vitti, Mario 1991 [1974] *Ideoloyiki litouryia tis ellinikis ithografias*, rev. edn. (Athens: Kedros).

Vizyinos, Yeoryios 1988 *My Mother's sin and other stories by Georgios Vizyenos*, trans. W.F. Wyatt (Hanover and London: University Press of New England).

Voutiras, Demosthenes 1994 *Apanta*, ed. V. Tsokopoulos, vol.1 (Athens: Delphini).

Voutouris, Pandelis 1995 *Os eis kathreptin...protasis kai ipothesis yia ton elliniki pezografia tou 19^{ou} aiona* (Athens: Nefeli).

Vryonis, Speros 1978 "Recent scholarship on continuity and discontinuity of culture: classical Greeks, Byzantines, Modern Greeks", in *The 'Past' in Medieval and Modern Greek culture*, ed. S. Vryonis (Malibu, CA: Undena Publications), pp.237–256.

Vryonis, Speros, ed. 1978 *The 'Past' in Medieval and Modern Greek culture*, (Malibu, CA: Undena Publications).

Vujakovic, Peter 1993 "Drawing on a Balkan dream", *Geographical* LXV/11: 38–40.

Vyzandios, K. 1972 *I Vavilonia*, ed. S. Evangelatos, 2nd edn. (Athens: Ermis).

Wagstaff, Malcom 1999, "Independent Greece: the search for a frontier, 1822–35", *Kambos: Cambridge Papers in Modern Greek* 7: 59–70.

Wallace, Alfred Russel 1880 *Island life: or, the phenomena and causes of insular faunas and floras, including a revision and attempted solution of the problem of geological climates* (London: Macmillan).

Webb, Timothy 1982 *English Romantic Hellenism, 1700–1824* (Manchester: Manchester University Press).

Weber, Eugen 1997 "L'Hexagone", in *Les Lieux de mémoire*, ed. P. Nora, vol.1 (Paris: Gallimard), pp.1171–1190. 1976 *Peasants into Frenchmen: the modernization of rural France, 1870–1914* (London: Chatto and Windus).

Wegener, Alfred L. 1924 *The Origins of continents and oceans*, trans. J.G.A. Skerl, intr. J. Evans (London: Methuen and Co).

Wheeler, Mark 1996 "Not so black as it's painted: the Balkan political heritage", in *The Changing shape of the Balkans*, eds. F.W. Carter and H.T. Norris (London: University College Press), pp.1–8.

Wilkinson, Henry R. 1951 *Maps and politics: a review of the ethnographic cartography of Macedonia* (Liverpool: Liverpool University Press).

Williams, Colin and Anthony D. Smith 1983 "The National construction of social space", *Progress in Human Geography* 7: 502–518.

Williams, J.R. 1988 *Goethe's Faust* (London: Allen and Unwin).

Williams, Raymond 1973 *The Country and the city* (London: Chatto and Windus).

Williams, Rosalind 1990 *Notes on the underground: an essay on technology, society, and the imagination* (Harvard, MA: MIT).

Wilson, William A. 1978 "The 'Kalevala' and Finnish politics", in *Folklore, nationalism, and politics*, ed. F.J. Oinas (Columbus, OH: Slavica), pp.51–75.

Wood, Joseph S. 1991 "'Build, therefore, your own world': the New England village as settlement ideal", *Annals of the Association of American Geographers* 81/1: 32–50.

Woodhouse, Christopher M. 1995 *Rhigas Velestinlis: the proto-martyr of the Greek revolution* (Athens: Denise Harvey). 1973 *Capodistria: the founder of Greek independence* (London: Oxford University Press).

Wyatt, William F. 1993 "Viziinos in Germany", *Modern Greek Studies Yearbook* 9: 281–296. 1985 "Andreas Karkavitsas's 'The Beggar and The Archaeologist'", *Modern Greek Studies Yearbook* 1: 114–130.

Xenopoulos, Grigorios 1892 *Stratiotika diiyimata* (Athens: Kasdonis).

Xenos, Stefanos Th. 1897 *Andronike: the heroine of the Greek Revolution*, trans. E.A. Grosvenor (Boston: Roberts Brothers).

Xydis, Stephen 1968 "Mediaeval origins of modern Greek nationalism", *Balkan Studies* 9: 1–2.

Yannopoulos, Periklis 1993 *Apanta*, ed. D. Lazoyiorgos-Ellinikos (Athens: Nea Thesis).

Ziolkowski, Theodore 1990 *German Romanticism and its institutions* (Princeton, NJ: Princeton University Press).

Index

Philippson, A. 46–7
Phillips, W. Alison 56
Pick, Daniel 108
Pitsipios, Iakovos 20, 50
Pittakis, Kyriakos 117
place-names 35, 140
poetry 44, 57, 126, 127
Polenz, Wilhelm von 93
Politi, Jina 135
Politis, Nikolaos 46–7, 51–2, 67,
    69–71, 73, 74, 82, 91–2, 93–4, 121,
    130
Pompeii 12
population, distribution of 65
provinces, division into 35, 83
Psycharis 52, 80–1, 86, 103, 148
Ptolemy 19
Pyrros, Dionysios 42

Quinet, Edgar 117
Quinn, Malcolm 135

racial superiority, ideas of 74, 109,
    144–5
Rados, Konstantinos N. 143
Raftopoulos, Perikles A. 103
railways, construction of 63–5, 141
Rangavis, Alexandros Rizos 23, 39,
    50, 59, 103, 122
Ratzel, Friedrich 40, 60, 81, 143, 145
rebuilding schemes 26, 34–5, 117
regional culture and diversity 30–1,
    32, 62–3, 69–70, 73–4, 77–8, 85–6,
    108–9
Renan, Ernest 148, 149
Renieris, Markos 47, 48, 49
Richetti, John 101
Riehl, Wilhelm Heinrich 72
Ritter, Karl 12, 81, 115–16, 141
Robinson Crusoe (Defoe) 101, 102–4
Rodd, Rennell 56, 66, 130
Rodokanakis, Th. P. 69
Rose, Jacqueline 131
Rose, W. Kinnaird 138
Ross, Ludwig 33
Rottmann, Carl 26, 28
Rouse, W.H.D. 71, 105
Rousseau, Jean-Jacques 6

Runciman, Stephen 120
rural life 30–1, 54–6, 65–8, 91–2
in fiction 60–1, 92–9, 107–8, 109–14
Russia 2, 49, 68, 93, 95, 140
wars with Turkey 14, 17, 140

Safarik, P.G. 140
Sahlins, Peter 42–3
Said, Edward 49
Saint-Simon, Claude Henri de 32, 59
Saint-Vincent, Bory de 32
Samos, archaeology of 118
Sand, Georges 92
Saripolos, Nikolaos 42, 48
Sathas, Yorgos 51
Sax, Karl 141
Scanderbeg (Albanian leader) 58
Schaubert, Eduard 34, 117
Schiller, Johann Christoph Friedrich
    von 128
Schinkel, Karl Friedrich 34, 117
Schlegel, August Wilhelm von 11
Schliemann, Heinrich 121, 122–3,
    125, 129, 131
Serao, Matilde 93
Serbia xi, 8, 39, 64, 138, 141, 145
Sikelianos, Angelos 44
Simon, Jules 76
Skliros, Yorgos 63
Skordelis, Vlasios 103, 119
Slavic languages 5–6, 35, 139, 140,
    141
Smith, Anthony 24
socialism 63, 68
Sofia, Princess 91
Sofianos, Nikolaos 18–19
Sokolis, Konstantinos S. 84–5
Souliotis-Nikolaidis, A. 84
Soutsos, Alexandros 23, 30
Soutsos, Ioannis 80
Soutsos, Panayiotis xiii, 22–5, 26, 28,
    29, 30, 59–60, 122
Spain 93
Stanford, Edward 141
state *vs.* nation x, 2, 83–4, 87, 147–8
Stathopoulos, Stavros 80
Stern, J.P. 18
Stevenson, Robert Louis 102

www.ingramcontent.com/pod-product-compliance
Lightning Source LLC
Chambersburg PA
CBHW050426280326
41932CB00013BA/2009